African Women Under Fire

African Women Under Fire

Literary Discourses in War and Conflict

Edited by Pauline Ada Uwakweh

LEXINGTON BOOKS
Lanham • Boulder • New York • London

Published by Lexington Books
An imprint of The Rowman & Littlefield Publishing Group, Inc.
4501 Forbes Boulevard, Suite 200, Lanham, Maryland 20706
www.rowman.com

Unit A, Whitacre Mews, 26-34 Stannary Street, London SE11 4AB

British Library Cataloguing in Publication Information Available

Library of Congress Cataloging-in-Publication Data
The hardback edition of this book was previously cataloged by the Library of Congress as follows:

Names: Uwakweh, Pauline Ada, editor.
Title: African women under fire : literary discourses in war and conflict / Pauline Ada Uwakweh.
Description: Lanham : Lexington Books, 2017. | Includes bibliographical references and index.
Identifiers: LCCN 2017018995 (print) | LCCN 2016059652 (ebook)
Subjects: LCSH: African literature (French)--Women authors--History and criticism. | African literature--Women authors--History and criticism. | War in literature. | Women in literature. | Refugees in literature. | Women--Violence against--Africa, Sub-Saharan. | Women and war--Africa, Sub-Saharan.
Classification: LCC PQ3980.5 (print) | LCC PQ3980.5 A32 2017 (ebook) | DDC 809/.89287096--dc23
LC record available at https://lccn.loc.gov/2017018995

ISBN 978-1-4985-2918-1 (cloth : alk. paper)
ISBN 978-1-4985-2920-4 (pbk. : alk. paper)
ISBN 978-1-4985-2919-8 (electronic)

Dedicated to all women, witnesses at the homefront and frontlines, who have dared to voice unspeakable violence.

Table of Contents

Foreword

Dr. Ada Uzoamaka Azodo

This book is a literary and gendered study of war and armed conflict along with their complicated toll on women and girls on the African continent and the globe as seen today in African women's writing. The title *African Women Under Fire* (the creative and destructive trope is eloquent!) and the subtitle "Literary Discourses in War and Conflict" draw scholars, activists and general readers' attention to the emergency situation of women and girls in peril, on a daily basis, due to the brutality of the violence of war and its aftermath. Gender and war brought together in this book implies that warfare and gender performance go hand in hand. This acceptation modifies currently held notions of masculinity and femininity.

It is precisely the recognition of the ontological link between war and gender that has made the focus of this book a study on the conditions of women and girls in varied armed conflict situations, conditions that include rape, ostracism, and stigmatization, to name only these few. Nonetheless, the flip side of the coin is that a wide range of implications and complexities of war, including its contexts, causes, and aftermaths at the universal and human levels are also analyzed and critiqued from a literary perspective, thanks to imagination. In so doing, silenced and voiceless women and girls regain their voices and speak up about the horrors of their experience, but also their endurance, resistance, resilience, survival, and coping mechanism in postwar times.

Therefore, this book is not only a chronicle on armed aggression and violence against women and girls in armed conflict areas; it is also a critical resource on how the endangered female passes from invisibility and passivity to agency. At the end, it deconstructs the traditional notion that gender roles in warfare are strictly defined, inevitable, and unchangeable.

Thus, the contributors to the volume have employed a variety of emerging theoretical frameworks to examine war, violence and trauma and their impacts on women's health. From the angle of ecocriticism, for example, the female body becomes a site for the scripting of the effects of war and violence in the environment. Eyewitness accounts from victims and perpetrators add to the corpus of war literature highlighted in the volume and bear witness to the sordid situation of women as internally and externally displaced persons, refugees at risk of or threatened with rape, homelessness, and other forms of sexual and nonsexual abuse.

At the intersections of patriarchy, poverty, and class, therefore, this book on war and conflict is a significant resource on gendered violence against women. It asks several cogent questions, the answers to which would afford women and girls the opportunity to seek redress for transgressions against their human rights, not merely their women's rights and reproductive rights, since they are affected as a category of human beings. First, is gender bias the reason for the growing male aggression against females in war? Second, what is the impact of armed aggression on men and women when treated as separate categories or together? Third, why is division of labor gendered in all world cultures? Fourth, what is the reason for male violence in war and peace times? Fifth, can women be as violent as men under warfare? Sixth, is gender performance in war and peace not about power play? Seventh, what would it take to stop violence in human society? Eighth, can reconceptualization of masculinity and femininity help males and females cope better with their identity problems? Ninth, how do changing political landscapes contribute to new sources of armed conflict and war on women nowadays?

Undoubtedly, it is the domain of literary analysis and interpretation to help humanity chart a new vision, a vision in theory. The reader will find in this anthology a contribution to the growing research on war and gender on women and girls' situations under armed conflict in Africa. The term gender has, subsequently, grown into a meme of sorts, through which the sordid rise in warfare and other forms of armed and unarmed aggression has been grappled, especially as it pertains to women and girls.

What is needed for the future, the editor of this book posits rightly, is a theory of trauma able to frame the emerging literature of violence in the twenty-first century, a century which is perhaps the worst yet in terms of incidents of sophisticated technological warfare in world history. Such a trauma theory will account for the complex and complicated war conditions and the culturally-rooted social stressors that engender armed conflicts in Africa. In addition, a new African feminist theory on women's agency will explore gender gap biases, the silences on women's roles in war, and erase the present dominance of androcentric representations of violence under war conditions. Next, expanding the ambit of war and violence will enable, in their new definitions, the inclusion of abduction, sexual slavery, and girl trafficking among the new trends on the continent. Finally, women's language and rhetoric of resistance and change should be reevaluated, so that female testimonies of war can better be understood and taken seriously in all considerations of worthwhile war literatures on the African continent.

Lastly, I concur with the editorial statement that university academics can benefit from the use of this book as a one-stop secondary resource. The book is interdisciplinary, cutting across the humanities, African studies, general studies, continuing studies, and women's and gender studies. Thus, readers interested in the causes, construction, and criticism on gender and war, the role of women and men in armed conflicts, and how gender shapes the system of warfare in human society can also derive a lot of benefit from the use of this book.

Indiana University Northwest
Gary Campus, October 1, 2016

Acknowledgments

African Women Under Fire: Literary Discourses in War and Conflict has barely covered the scope and complexities of wars and armed conflicts on the African continent. Indeed, the growth of literary production from different parts of the African continent, appropriately termed "harvests of war," certainly necessitates another collection of essays beyond this single book. Undoubtedly, the outpouring of war narratives, the emerging scholarship on trauma, and the demand for literary trauma theory suited to the African postcolonial contexts, have definitely found a base in Africa's literatures of war.

The idea for this book was engendered in 2014, in the wake of the audacious kidnapping of almost 300 schools girls in Chibok, northern Nigeria, by a militant group. This tragic incident was not unprecedented. Indeed, a similar occurrence goes back to 1996, in the small town Aboke in northern Uganda. As gendered violence reverberated globally, making headline news, the world held its breath at the increasing transgressions of women's human rights. It was not a surprise, therefore, that the CFP for *African Women Under Fire* generated a lot of interest and wide responses from scholars and researchers in various interdisciplinary fields. It is with utmost pleasure that I express my deep appreciation to many colleagues in various institutions, nationally and internationally, that responded enthusiastically to the call for papers.

I must state that every contributor to *African Women Under Fire* at that early stage shared with me the vision for this literary and critical exploration of African narratives of war and conflict devoted exclusively to women. Together, we all felt the need to capture the voice and experience of African women through their narratives and in their *own voices*. The female voice has not ceased to project its unique insight on women's daily existence and experience of crisis. It was your animated responses to my call that heightens the significance of this book. I am much obliged and grateful to you all for your time and effort.

The scholars whose work appear here bring fresh angles to the emerging narratives of war written by women from various sites of wars and armed conflicts. I, therefore, would like to extend my utmost gratitude to the contributors listed here: Dr. Jessie Sagawa (University of New Brunswick, Fredericton, Canada), Dr. Tendai Mangena (Department of English and Media Studies, Great Zimbabwe University), Dr. Melissa R. Root (Department of English, Metropolitan State University of Denver, Colorado), Ms. Emilie Diouf (African American and African Studies, Michigan State University), Dr. Moussa Issifou (English Department, North Carolina Agricultural and Technical State University), Dr. P. Julie Papaioannou (Department of Modern Languages and Cultures, University of Rochester), Dr. Paul N. Touré (French and Francophone Studies, Millikin University, Decatur, Illinois), and H. Nanjala Nyabola (Kenyan human rights advocate, writer, and political analyst).

Further, I am deeply grateful to the editorial peer reviewers from far and near, and across continents, for their collegial support. I hope that *African Women Under Fire,* in its final state, will be a fitting reward for your time and effort. At this instance, I would like to thank Dr. Maurice Vambe (English Studies, University of South Africa), Dr. Joya Uraizee (Department of English and International Studies, Saint Louis University), Dr. Heather Hewett (Department of English and Women's, Gender, and Sexuality Studies, State University of New York at New Paltz), Dr. Delphine Fongang (Dept. of Languages and Literatures, University of Wisconsin-Whitewater), Dr. Lily Mabura (Department of English, American University of Sharjah), Dr. Tanure Ojaide (Africana Studies Department, The University of North Carolina at Charlotte), Dr. Ann Beth Wiley (Dept. of English, University of Louisville), Dr. Obododimma Oha (Department of English, University of Ibadan, Nigeria), Dr. Nicki Hitchcott (Department of French and Francophone Studies, University of Nottingham, UK). Dr. Laura Murphy, (Department of English, Loyola University New Orleans), Dr. Alexandra Schultheis-Moore (University of North Carolina, Greensboro), Dr. Ayodeji Shittu (Department of English and Professional Communications, Redeemer's University, Ede, Nigeria), Dr. Amadou Fofana, (French and Francophone Studies, Willamette University, Salem, Oregon), Dr. Yianna Liatsos (School of Culture and Communication, University of Limerick, Limerick), Dr. Chielozona Eze (English Department, Northeastern Illinois University, Chicago), Dr. Ode Ogede (Department of Language and Literature, North Carolina Central University, Durham), Dr. Isidore Diala (Department of English and Literary Studies, Imo State University, Nigeria). Many thanks to Dr. Zoe Norridge (English and Comparative Literature, King's College London) for her kind recommendation, and to Dr. Ada Azodo (Women's and Gender Studies, Indiana University Northwest, Gary, Indiana) for her support in facilitating this critical discourse by writing the foreword.

Additionally, I extend warm appreciation to my international colleagues at Redeemer's University, Ede, Nigeria. My gratitude goes to Professor Z. Debo Adeyewa (Vice-Chancellor, Redeemer's University), Professor Edmund Bamiro (Dean, College of Humanities), Dr. Idowu Odebode (Chair, English Department), Dr. Ayodeji Shittu (Coordinator, Postgraduate program, Department of English), Professor 'Segun Adekoya (Department of English, Obafemi Awolowo University, Ile Ife, Nigeria), Dr. Adebola Adebileje (Reader and Director of General Studies,

Department of English), and many other fine ladies and gentlemen (space restricts me to name all), colleagues, friends and acquaintances alike, that made my brief residence at the serene campus of Redeemer's University a memorable experience. As a 2016 Fellow of the Carnegie African Diaspora Scholar's Program, my six weeks residency, filled with warmth and collegiality, was immensely vital to the successful completion of our collaborative Carnegie project, as well as this book project. Having six weeks to myself, devoted to nothing but writing, without the usual familial obligations, was a rarity that enabled me to meet the publisher's contractual deadline. I thank God for that invaluable opportunity. I am also immensely grateful to Professor Ademola Dasylva of the Department of English, University of Ibadan, Nigeria, for facilitating the Carnegie project and other collaborative initiatives between North Carolina A& T State University and Redeemer's University.

I appreciate my family, Professor Benjamin Obinero Uwakweh, both husband and brother, our offspring—Ekereoma (Eastern Michigan University), Agbo-oma (University of North Carolina, Greensboro), Ozioma (University of Cincinnati), and Abuoma (Vandalia Christian School)—for their prayers, blessings, and kind understanding of my long absence from the hearth. Thanks so much for your well wishes, and may God continually grant you increase in knowledge of Him. Special thanks to our dearest mothers, Lady Catherine Ulumma Onwubiko and Ugoeze Abigail-Clara Uwakweh for their sustaining love and persistent prayers. May God strengthen both of you. To Daberechi and Esther, our young sisters in the household, may God reward you with His abundant grace for all you do. Last, but not least, thanks to my friend Ms. Terri Williams, Administrative Assistant, College of Science and Technology, North Carolina A&T State University. I am continually grateful for your technical support, Terri. To all my readers, I trust that this critical discourse will provoke more enquiries into African women's literary harvests forged on the crucible of wars and armed conflicts.

I

Female, Victim, Agent: African Women in War and Conflict

Introduction

Exploring African Women and the War Experience—A Critical Update

Pauline Ada Uwakweh

Wars and armed conflicts have taken enormous toll on nations and human populations around the globe. In Africa alone, and since the last quarter of the twentieth century, the list of countries engaged in war and armed conflict has grown astronomically. A partial listing includes Nigeria, Liberia, Ivory Coast, Rwanda, Sierra-Leone, Zimbabwe, Somalia, Uganda, Libya, Central African Republic, etc. More recent additions to this catalogue are Mali, Egypt, Sudan, and South Sudan. It is doubtful whether any nation exists in Africa, today, that is yet untouched, directly or indirectly, by war or conflict and their tragic aftermath. While some scholars link Africa's armed conflicts to sectarian and ethnoreligious sentiments, others go beyond these obvious causes, and trace the roots to the continent's colonial and postcolonial history. Paul Zeleza (2008), for instance, asserts this viewpoint, while also underlining the dangers of protracted instability on Africa's development. He states:

> Violent conflicts of one type or another have afflicted Africa and exacted a heavy toll on the continent's societies, polities and economies, robbing them of their developmental potential and democratic possibilities. The causes of the conflicts are as complex as the challenges of resolving them are difficult. . . . Not only are African conflicts inseparable from the conflicts of the twentieth century—the most violent century in world history; many postcolonial conflicts are rooted in colonial conflicts. There is hardly any zone of conflict in contemporary Africa that cannot trace its sordid violence to colonial history and even the late nineteenth century. (1)

Ironically too, wars and armed conflicts have also engendered creative and artistic expressions. Without a doubt, African literature is being shaped by the new contexts of warfare, as well as the challenges of their aftermath. African writers have become not only the chroniclers of the war experience but also the "medium" by which its atrocities are exposed. They are witnesses with a mission to capture war's physical and psychological consequences, and more so, human resilience in adversity.

As Ernest Emenyonu (2008) aptly observes, literary artists translate the raw details of war into works of imagination with far reaching universal and human implications (xi).

Recognizing these facts about war and its representations, *African Women Under Fire: Literary Discourses in War and Conflict* focuses on African women's literary responses to wars and armed conflicts on the continent. Its primary aim is to extend this topical inquiry through fresh theoretical readings of narratives by women and about women in various contexts of crisis. Also, it offers scholarly research that simultaneously explores and updates constructs of war and conflict, while underpinning the emerging challenges for women in contemporary African societies. The book's gendered perspective is timely, considering the pervasive and protracted inter and intra ethnic wars and armed conflicts on the continent. Symbolically, the title, *African Women Under Fire* suggests the state of emergency which reflects the condition of women in contemporary global societies where wars and armed conflicts have become endemic. As a critical metaphor for this book, the title captures the sense of overwhelming tension and tragedy that continue to haunt the most vulnerable of the civilian population. Women (and their children) are literarily and symbolically being held hostage by debilitating social forces beyond their control.

Globally, violence against women is growing, as the ongoing incidents of male aggression on the female counterpart strongly indicate. In 2014, for instance, the world witnessed blatant abductions of school girls in Chibok, Nigeria; the rape and hanging of two teenage girls in India; the "honor" killing of a young woman in India, and the death sentence imposed on a newly married Sudanese woman.[1] These incidents initiated a global outcry among ordinary citizens, women, and civil rights organizations. They also raise pressing questions about sociocultural attitudes toward women in modern societies. What accounts for the growing male aggression and exploitation of women's human rights? In essence, what does it mean to be a female in the twenty-first century? December Green (1999) describes the features and implications of gender violence in this manner:

> Gender violence is commonly defined as violent acts (real or threatened) perpetrated on females because they are female. Whether gender violence operates as direct physical violence, threat, or intimidation, the intent is to perpetuate and promote hierarchical gender relations. It is manifested in several forms, all serving the same end: the preservation of male control over resources and power. Although it is commonly understood as the use of force and physical violence, gender violence may also include emotional and psychological abuse. (1–2)

African Women Under Fire extends Green's definition of violence in "normal" societies to include situations of crisis or armed conflicts where women are specifically targeted to fulfill ideological goals. In such instances, violence becomes not only an attempt to preserve male control but also a weapon of war itself. Indeed, several recent research on gender and war indicate that the female body has evidently become the site on which modern warfare is being waged.[2] A study by Victoria Brittain (2002) affirms the viewpoint that women and children have become favorite targets for armed aggression in contemporary warfare.[3]

> When we look at today's wars, we are looking at something that has a completely different shape from the wars in our history books, even the more modern wars like the Second World War and Vietnam, and so on. In those wars, major armies confronted each other; large numbers of young men got killed for the sake of an idea, an ideology. . . . But the wars I've been looking at over the past year are completely different in their style from this kind of template . . . the essential fact is that civilians, and specifically women, are now targets. (8)

Although none of the incidents mentioned above (Nigeria, India, Sudan) occurred in *war* contexts, the incidents, nonetheless, attest to the urgent need to redefine existing notions of war, armed conflict, and violence. These cases speak to the cogent need to investigate new sources and forms of gendered violence, as well as their impacts on the female. As insurgency shapes itself as a dominant force on the African political and cultural landscape, this grave situation necessitates new theoretical perspectives on the female experience. The Chibok incident evokes other catalogues of horror and gendered aggression on women and girls, for example, Uganda (1996), Sierra Leone (1991), Rwanda (1994), Sudan (1983–2005), and in several other African nations. A report, "Violence against Women: War's Overlooked Victims" (Bleasdale, 2011), documents statistical evidence for large scale violence perpetrated on women, not only in Africa, but also in Europe and Asia. In Africa alone, the estimated number of rape cases during the 1994 Rwandan Genocide and 1991–2002 war in Sierra Leone amounted to 500,000 and 50,000, respectively.[4] It seems, by these very accounts, that African war narratives of the future will be defined by the "violated female" experience. Gender violence is evidently integral to warfare stratagem, and minority, indigenous, refugee women, and girls have been isolated as the most vulnerable victims (Green 1999, 2).

Warfare is "gendered and sexualized" (5), states Alcinda Honwana (2011) in her ethnographic study of war's impact on child soldiers, especially girls. Using Angola and Mozambique as the focal site for her study of child soldiers in Africa, Honwana warns about the grave future consequences of rampant violence and abuse of children, especially girls. She asserts succinctly:

> Particularly damaging for future generations is the impact of war on girls. Disadvantaged even in peacetime, girls experience sexual abuse,

> rape, enslavement, and other tribulations during war. Children witness terrible atrocities and suffer from trauma. Children are deprived of education and basic healthcare. Wars and other forms of armed conflict have profound and lasting effects on young people. (2)

Unfortunately, and as Honwana also admits, silence and secrecy still shroud the experiences of women; their participation in wars and their experience of violence, exploitation, victimization, and the impact of these in post war societies are generally unaccounted for (79).

The issue of gender in war is an overarching one. Any study of contemporary wars and armed conflicts must account for the gender factor. These include, but are not limited to the following: perspectives and realities of women, men's experiences, gendered stereotypes, shifts and reconstructions of gender roles during and after wars, and most importantly, the silences, gendered coping and survival strategies. These points considered, *African Women Under Fire* privileges the female *voice* on Africa's wars and armed conflicts. When women depict their experience of crisis through their actions, and in their own voices, it is not only therapeutic, but also ensures an exclusive gendered perspective that offers unique analyses of the impacts of war on women and girls. Additionally, a gendered perspective provides insight into the varied modes (traditional and modern) by which women have engaged wars and conflicts, as well as their survival and coping mechanisms in the aftermath. Other less recognized and understudied sources of violence that impinge on the lives of females in conflict environments should also be noted. A few examples include—abductions, sex trafficking, forced marriages, familial ostracism, and social stigmatization. Additionally, the female voice informs on women's agency, their subversive and resistance praxis, as well as resilience in adversarial conditions. Notably, female agency in contexts of crisis runs contrary to persisting perceptions of victimhood. Thus, the female voice deconstructs the silences surrounding women's roles in wars, conflicts, and essentially, engages the consequences of their tragic circumstances.

THEMATIC UNDERCURRENTS AND BASIC QUESTIONS

While the thematic undercurrents of most research on women and war in African literary criticism focus on militarism, agency/victimhood, violence/rape, subalternity/subjectivity, memory/history, negotiation/resistance, trauma/healing, *African Women Under Fire* applies emerging theoretical perspectives that expand readings of existing issues. Reconceptualizing war[5] and armed conflict, reexamining trauma and its literary representations from an African postcolonial frame, and forms of therapeutic or healing practices peculiar to women, be they traditional, modern, or religious, are essential to understanding the gendered challenges in times of crisis. Also, since trauma, illnesses, alienation are important metaphors and constituents of war narratives, their health implications for women and children deserve more critical attention from scholars. Further, the ecocritical content of war narratives should engender more discussion among scholars and critics alike. Remarkably, this emergent critical theory promises to enrich women's literature by its focus on human relationships to nature and the environment in war or crisis. Does nature or the environment function as a space of refuge or accomplice in violence? In what ways does the forest, for example, constitute a space for gendered violence, considering that female (and males) abductees are held hostage in spaces where militant insurgents attempt to replicate "normal" communities? Studying the dynamics of patriarchy, power, oppression and their interrelationship with female subjectivity is necessary for understanding post war or conflict experiences of women and girls. Renewed inquiry into the making of woman's body as site of violence is cogent. These issues are accentuated in the chapters in this book.

African Women Under Fire facilitates reassessments of women's identities and its constructions in times of crisis. How does crisis disrupt women's traditional gender identity or roles as child bearers, mothers, wives, nurturers, etc.? What happens to female socialized identities when societies are at war or in conflict? What perceptions do societies have about ex-combatant females, especially in the aftermath? Are they held to the same social standards as in peacetime? Overall, how do wars and armed conflicts intersect with female identities, agency, and subjectivity? These are some of the issues that will foreground the analytical canvas of discourses in this book. The goal is to bring together emerging, relevant interdisciplinary and critical perspectives to bear on the representations of women in war and conflict in African literature. The collected essays in this book definitely enrich readings of African narratives of war and conflict, adding depth and breadth to the analyses of women's experiences.

WAR AND CONFLICT: LITERARY HARVESTS AND CRITICAL OVERVIEW

The importance of literary imagination in mediating social change cannot be overstated. African women writers lend their voices to condemning oppression, gendered violence, inequities, and all forms of social injustice, thereby engendering social transformation. They have assumed this role as part of their social responsibility as writers. However, gender gaps have been identified in African narratives of war. One example of such gaps is observed by Oike Machiko (2008).

> The reason why few 'authentic' works about war are written by women is that instead of describing terrible battlefields or the dirty politics behind them, they tend to delineate the home front and familiar everyday life in a plain, down-to-earth style using their own experiences as exemplified in *Never Again* by Flora Nwapa. Such works by women writers have not been paid serious critical attention except from feminist perspectives. (60)

While this critic acknowledges the differences in male and female narratives of war, as well as the preponderance of "autobiographical sketches" (60) in women's writings on war, it seems, however, that the unique female modes or styles of storytelling and "witnessing" about their war experiences have been glossed over. Consequently, what Machiko perceives as women's personal and "familiar everyday life" are excluded from a presumed male domain—the "terrible battlefields or the dirty politics behind them" (60). This viewpoint suggests, therefore, that the women writers' "down to earth style" is a narrative shortcoming. Such a limiting view of the content and style of women's war narratives seems to ignore the diversity of form, genres, substance, language, and style, through which African women artists are engaging their experience of war. It is, thus, necessary to account for the gender factor and its impact on women's literary production based on their war experiences, the changing contexts of wars and conflicts, and the diversity of women's creative representations of those experiences. How these new contexts contribute to redefining women's voices must also be taken into account.

Contrary to the presumed dearth in African women's writings on wars and conflicts, there has been demonstrable and appreciable growth since the last decade of the twentieth century. Earlier and notable narratives on war by African women include Assia Djebbar's *Children of the New World: A Novel of the Algerian War* (2005), Buchi Emecheta's *Destination Biafra* (1981), Flora Nwapa's *Never Again* (1975), Rose Adaure Njoku, *Withstand the Storm: War Memoirs of a Housewife* (1986). Pauline Onwubiko, *Running for Cover* (1988/2010). To this list have been added, other contemporary voices. These are as follows: Chimamanda Adichie, *Half of a Yellow Sun* (2006), Lenora Miano, *Dark Heart of the Night* (2010), Yvonne Vera, *The Stone Virgins* (2004), *Under the Tongue* (1996), *Without a Name* (1994) Goretti Kyomuhendo, *Waiting: A Novel of Uganda's Hidden War* (2007), Veronique Tadjo, *The Shadow of Imana: Travels in the Heart of Rwanda* (2002), Theodora Akachi, *Roses and Bullets* (2011), Hélène Cooper, *The House at Sugar Beach.* (2009), Marjorie Oludhe Macgoye, *The Present Moment* (2000). Another body of African war narratives written by non-Africans, mostly western journalists, freelance writers, members of charitable groups and missionary sympathizers, is also growing. This group often work as collaborators to publicize the experiences of victims in the postwar or post conflict African setting.

Individually female authored work, such as Elisabeth Combres's *Broken Memory: A Novel of Rwanda* (2007), Susan Minot's *Thirty Girls* (2012), and collaborative endeavors like *Girl Soldier: A Story of Hope for Northern Uganda's Children* (2007) which is part memoir and sociohistorical research, coauthored by Faith H. McDonnell and Grace Akallo, exemplify the contemporary trend and nature of mediated African narratives. Both Susan Minot and Faith McDonnell are westerners. Their authorship of African female trauma narratives heightens debates around the issue of mediation in many African war stories. How should these narrative accounts, in diverse forms, genres, and sometimes, hybrids of sociology, history, memoir, and fiction be read?

Robert Eaglestone (2008) discusses this issue while underlining the intricate parallels between Holocaust and African trauma literature. He observes that hybrid African trauma narratives complicate authorship and conventional genre; consequently, there is need for trauma and literary trauma theories that are relevant to postcolonial African literature. Incidentally, despite the occurrence of highly traumatic events in Africa that continue to generate creative work in various genres, there is, as yet, no specific trauma theory grown on native soil to deal with these emerging literatures of trauma. Eaglestone asserts the need for a clear theory for African trauma literature that considers the complex determining forces of traumatic conditions in the continent. He perceives lurking danger both in the concept of trauma and in replicating western theories of trauma for African narratives of war:

> [t]he term "African trauma literature" is problematic. It seems to reproduce a nineteenth-century clustering of the nations and regions of Africa into a single, mythical continent and passes over the various complexities and particular situations that range from, for example, civil war and military coups in Sierra Leone, to the work of the Truth and Reconciliation Commission in South Africa, to genocides in Darfur and Rwanda. It identifies Africa solely as a place of suffering. (75)

How, then, should African trauma literatures that speak about war and suffering be classified? Although Eagleston provides no alternative terminology, the problem of interpretive criteria remains far dire for African literary criticism than the terminology. African narratives that deal with trauma of all sorts demand a criteria of analysis. These concerns are made evident in Pauline Ada Uwakweh's assessment of *Girl Soldier* and *Thirty Girls*, two books in which coauthor and author, respectively, are Westerners. Taking these issues into account, and to facilitate a definition for African trauma literature, it would be necessary to consider certain wide ranging features that seem to be inherent in this body of literature. African trauma literature (ATL) would include literature in various hybrid genres and compositions, written by Africans and non-Africans, based on gendered experiences of violence in wars and armed conflicts, in which physical, psychological, and traumatic conditions arising from those experiences are represented, testified, or narrated; they exhibit therapeutic qualities, and express the narrator/subject's agency. Obviously, several African trauma literature do represent traumatic effects of violence in the aftermath or post-war/conflict setting. They account for both the traumatic conditions and social stressors that are culturally rooted in the African setting.

In contrast to the thriving narratives on war and armed conflicts by African women, African literary criticism may be slow in fully charting and updating concerns about the female in contexts of crisis. Although, studies on war and conflict in Africa abound, most are found in social science disciplines—sociology, anthropology, psychology, etc. A review of African literature with specific focus on women and war reveals a corpus of critical texts on war narratives. Some edited works focusing on war include Ernest Emenyonu's (2008) *War in African Literature Today vol.* 26, Charles Smith's (2008) *War and Conflict, Journal of African Literature no.* 5, and Flora Veit-Wild's and Dirk Naguschewski's (2005) *Body, Sexuality, and Gender: Versions and Subversions in African Literatures I, Matatu 29–30.* Incidentally, the above listed journals do not focus, exclusively, on the female experience of war. Although, Flora Veit-Wild and Dirk Naguschewski (2005) *Body, Sexuality, and Gender* unveils both the "cultural shifts in African societies" and the emerging openness to gender and sexuality issues (Agorde 2008, 166), it is only the book's final section titled "Violated Bodies" that pays a necessary, albeit token attention to African women's writings on war.

However, other significant studies on African women's writings on war have been published in *Research in African Literatures* (2012). Examples include Janice Spleth's (2012) "Civil War and Woman's Place in Leonora Miano's *L'Interieur de la Nuit* (*Dark Heart of the Night*)," and Zoe Norridge's (2012) "Sex as Synecdoche: Intimate Languages of Violence in Chimamanda Ngozi Adichie's *Half of Yellow Sun* and Aminatta Forna's *The Memory of Love.*" Another notable study, Jean-Marie Volet's (2001), "Francophone Women Writing in 1998–99 and Beyond: A Literary Feast in a Violent World," provides insight on the growing Francophone women's war literature. Pauline Ada Uwakweh's (2012) "Reconstructing Masculinity and Femininity in African War Narratives: The Youth in Chimamanda Adichie's *Half of a Yellow Sun* and Gorretti Kyomuhendo's *Waiting: A Novel of Uganda at War,*" published in *Journal of African Literature Association*, focuses on identity reconstructions among Africa's youth during periods of crises.

Remarkably, earlier work like Irene Staunton's (1990) *Mothers of the Revolution: The War Experience of Thirty Zimbabwean Women*, though not literary criticism, arguably, set the stage on the necessity to address and publicize Zimbabwean women's voices and contributions to the liberation wars. Interestingly, also, Régine Michelle Jean-Charles's (2014) *Con-*

flict Bodies: The Politics of Rape Representation in the Francophone Imaginary made a timely debut with its noteworthy transnational scope. Jean-Charles's study of gender violence is based on women's experiences of violence in both Africa and the African Diaspora; she draws remarkable parallels among cases in Rwanda, Democratic Republic of Congo (DRC), Haiti, and Guadeloupe. Her geographic breadth makes the point that gendered aggression transcends national boundaries.[6]

Thus, while scholarly articles on African women and the war experience may exist mostly in various disciplinary fields in the social sciences, for example, *African Women Under Fire* offers in a singular edited collection, literary criticism on women and the war experience, eye witness testimonials from victims and perpetrators, trauma, its representations, and impact on genre, visual representations of war, women refugee experiences, and other gendered complexities of war. Altogether, these critical perspectives on topical issues make this book a handy resource for scholars and researchers interested in representations of African women in contexts of crisis. The subject of women in war and armed conflict is one of the most exigent issues of the twenty-first century and, thus, deserves utmost attention. Bearing in mind the gaps in existing scholarship, and the need to update emerging challenges for females in conflict environments, *African Women Under Fire* is a necessary critical piece. Since the idea for this critical discourse was engendered by the possibilities of new insights and fresh readings of the African female narratives of war, certainly, only viable critical theories for such literature will effectively unpack the effects of crisis on women, their welfare, and that of society, in general.

African Women Under Fire focuses on reexamining the status of African women as female, victim, and agent. As such, chapters in this collection bring diverse theoretical perspectives on emerging issues surrounding African women and the war experience. The contributors have applied relevant interdisciplinary theories to fleshing out the gendered nuances in African women's narratives. Some of the issues articulated in the various chapters are striking. For instance, gender, a crucial category in studies about war foregrounds analyses in this book, thus, its intersections with patriarchy in war and post war societies, its significance in discourses on rape, violence, and its representations in narratives and visual media, trauma and its processing, are all informed by gender. Besides these, the contributors centralize the views of African feminists on women's agency in crisis, thereby debunking myths about women's passivity. Consequently, agency, realized individually or collectively, is underscored as the corollary to victimization. Gender gaps, biases, or silences around women's roles in wars, need to be redressed, for instance, in male representations of women's experience of rape and other forms of violence.

It is no coincidence that the Nigerian civil war, which lasted three years, from 1966 to 1970, is made the starting point for this critical discourse on women, war, and armed conflict in African literature. Of all African nations that have either gone through wars, or currently experiencing armed conflicts, the Nigerian civil war seems to have generated, perhaps, the most creative work in the Nigerian imaginary. The authors come from various backgrounds and walks of life, including Nigerian men and women, who were direct witnesses to the war, non-witnesses writing from research and oral memory garnered from eye witness accounts, military officials in the Nigerian or Biafran army, foreign journalists, mercenaries, among others.

Emecheta and Adichie are both non-witnesses to the war, yet they have made indelible impact on their readers through their creative discourse on this national tragedy. By bringing their feminist perspectives to bear on the Nigerian civil war story, they attained success by adding a gendered dimension that has been almost sidelined in accounts by male writers. Sagawa makes this case succinctly in her chapter, "At the Centre, Taking Charge: Disruptive Discourse and Female Agency in Buchi Emecheta's *Destination Biafra* and Chimamanda Ngozi Adichie's *Half of a Yellow Sun*." In her lucid, comparative examination of these two important female voices and their perspectives on women's place in the war story, Sagawa brings together in her analysis, many of the issues that emerge in contemporary discourses on war, especially as it relates to women's survival stratagems, experience of violence and its traumatic outcomes, gender role changes, and much more. Sagawa assumes the task of unsettling patriarchy in order to redress inherent biases in existing discourses on war. As she indicates, these biases also encompass representations of rape in accounts by male writers. Thus, her comparative analysis of two notable female writers both disrupts male biases while delineating mechanisms of female agency. Sagawa asserts that both female authors—Emecheta and Adichie—share a similar vision about the challenges women face in war situations. She demonstrates how the dynamics of male patriarchal power intersects with violence during war, and then plays out in rape incidents in the narratives. She makes a compelling argument against commonly held beliefs that women are only at risk during times of war. Other areas of disruptions include, not only patriarchy's discourses on war, but also prevailing myths about women's pacifism, and myths about masculinity.

Protracted conflicts and wars on the continent are rife. One of such is the Zimbabwean liberation struggles, also known as the *Chimurenga*. Unlike the Nigerian civil war which lasted for three years, the *Chimurenga* was a protracted indigenous effort to counter colonial yoke and achieve freedom of governance and self-determination. Having gained its independence in 1980, Zimbabwe is on record as one of Africa's new postcolonial nations, succeeded by South Sudan in 2011. Interestingly, Zimbabwean wars of liberation—the first and second *Chimurenga*—have become prominent sites of discourse that embody similar issues as are found in the Nigerian civil war, especially as it relates to women. The wars are united by common themes, the quest for self-determination, although their causes and outcomes differ. Similarly, gender biases abound in accounts of the liberation struggles as are found in the Nigerian war, or in any other conflicts and wars on the continent. Feminist writers and critics on the Zimbabwean war narratives note that women's voices and experiences have been negated, and thus call for a revised nationalist narrative on the liberation wars. Revisionism goals on Zimbabwean war historiography must acknowledge the importance of gender in understanding the full spectrum of this national incident.[7]

Tendai Mangena engages these gendered issues in her chapter, "An Attempt at Inclusion: Reading the War Theme in Black Zimbabwean Women Texts." Tackling the discursive arena of gendered writing in Zimbabwe, Mangena attributes to Black Zimbabwean women writers with the role of providing a "counter discourse" to male writings; by so doing, they subvert official nationalist narratives. Female discourses on war challenge the shortcomings of masculine narratives that downplay women's contribution to the liberation war. Such challenges counter masculinist writings on the Zimbabwean war. Mangena makes the case that narratives on the *Chimurenga* cannot be complete without women's roles accorded full recognition. Black Zimbabwean women writers are, therefore, engaged in artistic recreation that provides a comprehensive picture and understanding of national liberation. They are rewriting the liberation struggle to provide a more comprehensive picture free from gender gaps and less masculinist representations. In this regard, Mangena's observations corroborates Sagawa's on the gender gaps that pose challenges in the aftermath of wars and significantly hamper gender unity in the building of nations. Her assessment provokes questions by unveiling the dark side of nationalist narratives, and showing that not all proclaimed liberators are liberators, indeed.

Melissa Root's "The Female Body as Locus for National Trauma in the Fiction of Yvonne Vera" also focuses on the Zimbabwean liberation struggles as the source of creativity that directly underscores the importance of gender in the analysis of violence and traumatic effects. War, violence, and rape are very cogent issues for feminists, worldwide. Even more cogent for contemporary feminist scholars, globally, is the need to create better understanding of the worth of the female body. Why is the female body a site of violence in the era of modern warfare? Conflated as land and nation in the cultural and creative imaginary, why is the female body called forth to bear these burdens? From whence comes this conflation of female with the nation? Scholars, such as Regine Michelle Jean-Charles, address some of these questions in her recent book, *Conflict Bodies: The Politics of Rape Representation in the Francophone Imaginary* (2014).

Root tackles these serious questions in her study of Zimbabwean nationalist narratives by delving into detailed assessment of the traumatic effect of female violation. Illustrating the human and personal costs of wars through Vera's two novels, *Without a Name* (1994) and *Under the Tongue* (1996), Root makes the case that the trauma of the female body is symptomatic of the nation's rupture. Her focus on the fragmentation of the female body and identity as a result of rape reinforces the gendered aspects of war that is central to *African Women Under Fire*. Root analyzes the causes of female fragmentation, as well as Yvonne Vera's artistic integration of this metaphor within the narrative structures of her novels. She further underscores the point that as writer, Yvonne Vera assumes the task of mending ruptures, and offering the prospects for healing, so that the nation can function without gender divisive hindrances.

As a representational medium, film and other forms of visual media are recently gaining attention and momentum as platform for exposing and critiquing social evils, exploring African women's war experiences, as well as other gendered issues. In recent times, more films are engaging Africa's wars, the experiences of civilians, women, children, child soldiers, etc. In her chapter, "Fanta Nacro's *Night of Truth*: The Journey to the End of the Night," P. Julie Papaioannou's engagement with the impact of war and conflict through a "postcolonial transnational cinema narrative" is right on track. As Papaioannou observes, the film is Fanta Nacro's (2004) response to the 1994 Rwandan genocide and ethnic cleansing. While providing answers to key questions relating to the role of women in wars and conflicts, Papaioannou evaluates another gendered issue in this unique representational medium—the inversion of gender roles through the agency of women. Further, she taps into a gender issue rarely dealt with in literatures of war—women's potential or capacity for acts of horror on one hand, pacifism and healing, on the other hand. Her analysis debunks myths of women's victimhood, even as it unveils their motivations for horrible acts. What drives women to acts of horror? To explain, Papaioaonnou delves into the Kristevan notion of "feminine perversion" to examine the effects of disruption of motherhood on a female character. Using two female characters, Papaioaonnou illustrates how women's roles might debunk or counter stereotypical notions of women as "voiceless" or "muted" victims.

What is resilience, and how does it define women's ability to survive in times of crisis? What makes a resilient person different from others? How does a resilient person cope despite destabilizing conditions and traumas? Applying psychologist, Edith H. Grotberg's (2003) notion of resilience as "the human capacity to deal with, overcome, learn from, or even be transformed by the inevitable adversities of life," Paul Touré articulates the meaning of resilience through Miano's female characters. In the chapter, "Resilient Strategies and Reconstruction in Leonora Miano's Literary Writing," he provides answers to the questions above by exploring Miano's significant novels—*Dark Heart of the Night* (2005), *Contours of the Coming Day* (2006), *Scarlet Dawns Sankofa Cry* (2011). Conceiving these work as a study on human emotions, Toure investigates human nature and its ability to nurture strong resilient habits in times of political and social upheaval. He explains that women's resilience accounts for their agency and survival in times of instability, adding, however, that there is a notable correspondence between the female characters' display of positive or negative emotions and readers' attitude towards the characters. Hence, positive emotions generate positive reactions from readers and vice versa. Toure deftly articulates Miano's artistic oeuvre on the philosophy of self-reliance and resilience through her strong women characters.

Trauma and its effects have become focal to contemporary global literature and criticism on war and violence. Incidentally, almost every chapter in *African Women Under Fire* touches on this theme, especially as it relates to women's experiences in war and armed conflicts, or as refugees. Pauline Ada Uwakweh's "Memoir versus Fiction: Narrating Trauma in Faith McDonnell and Grace Akallo's *Girl Soldier: A Story of Hope for Northern Uganda's Children* and Susan Minot's *Thirty Girls*" shares a unique perspective on the effect of genre on trauma narratives. How does genre impact the representation of traumatic experiences, especially when the narratives are based on same traumatic incident as the 1996 abduction of school girls by the Lord Resistance Army (L.R.A) in Aboke, Uganda? Arguing that genre complicates traumatic representations, Uwakweh asserts that a critical look into the genre effect offers enormous value for understanding the memoir, *Girl Soldier* (2007), and the fiction, *Thirty Girls* (2014) written by Susan Minot, a Westerner. Uwakweh argues that in the fiction, Minot employs western post-traumatic stress symptoms to portray traumatic conditions in her protagonist, thus raising questions about replicating Western clinical symptoms for trauma in a different cultural setting. There are striking correspondences between Minot's portrayal of traumatic conditions and those outlined in Judith Lewis Herman's (1992) *Trauma and Recovery*—her conceptual framework for detecting PTSD and recovery for traumatized victims. In addition, Uwakweh discusses possible determining motives for differences in levels of traumatic incidents narrated in the memoir and represented in the fiction. This exploration of intersections between genres and trauma call for more attention to testimonial and African trauma narratives, especially by ex–child soldiers, to the nature of gendered violence in captivity and post captivity, and most importantly, to traumatic outcomes, cultural stressors, and the recovery processes. She insists that the growing area of African trauma narratives certainly deserves a homegrown interpretive criteria of analysis.

Emilie Diouf's "'I Just Wanted to Forget It All. But It Was Impossible': Umutesi and the Politics of Testimony in *Surviving the Slaughter: The Or-*

deal of a Rwandan Refugee in Zaire," examines the intersections of gender, ethnicity, displacement, rights discourses in post-genocide Rwanda, while also engaging the subversive potential of testimonial narratives in human rights advocacy. According to Diouf, testimony is gendered and political, and it also offers a persuasive platform for African women to seek redress for human rights transgressions. In this light, testimonies of "unspeakable" acts become manifestations of African women's agency. Focusing on one Hutu woman's testimonial on the Rwandan genocide, Diouf asserts that moral, aesthetic, and ethical aspects of culture are integral to testimonial narratives, and notes the possibility of ideological manipulations through testimony. Very few narratives of trauma focus on "perpetrator" testimonies. Thus, Marie Beatrice Umutesi's (2004) *Surviving the Slaughter*, offers a unique shift from "victim" to "perpetrator" account of the traumatic repercussions of the Rwandan genocide. Diouf's chapter also evokes crucial questions surrounding the sociocultural and political contexts of reproduction, reception, and circulation of African women's trauma narratives, as well as the validity of contemporary theories of trauma and witnessing, for African testimonial narratives. Further, by juxtaposing, especially, Felman's and Laub's (1992), theory of testimony and witnessing based on the Holocaust, with the Rwandan context, Diouf establishes the weaknesses of trauma witnessing that excludes the sociocultural and political contexts which, she argues, are central to understanding the survivor's experience of trauma. Notably, Diouf explains in this chapter why Umutesi's testimonial represents ongoing revisionist agenda to the Rwandan archival memory.

Moussa Issifou's "Victims' Narratives versus Perpetrators Testimonies: Understanding Violence against Women in Armed Conflicts in Africa" is a significant unveiling of the reasons behind growing male aggression on women, not only in Africa, but also, globally. It enriches emerging perspectives and ongoing scholarship on trauma and the therapeutic effect of testifying, telling, narrating, or witnessing about experiences of violence. The perpetrator "testimony" has not received much attention. Few have sought to understand the motives behind male acts of violence against women beyond the facts of its ideological motives. Although testimonies of victims of rape abound, very little information exist of the perpetrators themselves. Evidently, victimized women's testimonies on rape in DRC, Rwanda, Sudan, to mention a few, have become indelible markers of Africa's wars, ethnic cleansing, and genocide. Is gender bias at play in this instance? Issifou's chapter calls for more inquiry into the gender question by his focus on a neglected aspect of testimony based on war's impact on men and its gendered implications. While Issifou takes up the issue of violence against women as a crime and transgression of human rights, he also asks key questions. What motivates perpetrators of sexual violence? What drives male aggression on women, especially in times of war? How do myths of masculinity intersect with violence in war and peace times? He argues that answers to these questions have enormous merit for stopping violence on women. Issifou's explanations are backed by evidence, and his juxtaposition of victims' and perpetrators' testimonies highlight the causes of violence and effects on the victims, simultaneously. His analysis is strengthened by the "voices" of both parties, as they *open up* on the reasons behind their acts of violence and the traumatic effects. In as much as these violent crimes against women seem to contradict traditional expectations of men who are socialized to protect women, Issifou, nonetheless, traces war violence on women to its gendered roots in traditional African societies. He argues, cogently, that appropriate responses to violence against women requires better comprehension of the perpetrators' motives for violence.

The subject of refugees and their legal protection has always been a task reserved for national and international organizations. In contemporary times, however, there is an ongoing global refugee explosion. The reasons are not far to seek—political and economic insecurity, natural hazards, and manmade hazards, are few major causes to be blamed. Remarkably, tragic occurrences around refugees have propelled new ways of assessing their testimonies in public discourse. In the introduction to her book, *Asylum Speakers: Caribbean Refugees and Testimonial Discourse,* April Ann Shemak (2011) deliberates on the power of testimony in determining the fate of refugees seeking protection in other nations. Noting that "testimonial narrative and human rights discourse (can) become inflected through the literary" (3), Shemak asserts that "language can become a site of either comfort and sanctuary or expulsion and alienation. Those seeking asylum must become eloquent, persuasive speakers despite the enormous obstacles that can hinder testimony: trauma, memory, cultural differences, translation, and political ideologies" (3). Testimonies, especially those of African refugee women seeking protection in other nations as a result of conflicts and wars have rarely come under the spotlight in African literary criticism. They have seldom been analyzed as part of refugee women's agency and coping mechanisms.

In her chapter, Nanjala Nyabola brings new insights on this issue as well as the challenges refugee women face. How much is a refugee's narrative worth? In "Testimony as Text: 'Performative Vulnerability' and the Limits of Legalistic Approaches to Refugee Protection," Nyabola argues that refugee narratives have rarely been scrutinized for their artistic and psychological implications as platform on which women process trauma while seeking protection as refugees. Observing that refugee women's survival agency lies in their use of "selective storytelling" for processing trauma and accessing protection, Nyabola proposes the concept of "performative vulnerability" as a literary and analytical framework for understanding the embedded "truth" in their stories. She makes the assertion that tools of literature can be applied in legal discourse to analyze refugee narratives. Further, Nyabola explains how narratives of women fleeing from conflicts can be used "to critique the legalistic approach" to their refugee status, while also informing on the survival strategies that women deploy as a means for accessing protection. Her succinct attention to the discourses of refugees, undoubtedly, defines an emerging critical pathway in the study of African war narratives.

Overall, *African Women Under Fire* engages old and new concepts in fresh and intellectually enriching ways. It recognizes that modern warfare and that of the future are being fought not only on battlefields and home fields (physical spaces), but also technologically and psychologically. Certainly, technology is redefining warfare through the media by its immediacy in reaching mass audiences. It is necessary to expand definitions of wars and conflicts to include abduction, forced sexual slavery, girl trafficking, and other atrocities that victimize the female. Even more urgent is the need for new readings of trauma that uncover traumatic aftermath of violence and rape in the female experience, in addition to the trauma arising from imposed motherhood, parenting a child of rape, and the stigmatization or ostracism that extends to the children born of rape. Also, women's language, rhetoric of resistance, and quest for change in their social conditions need deeper exploration.

Lastly, African writers and literary critics must, of necessity, continue to account for the changing political and economic terrain on the African continent and how emerging events facilitate new sources of conflicts and aggression toward women. Essentially, this book promises in one text, the full spectrum of the female, under fire in our unstable times. It brings invaluable insight and breadth to the growing research on women, war, and conflict in Africa. The aftermath of wars and conflicts initiates new forms of violence and related gender challenges, thus the chapters establish compelling evidence for the significance of gender in the analyses of contemporary warfare and conflict. Without a doubt, articulating war's consequences for women and children remains a major challenge for critics, policy makers, and human rights organizations. There is a need for deeper understanding of the new sources of violence and male aggression on women, the gendered challenges of reintegration in the aftermath, and most importantly, the future consequences of gendered violence for the African continent. *African Women Under Fire* is intended for scholars, researchers, instructors, students of literature in the humanities, women's studies, liberal studies, and African Studies at both undergraduate and graduate levels. It also offers interdisciplinary value, and general readers interested in literary representations of women's experience in war and conflict will find this book invaluable.

REFERENCES

Adichie, Chimamanda. 2006. *Half of a Yellow Sun*. New York: Anchor.

Agorde, Wisdom. 2008. Review of *Body, Sexuality, and Gender: Versions and Subversions in African Literatures I, Matatu 29–30,* by Flora Veit-Wild and Dirk Naguschewski. In *War in African Literature Today* 26, edited by Emenyonu Ernest et al. 166–68.
Akachi, Theodora. 2011. *Roses and Bullets.* Lagos, Nigeria: Jalaa Writers' Collective.
Bleasdale, Marcus 2011. "Violence Against Women: War's Overlooked Victims." January 13. Accessed July 2, 2014. http://www.economist.com/node/17900482.
Brittain, Victoria. 2002. "Women in War and Crisis Zones: One Key to Africa's Wars of Underdevelopment." Crisis States Programme. Development Research Center, DESTIN, LSE, London. 1–12. Accessed July 2, 2014. http://www.eprints.lse.ac.uk/28270.
Bryce, Jane. 1991. "Conflict and Contradiction in the Women's Writing on the Nigerian Civil War." *African Languages and Culture* 4 (1): 29–42.
Combres, Elizabeth. 2009. *Broken Memory: A Novel of Rwanda.* Translated by Shelley Tanaka. Toronto: Groundwood Books.
Cooper, Helene. 2009. *The House at Sugar Beach.* New York: Simon and Schuster.
Cubilie, Anne. 2005. *Women Witnessing Terror: Testimony and the Cultural Politics of Human Rights.* New York: Fordham University Press, 2005.
Djebbar, Assia. 2005. *Children of the New World: A Novel of the Algerian War.* Translated by Marjolijn de Jager. New York: Feminist Press.
Eaglestone, Robert. 2008. "You Would Not Add to My Suffering If You Knew What I Have Seen': Holocaust Testimony and Contemporary African Trauma Literature." *Studies in the Novel* 40 (1–2): 72–85.
Emecheta, Buchi. 1982. *Destination Biafra.* Portsmouth: Heinemann.
Emenyonu, Ernest. 2008. *"War in African Literature: Literary Harvests, Human Tragedies."* In *War in African Literature Today* 26, edited by Ernest Emenyonu et al. xi–xiv.
Felman, Shoshana and Laub, Dori. 1992. *Testimony: Crises of Witnessing in Literature, Psychoanalysis and History.* New York: Routledge.
Green, December. 1999. *Gender Violence in Africa: African Women's Responses.* New York: St. Martin's Press.
Green, Llezlie. 2002. "Sexual Violence and Genocide against Tutsi Women." *Race, Racism, and Law.* http://academic.udayton.edu/race/06hrights/georegions/africa/Rwanda01.htm.
Grotberg, Edith H. 2003. *Resilience for Today: Gaining Strength from Adversity.* Westport, CT: Praeger.
Guilbert, Kieran. 2016. "#BringBackOurGirls: 10 key facts", *Mail & Guardian Africa,* October 13, 2016. http://mgafrica.com/article/2016–10–13-bringbackourgirls-10-key-facts/. Accessed October 16.
Herman, Judith Lewis 1992/1997. *Trauma and Recovery: The Aftermath of Violence—From Domestic Abuse to Political Terror.* New York: Basic Books.
Honwana, Alcinda. 2011. *The Ethnography of Political Violence: Child Soldiers in Africa.* Philadelphia: University of Pennsylvania Press, ProQuest. Accessed June 30, 2016. http://site.ebrary.com.ncat.idm.oclc.org/lib/ncat/reader.action?docID=10491974.
Ikuomola, Adediran Daniel. 2012. "The Nigerian Civil War of 1967 and the Stigmatization of Children Born of Rape Victims in Edo State." In *Rape in Wartime,* edited by Raphaelle Branche and Fabrice Virgili. New York: Palgrave McMillan, 169–83. Accessed June 2014. http://www.palgrave.com/PDFs/9780230363991.
Jean-Charles, Regine Michelle. 2014. *Conflict Bodies: The Politics of Rape Representation in the Francophone Imaginary.* Columbus: The Ohio State University Press.
Kaufman, Joyce P. 2010. *Women and War: Gender Identity and Activism in Times of Conflict.* Sterling, VA: Kumarian Press.
Kyomuhendo, Goretti. 2007. *Waiting: A Novel of Uganda at War.* New York: The Feminist Press.
Macgoye, Marjorie Oludhe. 2000. *The Present Moment.* New York: Feminist Press.
Machiko, Oike. 2008. "Becoming a Feminist Writer: Representations of the Subaltern in Buchi Emecheta's *Destination Biafra.*" In *War in African Literature Today* 26, edited by Emenyonu Ernest et al. 60–70.

Marcotte, Amanda. 2014. "Officials in India Don't Seem too Bothered about the Gang Rape and Murder of Two Teenage Girls." June 2. Accessed July 2, 2014. http://www.slate.com/blogs/xx_factor/2014/06/02/teenage_girls_are_raped_and_murdered_in_india_and_an_official_responds_what.html.

McDonnell, Faith J. H. and Grace Akallo. 2007. *Girl Soldier: A Story of Hope for Northern Uganda's Children.* Grand Rapids, MI: Chosen Books.

Metz, Steven. 2000. "Armed Conflict in the 21st Century: The Information Revolution and Post Modern Warfare." Accessed September 22, 2016 http://www.strategicstudiesinstitute.army.mil.pdffiles/pub/226.pdf.

Miano, Lenora. 2010. *Dark Heart of the Night.* Translated by Tamsin Black. Lincoln: University of Nebraska Press.

———. 2013. *The Season of Shadow: A Novel.* Paris: Grasset.

Minot, Susan. 2014. *Thirty Girls.* New York: Knopf.

Nacro, Fanta Régina. 2004. *The Night of Truth (La Nuit de la vérité).* 100 min. Burkina Faso/France, distr. Global Filn Initiative, USA, Acrobates Film, France.

Njoku, Rose Adaure. 1986. *Withstand the Storm: War Memoirs of a Housewife.* Onitsha: Africana-FEP.

Norridge, Zoe. 2012. "Sex as Synecdoche: Intimate Languages of Violence in Chimamanda Ngozi Adichie's *Half of a Yellow Sun* and Aminatta Forna's *The Memory of Love*." *Research in African Literatures* vol. 43.2 (Summer): 18–39.

Nwahunanya, Chinyere. 1997. *A Harvest from Tragedy: Critical Perspectives on Nigerian Civil War Literature.* Owerri: Springfield Press.

Nwapa, Flora. 1992. *Never Again.* Trenton: Africa World Press.

Onwubiko, Pauline. 1988/2010. *Running for Cover.* Onitsha: Africana First Publishers.

Shemak, April. 2010. *Asylum Speakers: Caribbean Refugees and Testimonial Discourse.* New York: Fordham University Press. http://public.eblib.com/choice/publicfullrecord.aspx?p=3239540.

Smith, Charles, ed. 2008. *War and Conflict: Journal of African Literature*. Vol. 5.

Spleth, Janice. 2012. "Civil War and Woman's Place in Lenora Miano's *L'Interieur de la Nuit* (*Dark Heart of the Night*)." *RAL* 43.1: 89–100.

Staunton, Irene. 1990. *Mothers of the Revolution: The War Experience of Thirty Zimbabwean Women*. Bloomington: Indian University Press.

Tadjo, Veronique. 2000. *The Shadow of Imana: Travels in the Heart of Rwanda,* translated by Veronique Wakerley. Oxford: Heinemann, African Writers Series.

Tal, Kali. 1996. *Worlds of Hurt: Reading the Literatures of Trauma.* New York: Cambridge University Press.

Umutesi, Marie Beatrice. 2004. *Surviving the Slaughter: The Ordeal of a Rwandan Refugee in Zaire.* Translated by Julia Emerson. Madison: University of Wisconsin Press.

Uwakweh, Pauline Ada. 2012. "Reconstructing Masculinity and Femininity in African War Narratives: The Youth in Chimamanda Adichie's *Half of a Yellow Sun* and Goretti Kyomuhendo's *Waiting: A Novel of Uganda at War*." *Journal of African Literature Association (JALA)* 7.1: 82–106.

Veit-Wild, Flora and Naguschewski, Dirk. 2005. *Body, Sexuality, and Gender: Versions and Subversions in African Literatures I, Matatu* 29–30. Amsterdam: Rodopi.

Vera, Yvonne. 2004. *The Stone Virgins.* New York: Farrar, Straus & Giroux.

———. *Without a Name.* 2002. New York: Farrar, Straus & Giroux.

———. *Under the Tongue.* 2002. New York: Farrar, Straus & Giroux.

Volet, Jean-Marie. 2001. "Francophone Women Writing in 1998–1999 and Beyond: A Literary Feast in a Violent World." *RAL* 32.4: 187–200.

Zeleza, Paul T. 2008. "The Causes and Costs of War in Africa: From Liberation Struggles to the 'War on Terror.'" In *The Roots of African Conflicts: The Causes and Costs,* edited by Nhema Alfred G. and Paul Tiyambe Zeleza. Athens: Ohio University Press.

NOTES

1. Globally, violence on women continues to be the gendered scourge. To date, most of the 270 school girls abducted from Chibok by the terrorist group, Boko Haram, on April 14, 2014, have not been found. For information and update on this case, see for example, Kieran Guilbert, "#BringBackOurGirls: 10 key facts." October 13, 2016. http://mgafrica.com/article/2016-10-13-bringbackourgirls-10-key-facts/. Other incidents of gendered aggression have made headline news across the globe. For instance, in May 2014, immediately following the abductions in Nigeria, two teenage girls were gang raped and murdered in India. The inaction of the officials was as disturbing as the incident, itself, according to Amanda Marcotte in "Officials in India Don't Seem Too Bothered about the Gang Rape and Murder of Two Teenage Girl", *Slate Magazine*, June 2, 2014. http://www.slate.com/blogs/xx_factor/2014/06/02/teenage_girls_are_raped_and_murdered_in_india_and_an_official_responds_what.html.

2. The world has witnessed series of genocide involving "ethnic cleansing" warfare that target women. Examples include Dafur, Sudan (2003), Rwanda (1994), and Bosnia (1992–1995). For insight on strategies that aided and perpetuated sexual violence in the Rwandan Genocide (2002), see for example, Llezlie L. Green, "Sexual Violence and Genocide Against Tutsi Women." http://academic.udayton.edu/race/06hrights/georegions/africa/Rwanda01.htm.

3. See "Women in War and Crisis Zones: One Key to Africa's Wars of Underdevelopment." Working Paper No. 21. Crisis States Programme, Development Research Center, LSE, 2002. Ironically, and in contrast to the "large scale crime," the push to punish male aggressors in postwar/conflict societies and bring justice to victims is very slow. Notably, the first major summit to tackle this challenge was the "The Global Summit to End Sexual Violence in Conflict" which was held in London, June 10–13, 2014. Some goals of the Summit, included shattering the culture of impunity, supporting survivors, changing attitudes, and creating public awareness. See website—https://www.gov.uk/government/topical-events/sexual-violence-in-conflict/about.

4. See Marcus Bleasdale's (2011), "Violence against Women: Wars Overlooked Victims." As the culture of silence over rape is being gradually lifted, the enormity of the crime is also being exposed. According to Bleasdale, "As the reporting of rape has improved, the scale of the crime has become more horrifyingly apparent. . . . And with the Bosnian war of the 1990s came the widespread recognition that rape has been used systematically as a weapon of war and that it must be punished as an egregious crime. In 2008 the UN Security Council officially acknowledged that rape has been used as a tool of war. With these kinds of resolutions and global campaigns against rape in war, the world has become more sensitive." *The Economist.* July 13, 2011. http://www.economist.com/node/17900482.

5. Steven Metz, "Armed Conflict in the 21st Century: The Information Revolution and Post Modern Warfare," April 2000. This is a significant study on the changing nature of warfare and armed conflicts as defined by insurgency, technological, and psychological strategies used by state and non-state combatants. http://www.strategicstudiesinstitute.army.mil/pdffiles/pub226.pdf.

6. Significant work on gendered violence in war include Cubilié, Anne (2005) *Women Witnessing Terror: Testimony and the Cultural Politics of Human Rights*; Kali Tal (1996) *Worlds of Hurt: Reading the Literatures of Trauma*; Joyce Kaufman and Kristen P. Williams (2010) *Women and War: Gender Identity and Activism in Times of Conflict*.

7. Early attempts to retrieve and centralize those voices are exemplified by Irene Staunton's (1990) *Mothers of the Revolution*. The importance of feminist analysis in deconstructing biases in narratives of war and liberation struggles cannot be underestimated. In recent times, movies and documentaries add significant dimension to women's narratives on the war experience.

ONE

At the Center, Taking Charge

Disruptive Discourse and Female Agency in Buchi Emecheta's Destination Biafra *and Chimamanda Ngozi Adichie's* Half of a Yellow Sun

Jessie Sagawa

The Nigerian civil war lasted from 1966 to 1970 and has been the subject of several books, both historical and fictional (McLuckie 1987, 510). Buchi Emecheta's *Destination Biafra* was first published in 1982 and Chimamanda Ngozi Adichie's *Half of a Yellow Sun* was first published in 2006. Critics of *Half a Yellow Sun* have remarked on Adichie's debt to Chinua Achebe (VanZanten 2015, 86) but few have acknowledged a similar debt to Buchi Emecheta. Although the two books are separated by several years, they are strikingly similar. Both use allegory as a fictional technique to tell the story of the civil war, and both employ multiple perspectives filtered through different characters. What ties them together is that they unsettle patriarchy by disrupting its discourses of war and by using the female protagonists to explore gender and agency. Throughout the two novels, the authors tackle similar challenges but do so in ways that preserve the story's uniqueness.

Emecheta's *Destination Biafra* is an allegorical rendering of the story of the Nigerian civil war and the events immediately preceding it. It revolves around Debbie Ogedemgbe, an officer in the Nigerian army and the daughter of the finance minister who is assassinated during the first coup d'etat.[1] Emecheta chooses a protagonist who is not from Nigeria's three major ethnic groups: Hausa, Yoruba, or Igbo; Debbie is a member of the Itsekiri, a minority ethnic group. Emecheta's choice of protagonist is driven by the desire to inject a neutral and unifying voice into the conflict. Adams (2001) expresses a similar view when she states: "As a person who is not a member of any of the major tribes, Debbie is removed from the calls of ethnic nationalism that have split the country. Debbie's desire to see Biafra brought to fruition is thus not a desire to see the rise of an Igbo hegemony" (292).

From time to time, the narrative also loops to focus on the leaders of Biafra and Nigeria respectively, Chijioke and Sakah Momoh in real life, General Chukwuemeka Odumegwu Ojukwu and General Yakubu Gowon—who, in the fictional account, are also part of the original coup plotters. At times, the focus shifts onto Debbie's British boyfriend, Alan Grey, a metaphor for British interests and continued involvement, whose machinations are mainly responsible for the war. This revolving perspective has led one reviewer to claim that the novel has no perspective and to indict the novel for the use of what he terms "clumsy language" and an unclear message (Berner 1983, 160). Obioma Nnaemeka (1997a) concurs with Ernest Emenyonu (1991) that "the great Nigerian novel is yet to be written" (as cited in 1997a, 262). However, she does not echo Berner's negative assessment above: "I would not go so far as to say the result is awful" (240). A more robust endorsement comes from Ann Marie Adams (2001): "*Destination Biafra,* perhaps more than any other Anglophone work, attempts to redress the gendered bias of discourse on the war as well the "gender" of military warfare itself" (288). The title, *Destination Biafra,* does not refer to the geographic one located in the eastern part of Nigeria. It stands for an ideal nation where the state machinery will function smoothly unencumbered by the corruption and dysfunction already at work in the new state.

By contrast, Adichie situates her narrative among characters who are located outside the locus of power and among the Igbo intelligentsia. Set in Biafra, the omniscient narrative viewpoint of *Half of a Yellow Sun* oscillates mainly between Olanna, an Igbo woman lecturer at the University in Nsukka, and Ugwu, a young man who is employed as Odenigbo's housekeeper and cook. Although these two are at the centre, at times the narrative shifts to focus on Olanna's boyfriend, Odenigbo, her twin sister, Kainene, and Kainene's British boyfriend, Richard Churchill. This may be the reason why Hallsworth (2006) feels that *Half of a Yellow Sun* "does not merit the same extravagant praise as the first" (132). She finds that, "the story line is not as well developed as the setting and the characters fail to emerge fully" (132). Her conclusion: "Not as great as the sum of its parts" (132). In her review of the novel, White (2007) notes the use of twinning as a literary technique (10). In her opinion, Ugwu is paired with Odenigbo, Olanna with Kainene, and Richard with Madu. However, I believe that the Richard-Madu pairing works to some extent, but pairing Richard and Ugwu as authors is more persuasive. The title, *Half of a Yellow Sun* references the Biafran flag which symbolically represents the breakaway, short-lived nation of Biafra.

Patriarchy has fostered certain discourses about war. First, war is traditionally seen as a male domain. As Elshtain (1987) rightly points out, society has been socialized to believe that "Men fight as avatars of a nation's sanctioned violence. Women work and weep and sometimes protest within the frame of discursive practices that turn one out, militant mother and pacific protestor alike, as the collective "other" to the male warrior" (3–4). Elshtain asserts that women's attitudes to war are not identical: "We in the West are the heirs of a tradition that assumes an affinity between women and peace, men and war, a tradition that consists of culturally transmitted myths and memories" (4). She uses two Hegelian archetypes or personas to sketch the gendered dichotomy of how men and women relate to war:

> Just Warriors and Beautiful Souls. Man constructed as violent, whether eagerly and inevitably or reluctantly and tragically; woman as nonviolent offering succor and compassion: these tropes on the social identities of men and women, past and present do not denote what men and women are in time of war, but function instead to recreate and secure women's location as noncombatants and men's as warriors. (4)

Elshtain maintains that this view of war is flawed in that it does not reflect real life. It fails to reflect the diverse views of war present among men and women. Not all men are eager to go to war; by the same token, neither are all women pacific nurturers. Although she suggests that these ideas proliferate in the West, her observations apply just as fully to Nigeria, a former colony of Britain and whose writers have been educated in the same western tradition. In fact, Emecheta has lived in Britain since she was eighteen and Adichie divides her time between the United States and Nigeria (Anyadike 2008, 141). Indeed, in the novels, the two writers interrogate and disrupt the same discourse.

In *Destination Biafra*, some of the women are fully supportive of the war. After secession, Biafran women compose songs praising their leaders. Once they hear that women are allowed in the army, many of the women in Biafra go to enlist. By comparison fewer women in the rest of Nigeria are interested in enlisting (122). Later, after their town is overrun by soldiers, a group of women mobilize and create a community which they guard ferociously against soldiers. As their angry response to Biafran soldiers who are looking for recruits shows, they are caught in the crossfire: "Biafra, Biafra, what is Biafra? You killed our man, from this part, Nwokolo; the Nigerian soldiers came and killed what your soldiers left" (218). For these women, neither side is safe.

Similarly, bellicose tendencies are evident in Elizabeth, the wife of Nigeria's leader. She is passionate in her bitterness on the topic of Biafra. When her husband and Alan worry about the possible loss of life in

Biafra, she has no compassion. Her response is harsh, dismissive, and lacking in empathy. She blames it on the Igbo "Can't they see? Why should they support Abosi blindly like that? He doesn't even belong to their world. He is too rich, has too much education and belongs to too many international clubs" (189). Considering that she and her husband have amassed great wealth in a short time, her words are hypocritical. After her husband dismissively attributes her opinions to her pregnancy, she interrupts his and Alan's discussion with a comment that labels young Biafran lives as expendable: "those that die in Biafra are only babies Captain. Think of the sixteen- and seventeen-year-olds we Nigerian mothers are losing. Anyway, don't you know that those people breed like rats? They will soon replace their dead babies" (190). The callousness and irony of these words is especially striking, because she is expecting to give birth at any time.

"Any piece of written literature on the Nigerian Civil War, especially by writers from the Biafran side which does not embody the war songs which, at the time, were 'weapons' of the war stands to be regarded as an inauthentic representation of the truth of fiction" declares Nwachukwu-Agbada (1996, 525). Although his words are written in condemnation of Emecheta's *Destination Biafra* and in praise of Chukwuemeka Ike's *Sunset at Dawn*, they would be equally laudatory of *Half of a Yellow Sun* which includes a few songs as well as a verse from the Biafran anthem. Except for dissenters like Alice, support for Biafra's war efforts is strong among the women in *Half of a Yellow Sun*. Whenever Biafra is victorious, they compose and sing songs that predict victory for their nation (332). This is in keeping with Nwachukwu-Agbada's (1996) findings that Biafran war songs are used to mobilize support for the leader and soldiers and to condemn the enemy (525). In *Half of a Yellow Sun*, this commitment to the war effort is evident in that anyone who does not participate is written off as a "sabo" (saboteur), a despicable person. The Biafrans believe such people are undermining the cause or, worse, spying on behalf of the enemy. The reclusive Alice is considered a "sabo."

The treatment meted out to those suspected of such betrayal is demonstrated when two women refugees fleeing the war are confronted. They are pushed, spat on, jeered, and stoned to shouts of, "Sabo! God punish you! Sabo!" (377). Mama Oji suggests an even more draconian punishment that was known as "necklacing" during the South Africa's anti-apartheid struggle: "They should throw tyres round their necks and burn them . . . They should burn every single saboteur" (377). Considering that ordinarily, these citizens would not delight in this, war is indeed a dehumanizing factor. Later, one woman hears that the Biafran army has had some successes and her response is, "Our boys are showing them," the same pride that will be expressed when the Biafran side unleashes the dreaded *ogbunigwe* resulting in serious loss of life on the Nigerian side.

Contrary to patriarchal discourse which presents men as fearless and eager to march to war, most of the men in *Half of a Yellow Sun* do not measure up. Odenigbo and his future wife, Olanna, symbolize the role played by the intellectual elite in the build up to secession. As the war progresses, Odenigbo, is gradually reduced both in physique and standing. When Ugwu first meets Odenigbo, whom he insists on calling "Master," the latter is an imposing figure: "he filled the armchair, his thick hair that stood high on his head, his muscled arms his broad shoulders" (5). Olanna adores him, yet her twin sister pronounces: "You've never even accepted that the man is ugly" (388). He is an intellectual, yet he fails to recognize the country's descent into war. As the war continues, however, he is stripped of many of the attributes Olanna finds so attractive. Adept at theorizing and argumentation, he is not as pragmatic during wartime.

Odenigbo also lacks moral strength, and he betrays Olanna twice. First, through his mother's scheming, he betrays Olanna by sleeping with Amala, the girl his mother hand-picked to supplant Olanna, and getting her with child. After he is married to Olanna, he betrays her again with Alice, their next door neighbour. Grief emasculates him even more. Already disempowered by the war, his mother's death sends him into depression, and he is unable to deal with his loss and feelings of guilt. At the time when his family needs him most, he becomes an alcoholic. The gender roles are reversed with Olanna taking on the stronger role of comforter. He is the embodiment of abjection as she comes home and finds him seated on the bed, "his back hunched, his shoulders heaving silently" (330). She consoles, holds and supports him while he grieves (330–31). Adichie overturns societal gender roles and norms of manliness; she suggests a descent into childhood. This metonymic association between the grieving Odenigbo and a child is clinched by Olanna's feeling that his sobs are reminiscent of his daughter's, Baby (331). It is only after this crying session that he can resume his manly responsibilities and ultimately acknowledge her strength (392). This acknowledgment cements the notion that Olanna has grown in strength while he has been diminished.

Kainene's boyfriend, Richard, also evolves as the war progresses. Unlike *Destination Biafra's* Alan Grey, he has chosen to side with Biafra instead of manipulating both sides. Although he is presented positively most of the time, he does represent Britain's plundering of Biafra's as yet unrecognized cultural riches as he goes around the country writing about art, particularly roped baskets. His surname, Churchill, evoking that of Britain's wartime leader during World War II, conjures images of bravery on the battlefield. Yet he, like Odenigbo, is reduced in stature even as the narrative begins.

His affair with Kainene begins while he is already in a relationship of convenience with Susan, a British woman. Instead of sorting out things with her first, he secretly carries on with Kainene and only reveals the relationship when it suits him. This moral weakness appears to manifest itself in erectile dysfunction as he fails to make love to Kainene despite his being attracted to her. Later, when the relationship is established, this moral weakness will reappear as he betrays her with her closest relative: her twin. Indeed, from the metonymic associations he makes between Kainene and the roped pot, she seems to fascinate him, because he finds her exotic.[2] Indeed, one may argue, given his sexual problems at the onset, the pot excites him more than she does, hence his decision not to tell her how deeply it stirs him (62).

At the stylistic level, Richard appears to provide a foil for Adichie's disruption of gender discourse in *Half of a Yellow Sun.* As the war progresses, he does not emulate the historical Churchill. Instead, like Odenigbo, Richard is further diminished in stature. After witnessing the massacre of Igbos at the airport in Kano, he wets his pants and vomits (63). Later, at Susan's house, he cries while her equanimity implies this is not news to her. Further, after Biafra's secession is announced, he trembles, while Kainene is stoic. Later, her disappearance initially reduces him to tears, not action. Through this, Adichie shows that, contrary to society's belief, gender does not determine character.

Despite this unattractive dimension, there are redeemable qualities in Richard. Unlike *Destination Biafra*'s Alan Grey, Richard evolves. As Anyadike (2008) notes, he "undergoes the full processes of wooing and genuinely feeling the anxieties and jealousies of falling in love before he happily gets engaged to a cynical Nigerian girl, Kainene" (143) He changes from an expatriate who is only there to exploit Igbo-Ukwu art, to someone who considers himself a Biafran. As has been pointed out, his decision to abandon his manuscript about the war and encourage Ugwu to write instead is an acknowledgment that the story is best told by native Biafrans (143). He also matures: by the end of the war, he can chronicle the atrocities being committed without breaking down. Anyadike sees the positive portrayal of Richard as potential for more interaction between Nigerians and Britons (147). I believe that an even greater possibility exists. The inference here is that a new, renegotiated, and mutually beneficial relationship with a Britain that is willing to acknowledge the humanity and sovereignty of a reunited Nigeria is possible.

Some women in the novel make a direct connection between serving in the army and male prowess. After Mama Oji's husband deserts the army, she frequently berates and questions his manliness: "You castrated sheep! You call yourself a man, and yet you deserted the army!" (327–28). She also threatens to report him to the soldiers. In her eyes, and in those of the society, his actions are inconsistent with patriotism and society's standards of manliness. She equally has no problems scolding and exposing Pastor Ambrose, a lay man who has assumed the role of a clergyman to avoid being conscripted. She contemptuously refers to his prayers as "babbling" and tells him to go and enlist (337). For her, participating in the war effort supersedes everything.

That certain women may desire a more active role in war is not even entertained by patriarchal discourses of war. Despite having pasts in which women actively participated in military activity, as well as in the fight for independence, many African countries are only starting to recruit women as soldiers.[3] Buchi Emecheta is ahead of her time when she introduces women with military careers: the female protagonist in *Destination Biafra*, Debbie Ogedemgbe, and her friend, Babs Teteku. In choosing to make her protagonist an army officer at a time when women in combat were mostly unheard of, Emecheta's decision disrupts the normative discourse that sees women as simply passive participants in war. Ogunyemi (1996) rightly terms her choice "subversive" (57). Even Debbie admits that her decision is unconventional. She is the first to acknowledge that her situation will be complicated by her social status and gender. The reaction to her decision only confirms her fears: it ranges from outright dismissal to derisive laughter. She is either dismissed or viewed as a sex symbol. Abosi, her childhood friend and an army officer, sees her more as a sex symbol than as a potential soldier: "You would certainly add glamour to our regiment" (55). Her British boyfriend, Alan Grey, is not supportive either: he suggests that she should focus on peacemaking. Later, when the war begins, she has no option but to engage in peacemaking.

Her experience of life as a soldier is riddled with humiliation. As a Nigerian soldier, she should enjoy the same privileges as her male colleagues. However, her status is negated even as she is entrusted with the mission of dissuading Abosi from seceding. She is not advised to use her intellect, Momoh wants her to "use her feminine wiles" (118). Her uniform does not protect her from humiliations that other women undergo, in fact, at times it subjects her to more. Salihu Lawal, the soldier who drives her to the meeting where she receives her assignment, does not see her as a fellow soldier; in his eyes she is "nothing but a woman, an ordinary woman" (167). Her humiliation stems from his desire to reinforce what he sees as her inferiority by virtue of her gender; the men she has to deal with are still stuck in patriarchal discourse that sees woman as other. Not surprisingly, both her missions as soldier and envoy fail: even as she pleads with Abosi to put the people's interests before his pride, he constantly reiterates that she is a woman (227–28). By implication, whatever she recommends is suspect, not on its merits, but because of her gender. Fascinatingly, Adichie, writing over twenty years later, is seemingly silent on the topic of women in combat. Seemingly is the right word, because she briefly touches on it through the characterization of Phyllis Okafor. She invites Richard to attend a talk by Ojukwu who has come to seek support for secession. Ojukwu whips the group he is addressing into a frenzy as they demand arms to defend their homeland.

When Richard looks around, he realizes that Phyllis is one of the people with hand raised demanding guns from Ojukwu. Given the involvement of women in nontraditional areas, it is surprising that Phyllis' character is not developed. Adichie's decision may stem from a desire to anchor her characterization in the general social conditions obtaining at that time.

In *On Violence,* Hannah Arendt (1969) distinguishes between power and violence but concedes, "Power and violence, though they are distinct phenomena, usually appear together" (52). Since war is an exercise in power and powerlessness, it is not surprising that violence against women emerges as a major theme in both novels. In her book, *Women and War,* Vickers (1993) observes, "rape, torture and killing are not the only horrors suffered by women in times of conflict. Most women's experience of war is not as combatants or activists, but as civilians caught in the crossfire" (23–24). Traditionally, such violence is presupposed to occur between men on one side of the conflict and women on the opposing side. Emecheta and Adichie disrupt this notion in their handling of the topic.

In *Destination Biafra,* the spectre of violence against women appears at the onset of the first coup. Samuel Ogedemgbe, the finance minister has been subdued, but his wife is being ordered to undress for a soldier's amusement. Although he is eventually stopped by his superior, this does not stop the other soldiers from fondling her daughter and their colleague, Debbie (61). That being a soldier does not shield her is a harbinger of the atrocities to come. Intriguingly, having experienced the brutality of the soldiers on a familial and personal level, an armed Debbie has no second thoughts about brutalizing others. Through this incident, Emecheta indicts the process by which people are turned into soldiers as too dehumanizing. A soldier who has been brutalized cannot act humanely.

After the first coup, suspicions that corrupt Igbo politicians were spared while those from other regions were not, fuel hatred and attacks against Igbos. In a country riven by ethnic cliques, this unwittingly becomes evidence of Igbo hegemonic ambitions. Citizens who had no input on the decision to go to war become scapegoats. For the women, gender becomes a signifier for sexual violence. The owner of the Yankee Bar, Area Mama, is stripped naked, dragged, and has her feet torn in different directions (82–83). Another woman, Regina, is unable to escape with her boyfriend and is hacked into pieces. Ugoji, her boyfriend, escapes and eventually reaches the railway station. He finds that Igbo women returning to the East have been mutilated: "Nearly all the women were without one breast. The very old ones had only one eye each" (84). The choice of organs for mutilation is deliberate: the young women's breasts are targeted as a way of reducing their sexual attractiveness and their potential to produce and nurture more Biafran soldiers. Although they are not so labelled, these mutilations are forerunners of ethnic cleansing. As Debbie and her mother travel to their home in the midwest, there is an act of ethnic cleansing. Their group is attacked by Nigerian soldiers who haul a pregnant woman into the bush, where she is possibly raped and then mutilated. According to the survivors, the soldiers disembowelled her and killed her unborn child saying, "Who knows, he might live to be another Abosi'" (128). This is an act of ethnic cleansing, because by targeting a fetus, they are threatening the perpetuation of Igbo ethnicity.

Violence against women crops up in *Half of a Yellow Sun* as well. Olanna's uncle lives in the North with his family. Her cousin, Arize, is with child and almost due. When the attacks begin, most of the family is killed. Olanna, who was visiting, escapes with Mohammed's help, only to encounter psychic trauma on the train. A woman carrying a calabash which Olanna caresses in awe invites her to look inside where horror awaits: "She saw the little girl's head with the ashy-grey skin and the plaited hair and rolled-back eyes and open mouth" (149). Obviously the violence is not restricted to women, it extends to little girls, too. Olanna has not been physically harmed, but she has suffered psychic damage. When she returns to Nsukka, she is subject to blackouts and is bedridden for a long time.

Rape is violence against women, but it is discussed separately, because it warrants its own space. Since time immemorial, this crime has been used as a military strategy. In her December 8 article, Smith-Spark (2004) maintains that rape has been justified as "the spoils of war" or as "something that is inevitable when men are deprived of female companionship for prolonged periods" ("How"). Indeed, as early as eighth century BC, the Roman historian Livy recounts how, having failed to convince his neighbors to consent to marry off their daughters to the youths from his city state, Romulus invited the neighboring city states to a celebration in honor of some god and, during the ceremony, his men grabbed the women. Reportedly, Romulus visited the women the next morning and blamed the whole incident on their fathers, arguing that the whole issue would have been avoided had their fathers complied. He further assured them:

> Now they would have the status of wives with all the material rewards and civil rights of citizenship and they would have children, than which nothing is dearer. They should cool their anger and give their hearts to the men who had already taken their bodies. A good relationship often begins with an offence, he said. (Livy, as cited in Leftkowitz and Fant 2006, 177–78)

As outrageous as Romulus' words sound, in some respects history appears to repeat itself. In 2014, the terrorist group Boko Haram committed a similar outrage on the young women of Chibok, Nigeria. To date, their parents' pleas for their safe return and the worldwide condemnation of this crime have been ignored. The terrorists' declaration that the young women will become wives for members of the group makes them vulnerable to a crime against humanity: rape (Smith 2015). Sadly, in this June

29, 2015 post, Dominic Smith cites evidence that rape (this) and worse has happened. As reported, "Captives are subjected to rape, torture, forced marriage and religious conversion" (*The Guardian*, 2015).

According to Andrew Osborn's February 28, 2001 article, rape was included in the general category of crimes against humanity in trials during the Second World War but was only recognized as a separate war crime in 2001. Finally, in 2008 the United Nations passed resolution 180 declaring rape a weapon of war. The implications for perpetrators and victims are enormous in that perpetrators and those who abet them can be held to account. In its statement on rape, the Global Justice Centre considers it "the most powerful, cost-effective weapon available for destroying the lives of "enemy" women, families, and entire communities; demoralizing enemy force; and, in some cases, accomplishing genocide" ("How the Laws"). The Global Centre also notes that "no state has ever been held accountable for the use of rape as a prohibited weapon of war" ("How the Laws"). However with leaders of countries and individuals being held responsible for crimes of rape at the International Criminal Court (ICC), there is cause for optimism.

Obioma Nnaemeka (1997a) sees a difference between the way that male and female authors depict rape. She maintains that the former "focus on consensual sex and raise moral questions about the promiscuity of girls during the war, women writers foreground painful and graphic depictions of sexual violence and rape as a weapon of war" (255). Emecheta and Adichie tackle the issue of wartime rape and in doing so they disrupt patriarchy's commonly held notions about it. Their depictions suggest that rape is more about power and control than anything else, and part of that control is using rape as punishment.

In *Destination Biafra,* the protagonist, Debbie, and the women travelling with her are attacked, because two men travelling with them are overheard hailing Biafra. Identifying herself as part of the Nigerian army angers her attackers, but turning her gun on them inflames them more. She is aware that her rape is a form of punishment for breaching the gender divide. After she surrenders the gun, they quickly take advantage of her perceived powerlessness. After she hears her mother being slapped, Debbie kicks one of the soldiers holding her; they retaliate by gang-raping her. Emecheta (1982) ensures that readers see the rape from the victim's point of view, not the perpetrator's: "She could make out the figure of the leader referred to as Bale on top of her, then she knew it was somebody else, then another person. . . . She felt herself bleeding, though her head was still clear. Pain shot all over her body like arrows" (122). Thereafter, she loses consciousness and only regains it the next day. In spite of her mother's support, the physical pain and trauma last longer.

Through the second rape, Emecheta debunks the spoils-of-war notion of rape. After the lorry they are travelling in is ambushed by Nigerian soldiers, it becomes evident that revenge is behind their decision to rape the women. After all the men travelling with them are shot, they are ethnically slurred as "Yarmirin Igbo bastards" (163). As far as the soldiers are concerned, the women are just an extension of their men. Raping the women is tantamount to defeating and emasculating their men. This echoes Stimpson's (1989) view that "Men rape what other men possess" (78). However, the officer who rapes Debbie knows that she is a colleague travelling to the East on government business. That does not deter him from ordering his soldiers to send her to him. Once she is in his presence, his words show that he resents her, because her boyfriend is white, "You are still his plaything then, are you? You are all saboteurs, selling our country to the foreign powers" (166). He rapes her violently and, when he is done, he slaps her for being "dry as the desert and as unappetizing as a great-great grandmother" (167). However, once she reveals that she has also been raped by the other soldiers, he expresses his distress by invoking the name of his God, "Allah, Allah." He feels no remorse, just dismay that he has scavenged on other men's leftovers.

Later in the novel, the Irish nuns who have been tending to refugees are also raped and killed indiscriminately. In this instance, Adams (2001) succinct observation says it better, "In this work, rape is not used as a metaphor to depict how one side/interest/country is harming another; rather, it is seen as a horrifying yet common occurrence in warfare. Both Federal and Biafran sources are guilty" (295). Emecheta shows that the effects of rape extend beyond the mental and physical pain, Debbie is further victimized by her boyfriend's rejection, but she and the women will carry these physical and psychic traumas beyond the war, if not for ever.

Rape in *Half of a Yellow Sun* also debunks the notion that in war only women on the opposing side are endangered. After Ugwu is conscripted into the Biafran army, he joins his fellow soldiers on a trip to a tavern to celebrate some of their victories. Although the young woman who serves them is Biafran too, she is raped. As in Emecheta's *Destination Biafra,* Adichie's (2006) account of the rape is very graphic:

> The bar girl was on her back on the floor, her wrapper bunched up at her waist her shoulders held down by a soldier, her legs wide, wide ajar. She was sobbing, 'Please, please, *biko.*' Her blouse was still on. Between her legs, High-tech was moving. His thrusts were jerky, his small buttocks darker coloured than his legs. The soldiers were cheering. (365)

Ugwu's initial reluctance to participate disappears once the others challenge his manliness. He joins, undeterred by her dryness and tension, which signify her unwillingness. The hatred he sees in her eyes and his guilt only haunt him afterwards. If he does not fully appreciate the enormity of his actions, he will at the karmic moment when he learns that not only has his sister been violated through a gang rape by five soldiers, she has also been severely beaten and disfigured (421). These rapes do not only symbolize the violation of these women, but also, they are an abomination (Nnaemeka 1997a, 256), a violation of the realm of the earth goddess, Ani. In retribution, the earth refuses to yield provisions, thus plunging the fictional Biafra into famine and defeat.

If the two authors disrupt patriarchal discourses of war, they are just as disruptive when it comes to women's agency. There has been plenty of discussion around female agency. Traditionally, western feminists have seen agency as embodying "choice, empowerment, and voice." The issue of voice, or the power to speak out against oppression, has been problematic for feminists, because some equate voicelessness with powerlessness. Proponents of this position believe that without voice, women gcannot have agency. However, non-Western feminists have rightly expressed concern that a too rigid definition neglects some women whose contexts may exclude some of these elements. Noting that some women have participated in struggle only to have their voices overwhelmed by their more vocal male compatriots, Gayatri Chakravorty Spivak (2010 Appendix) worries that, "[I]f, in the context of colonial production, the subaltern has no history, and cannot speak, the subaltern as female is even more deeply in shadow" (257).

Her thinking is echoed by other scholars who argue that sometimes there is power in some forms of silence. For example, Sagawa and Robbins assert that although slaves were denied voice by laws that prevented them from writing, Mary Prince influenced the abolition of slavery by dictating her story to an amanuensis (2011, 8–9). Furthermore, DoVeanna Fulton (2006) maintains that Black women resorted to orality as a way of combatting voicelessness. This resonates with Angela Davis' (1999) claims that blues were used in African-American society for similar purposes. Renowned theorist, Obioma Nnaemeka (1997a, 1997b) warns that it is advisable to distinguish between "to be silent" and "to be silenced" (4). In other words, there is a significant difference between choice, as connoted by the former, and compulsion as implied by the latter.[4] This may explain why more recent definitions do not include voice. For instance, Ahearn (2001) defines agency as "the socio-culturally mediated capacity to act" (112), and Isaacs (2002) explains feminist agency as "women's ability to be effective agents against their own oppression" (129). In other words, and considering these perspectives, feminist agency needs to be fluidly constituted to accommodate the varied contexts and realities for women.[5]

The need for this fluidity is apparent when it comes to women in African literature. Several critics have looked at the characterization of women in writings by male and female authors. Many have noted that in early writing by men, women are presented as lacking agency. Critic after critic has noted that women are generally presented in caricature or in subordinate roles that consign them to the margins of narrative.[6] The same critics and others concede that there have been improvements in portrayal with the passage of time. When it comes to women writers, however, there is agreement that women writers have generally been more realistic in their depictions.[7] In her introduction to the second part of the influential *Ngambika: Studies of Women in African Literature,* Graves (Davies and Graves 1986) highlights that papers in that section focus on the African woman "Functioning as her own spokesperson and agent" (115).

The women in *Destination Biafra* and *Half of a Yellow Sun* face many challenges, but ultimately, this results in their finding ways to address and overcome the challenges. In *Destination Biafra,* one of the issues that Emecheta explores is denial of agency through the act of rape. As the discussion above has shown, Debbie is raped more than once. This can be physically and psychically debilitating. As Jean-Charles (2014) explains, "the act of rape compromises or, more accurately, snatches power from the individual in ways that are both physical and psychological" (39). Ordinarily, the experience would traumatize anyone, and Debbie is no exception. She is traumatized by the incidents, but they fail to deter her from fulfilling her mission. Although she fails to dissuade Abosi from seceding, her arrival in Biafra is a success. She has refused to surrender her agency to the rapists. She not only succeeds in arriving in Biafra, but also acts as an envoy tasked with seeking aid in Britain on behalf of Biafra.

Because patriarchy views women who display agency as threatening, some wives suppress their agency in order to appear submissive to their husbands. The wives of the old politicians exemplify this suppressed agency. While their husbands are in office, the women focus on fulfilling their role as wives. They are presented as women who simply exist to tend to their families, particularly their husbands. Their autonomy is suppressed in the interests of the family. With the coming of war, these women respond to challenges in ways that reveal that they have had agency all along.

Stella, Debbie's mother in *Destination Biafra,* is initially portrayed as a shallow woman who is obsessed with superficial issues; this view is highlighted by Mrs. Teteku's envious concession that her friend was, "the best dressed wife of the whole lot." (15). Alan, Debbie's boyfriend, confirms Stella's fixation on mindless conspicuous consumption when he says, "She swept the streets of London with her trails of velvet" (13). Her appearance is described as immaculate. Although she is an astute businesswoman operating an alcohol importation business, she is totally eclipsed by a husband whose primary concern is his economic well-being. She only runs the business with his control and approval. However, the day that he is abducted and killed marks the beginning of the outward manifestation of her agency: she resists the soldier's attempt to undress her (60). Debbie, who has internalised the view that Stella is a powerless and helpless woman, believes that she will have to look after her, henceforth. However, the roles are reversed on the road: it is Stella who stands up to the soldiers and tries to prevent her daughter's rape by offering herself as a replacement. Although she fails to save her daughter, she comforts Debbie after the gang rape. She is also the one who speaks out in an effort to obtain justice for her daughter, and stops only after Debbie convinces her that the effort is futile. Eventually, once she arrives and settles in her hometown, she initiates commerce, supplying goods to her besieged friends in Biafra. Although her actions do not rise to the level of Harriet Tubman's operation of the Underground Railroad, she assists those who seek to escape the siege in Biafra.

Her friend, Rosita, Mrs. Ozimba, is another seemingly disempowered wife. An unsung political analyst, she has strong opinions about the political situation; in fact, she astutely sees the flaws in the political choices that are being made, "I can see no peace in this country with this kind of treachery" (23). Her husband dismisses her observations although his assistant finds them insightful. The husband implies she is out of her depth when, in reality, he is the one who has miscalculated. He opts to side with Biafra after secession even when his wife, who sees beyond the hypocrisy in their leader, Abosi, suggests they leave. He overrules her and scolds her for being disloyal. Rather than engage in arguments, her response signals the outward exercise of her agency and the beginning of resistance. Her thoughts indicate that, unlike her husband, she has no faith in Biafra. Although she is silent, her thoughts are those of a woman who has felt silenced in the marriage but will be silent no longer: "As she looked at her husband, fury swelled her throat, making her look momentarily as ugly as a toad. Many, many things which she would have liked to tell this man forced themselves back into her belly like a lump of vomit that would not come out" (215). No longer ceding authority to the husband on all issues, she secretly arranges for their sons to be smuggled out of Biafra and sent to safety in England. Ultimately, when he finally realizes that the leader he has trusted plans to kill him, Ozimba acknowledges that his wife was more politically astute and has been right all along. She successfully arranges their escape and safe passage to England. That he willingly entrusts all arrangements to her suggests that he is finally recognizing her abilities.

Income generation is one way that women can exercise agency. Mrs. Eze, a politician's wife too, decides to reduce her reliance on her husband. Having also lost faith in Biafra and looking for a way out, she agrees to Stella Ogedemgbe's proposal that they start trading. That she is similarly constrained is evident from their decision to do so, secretly. However, the wisdom in their actions is clear from their husbands' mutual admission—albeit not to the wives—that the wives made the correct decision. It is this newfound confidence in her ability that enables Dr. Eze to entrust her with smuggling their family, as well as two orphaned boys, out of Biafra

(216). His decision is an acknowledgement of, and confidence in, her ability to make the best decisions for the family.

It is not the politicians' wives alone who display agency in their actions. The war has overturned normative gender roles. Women are now assuming responsibilities that would ordinarily be the territory of men. They are digging graves and burying the dead, building shelters and protecting their families. In dedicating *Destination Biafra* not only to her nieces, Buchi and Ndidi Emecheta who died of starvation, but also to women and children from Ibuza who perished in a fire at Nkpotu Ukpe, Emecheta acknowledges the weight of responsibility that women contend with in wartime. They are not only responsible for saving themselves, but also their children: in some instances, this may reduce chances of survival for both.

Half of a Yellow Sun also addresses issues of agency. Olanna and her twin sister already have agency. Highly educated and very accomplished in education and business, respectively, their views on marriage are unconventional. Having resisted their parents' efforts to use them to secure political favours, Olanna starts living with Odenigbo before they marry and Kainene opts for cohabitation. With the start of the war, they, as well as the women in their community, become more adept at negotiating and coping with the challenges presented by their changed circumstances. For Olanna, one of those is empowering students whose studies have been interrupted by ensuring them continuity in learning (291). With only Ugwu and Mrs Muokelu helping, the school is understaffed and lacking resources, but this does not deter her. Even when Mrs. Muokelu's domestic situation forces her to leave and start a trade, Olanna continues to run the school with the assistance of Ugwu only.

In addition to running the school, Olanna learns to make soap. After Mrs. Muokelu insults Olanna by comparing her sister to a prostitute, the relationship between them is strained. To make amends, Mrs. Muokelu teaches Olanna how to make soap using the locally available ingredients of palm oil and ash. Although an initially unimpressed and dismissive Olanna sees it as an attempt to curry favour, over time, she begins to appreciate the knowledge. In a country where access to imported resources is fast disappearing, knowing how to make soap will help.

She also learns to provide for her family. At the onset of their reaction, Odenigbo's mother is very hostile to Olanna. Although Olanna has been very nice to her, his mother slaps her and accuses her of having been wet-nursed and raised by nannies. The implication here is that having not been raised traditionally, Olanna will not make a capable wife for her son. That accusation is proved wrong with the beginning of the war. Although she has never had to forage for food, Olanna becomes a very determined provider for her family. She not only stands in food lines, but also, she fights to keep scant rations when others try to take them from her.

Agency can be individual or collective. Collective agency can be exercised on behalf of members of a group or for others who are not in a position to exercise their own. In *Half of a Yellow Sun*, when Igbos are being forcibly repatriated to their homeland in the East, the university women's association organizes food donations for the refugees (158). With women's intuition, they realize that food will be a challenge. They organize food donations for the refugees (158). As the prospect for war becomes more likely, they organize a seminar to share tips on how to cope during wartime. Furthermore, once the war begins, Olanna joins the village women to help with sewing clothing and accessories for the soldiers (185). By contrast, the men are doing little to prepare.

Kainene also goes through a transformative process. As a hard working businesswoman, her focus has been on personal success. However, during the war her energies are directed towards working with those displaced by the war. She exercises resistant feminist agency after she discovers that one of the priests she has been working with has been sexually exploiting the girls and has got one of them with child. She physically confronts him, pushing at his chest and shoving him. She also reprimands his fellow priest for not intervening and expels them both (398). Her actions are revolutionary, especially, because she is challenging priests, men in whom heavenly authority is believed to be vested. For the women, the battlefront is not only on the field but even in the temporary places that are supposed to offer refuge. The enemy is not only their Nigerian foe but also their Igbo compatriots. The church, the last refuge for the displaced and disempowered, has become as dangerous as the soldiers. This attests to war's capacity to bring out the worst in people and to distort structures that normally operate for the good of those deemed the most powerless.

Although patriarchy glosses over the role of women in wartime, *Half a Yellow Sun* suggests that they can be agents in initiating peacemaking. While the men are fighting, the women engage in trade across enemy lines, or what they call *afia attack*. *Afia attack* has a lot of potential for peacemaking, because the women interact as trading partners, not enemies. Kainene's decision to engage in it is an instance of resistant agency. As it gets progressively harder to find provisions, she decides to engage in cross-border trading and hopes to find a market for crafts that are made at the refugee camp. Underlining the danger, Odenigbo reminds her that she will be trading with the enemy and can be shot. Her blunt response not only corrects him but also asserts a different outlook, a reassessment of the war itself and an attempt to right what the men have destroyed: "I am trading with illiterate Nigerian women who have what we need" (403). Her failure to return does not indicate a failure in agency; it is allegorical. In her convincing analysis of the characters, White (2007) has rightly taken Olanna and Kainene as metaphors for Nigeria and Biafra. The evidence is persuasive. As twins, they are seemingly one, yet they are very different in build and in looks. While Olanna is curvaceous, her sister is more androgynous. Both are very independent, as attested by their attitudes towards marriage. Kainene thinks Olanna is the beautiful one but feels that they are both commodities, namely meat (59). Although she sees herself as the ugly sister, it is her beautiful sister who trespasses on her relationship with Richard. I read this trespassing as an allegorical comment on the wartime Nigerian government's decision to partition the country in a way that wrests control over oil out of Igbo hands. If so, her disappearance by the end of the narrative mirrors the disappearance of the state of Biafra as the secessionists surrender.

This chapter has examined how two Nigerian women writers have disrupted the patriarchal discourses and stereotypes of war that have been passed down to society over the ages. They have shown that contrary to conventional beliefs, not all men are eager to go to war, and that some are unwilling to take up arms. They have also demonstrated that not all women are pacifists reduced to looking after the home and nurturing the family. They also confirm that some women are bellicose, whether it is wanting to join the army as soldiers as in the case of *Destination Biafra*'s Debbie Ogedemgbe and Babs Teteku, or *Half a Yellow Sun*'s Phyllis Okafor, or whether it is supporting the leaders and soldiers during wartime in both novels. Their writings also prove that in issues of war, women are not always the passive participants they are assumed to be.

These are not the only issues the writers tackle. The novels have shown that wartime violence is gendered and that women are singled out for specific types of violence. They are either killed or spared with mutilations or trauma. Regarding wartime rape, the writers have disrupted some prevailing discourses. First, they have debunked the idea that women are raped only as spoils of war by showing that rapist soldiers do not target women on the enemy side only, even those on their side are at risk. They have also shown that rape is an issue of exerting power and control, especially on women who are seen as a threat to the prevailing gender relations.

The writers also address the issue of female agency in wartime. They have revealed that sometimes agency can be suppressed or overt, individual or collective. In each novel, women reveal hidden capacities to confront oppressive conditions. Whether it is the affluent politicians' wives in *Destination Biafra* revealing their hitherto hidden capacity to address and successfully overcome challenges, women digging graves to bury the dead, or women trying to cross into Biafra with children but without husbands, women are rising to the challenge. The same is true for *Half of a Yellow Sun* which also reveals female agency as women rearrange their priorities to address issues arising from upheavals caused by the war. Olanna learns to make her own soap using local materials. She becomes the bulwark against which her family, especially her husband, leans for support. She proves her mother-in-law wrong by providing nurture for her family and also participates in community renewal and support. Her twin is just as empowered, helping refugees and engaging in cross border commerce.

REFERENCES

Adams, Ann Marie. 2001. "It's a Woman's War: Engendering Conflict in Buchi Emecheta's *Destination Biafra*." *Callaloo*. 24.1: 287–300.

Adichie, Chimamanda Ngozi, 2006. *Half of A Yellow Sun*. London: Harper Perennial.

Ahearn, Laura M. 2001. "Language and Agency." *Annual Review of Anthropology*. 30.1: 109–37.

Anyadike, Chima. 2008. "The Global North in *Achebe's Arrow of God* and Adichie's *Half of a Yellow Sun*." *The Global South*. 2.2: 139–49.

Arendt, Hannah. 1969. *On Violence*. New York: Harcourt Brace.

Banyiwa-Horne Naana. 1986. "African Womanhood: the Contrasting Perspectives of Flora Nwapa's *Efuru* and Elechi Amadi's *The Concubine*." In *Ngambika*: *Studies of Women in African Literature,* edited by Carol Boyce-Davies and Anne Adams Graves, 119–29. Trenton, NJ: Africa World Press.

Berner, Robert L. 1983. "Nigeria." Review of *Destination Biafra* by Buchi Emecheta. *World Literature Today*. 57.1: 160.

Davies, Carole Boyce and Anne Adams Graves. Ed. 1986. *Ngambika: Studies of Women in African Literature,* Trenton, NJ: Africa World Press.

Davis, Angela Y. 1999. *Blues Legacies and Black Feminism*. New York: Vintage Books.

Elshtain, Jean Bethke. 1987. *Women and War*. New York: Basic Books Inc.

Emecheta, Buchi. *Destination Biafra*. 1982. Oxford: Heinemann Educational Books.

Emenyonu, Ernest. 1991. "The Nigerian Civil War and the Nigerian Novel: The Writer as Historical Witness." in *Studies on the Nigerian Novel,* edited by Ernest Emenyonu, 89–105. Ibadan: Heinemann.

Fubara, Angela M. 2012. "Metamorphosing Female Characters in Select Achebe's Novels: Women as Signposts." In *Achebe's Women: Imagism and Power*, edited by Helen Chukwuma, 101–10. Trenton, NJ: Africa World Press.

Fulton, DoVeanna S. 2006. *Speaking Power: Black Feminist Orality in Women's Narratives of Slavery*. New York: State University of New York.

Global Justice Centre. "How the Laws of War Fail Women: The Inexcusable Failure to Hold States Accountable For the Use of Rape as an Unlawful Weapon and Tactic of War." Web.

Hallsworth, Caroline. 2006. "Half of a Yellow Sun." Review of *Half of a Yellow Sun* by Chimamanda Ngozi Adichie. *Library Journal*. 131.14: 132.

Isaacs, Tracy. 2002. "Feminism and Agency." *Canadian Journal of Philosophy*. Vol. 32, Iss. sup1, 129–54.

Jean-Charles, Regine Michelle. 2014. "Toward a Victim-Survivor Narrative: Rape and Form in Yvonne Vera's *Under the Tongue* and Calixthe Beyala's *Tu t'appelleras Tanga*" Research in African Literatures. 45, no.1: 39–62. EBSCO HOST. Academic Search Premier. DOI: 10.2979/reseafrilite.45.1.39

Jones, Eldred Durosimi. Ed. 1987. *Women In African Literature Today*. Trenton, NJ: Africa World Press.

Lefkowitz, Mary R., and Maureen B. Fant. 2005. *Women's Life in Greece and Rome. A Sourcebook in Translation*.3rd ed. Baltimore, MD: Johns Hopkins.

McLuckie, Craig W. 1987. "A Preliminary Checklist of Primary and Secondary Sources on the Nigerian Civil War/Biafran War Literature." *Research in African Literatures*. 18.4: 510–27.

Nnaemeka, Obioma. 1997a. "Fighting on All Fronts: Gendered Spaces, Ethnic Boundaries and the Nigerian Civil War." *Dialectical Anthropology* 22.3/4: 235–63.

———. 1997b. Ed. *The Politics of Mothering Womanhood Identity and Resistance in African Literature.* New York: Routledge.

———. 1997c. "Introduction: Imag(in)ing Knowledge, Power, and Subversion in the Margins." In *The Politics of Mothering Womanhood Identity and Resistance in African Literature,* ed. Obioma Nnaemeka, 1–25. New York: Routledge.

Norridge, Zoe. "Sex as Synecdoche: Intimate Languages of Violence in Chimamanda Ngozi Adichie's *Half a Yellow Moon* and Aminatta Forna's *The Memory of Love.*" *Research in African Literatures.* 43.2: 18–39.

Nwachukwu-Agbada, J.O.J. 1996. "Lore from Fiction: Praise and Protest in Biafran War Songs." *Anthropos.* Bd. 91, H. 4.6: 525–34.

Ogundipe-Leslie, Molara. 1994. *Re-Creating Ourselves: African Women and Critical Transformations.* Trenton, NJ: Africa World Press.

Ogunyemi, Chikwenye Okonjo. 1996. *African Wo/Man Palava: The Nigerian Novel by Women.* Chicago: University of Chicago Press.

Osborn, Andrew. 2001. "Mass Rape Ruled A War Crime." *The Guardian.* June 28, 2015.

Sagawa, Jessie and Wendy Robbins. 2011. "Resister and Rebel Storytellers: Slave Narratives and Neo-Slave Novels by and/or about Women Connected to Canada." *Postcolonial Text* 6.4. 1–21.

Smith, Dominic. 2015. "Schoolgirls Kidnapped by Boko Haram 'Brainwashed to Fight for Group.'" *Guardian.* http://www.theguardian.com/world/2015/jun/29/schoolgirls-kidnapped-boko-haram-brainwashed-fight-group.

Smith, Esther Y. 1986. "Images of Women in African Literature: Some Examples of Inequality in the Colonial Period." In *Ngambika,* edited by Carole Boyce Davies and Anne Adams Graves, 27–44.

Smith-Spark, Laura. 2004. "How Did Rape Become a Weapon of War?" *BBC News.* http:/news.bbc.co.uk/go/pr/fr/-/2/hi/in_depth/4078677.stm.

Spivak, Gayatri Chakravorty. 2010. "Can the Subaltern Speak? Reflections on an Idea." Appendix. Rosalind Morris and Gayatri Chakravorty Spivak. *Can the Subaltern Speak?: Reflections on the History of an Idea.* New York: Columbia UP. Press. *eBook Academic Collection (EBSCOhost),* EBSCO*host* (accessed January 30, 2016).

Stimpson, Catherine. 1988. "Shakespeare and the Soil of Rape." *Where the Meanings Are: Feminism and Cultural Spaces.* New York: Routledge.

The Office of the United Nations High Commissioner for Refugees. "Rape: Weapon of War." Web.

The Washington Post. 2013. "Map: Which Countries Allow Women in Front-line Combat Roles?" http://mgafrica.com/article/2014–09–25.

Van Der Wolf, Marthe. 2014. "Africa's Female Fighters: They Bled and Died on the Battlefields of Freedom—and were Forgotten After Victory." *Mail and Guardian, Africa.* http://mgafrica.com/article/2014–09–25

Van Zanten, Susan. 2015. "The Headstrong Historian": Writing with Things Fall Apart" *Research in African Literatures.* 46.2: 85–103.

Vickers, Jeanne. 1993. *Women and War.* London: Zed Books.

White, E. Frances. 2007. While the World Watched. Rev of *Half of a Yellow Sun* by Chimamanda Ngozi Adichie. *Women's Review of Books.* 24.3: 10–11.

NOTES

1. Intriguingly, Ogunyemi (1996) suggests that the name Debbie is an acronym for the title, *Destination Biafra.*

2. Zoe Norridge (2012, 23) provides a similar reading of this incident.

3. According to a Washington Post (2013) map, only Eritrea formally allows women to serve in combat, and only South Africa formally allows women to serve in major military roles such as fighter pilots. However, Marthe Van Der Wolf debunks this: "Up to 30 percent of the total forces in Tigray and Eritrean liberation movements were women." She notes that these women, as well as those in Mozambique, Zimbabwe,

and Rwanda served in combat. However, once the fighting ended, their roles were scaled back. Some exceptions are Zimbabwean Joise Mujuru who served as Vice President before she was fired and expelled from the party and Rwandan Rose Kabuye who held high ranking positions before she was fired by President Kagame.

4. Ogundipe-Leslie (1994) has expressed frustration at some critics' tendency to label African women voiceless. She wonders, "Are African women voiceless or do we fail to look for their voices where we may find them, in the sites and forms in which these voices are uttered?" 11.

5. Writings by feminist theorists of African literature demonstrate this seeming contradiction and the need for fluidity. The renowned critic Obioma Nnaemeka (1997a) takes issue with Nigerian women writers for privileging certain voices at the expense of others, yet she rightly observes the difference between being silent and being silenced.

6. See Molara Ogundipe-Leslie, 6–7, Mineke Schipper, 45, Esther Y. Smith, 33–37, Juliana Makuchi Nfah-Abenyi, 4–5, Fubara, 102, Carole Boyce Davies, 85, Naana Banyiwa-Horne, 120.

7. See Chikwenye Okonjo Ogunyemi's *African Wo/ManPalava,* Juliana Makuchi Nfah-Abenyi, Naana Banyiwa-Horn.

TWO

An Attempt at Inclusion

Reading the War Theme in Selected Black Zimbabwean Women Texts[1]

Tendai Mangena

Blacks fought two important wars against white colonialists in Rhodesia, which are popularly known as First and Second Chimurenga, respectively. *Chimurenga* is a Shona word for war. First Chimurenga was the 1896–1897 initial anti-colonial struggle, whereas the Second Chimurenga was fought from 1966 to 1979, with Zimbabwe gaining its political independence from British rule in 1980. The Second Chimurenga became an important literary event for both white and black Zimbabwean writers. As argued by Hochbruck (1996), the Second Chimurenga is one of the wars in the world, which "grew in telling" (161). The Second Chimurenga remains a highly contested literary theme, with many versions coming from authors belonging to different social classes (inclusive of race and gender). Texts written by white writers are mainly "based on the Rhodesian chronotope" (Primorac 2006, 128) and continue in the ideology that "others" the African and sustains colonial domination. Examples of such texts, include Peter Stiff's *The Rain Goddess* (1976), Robert Early's *A Time of Madness* (1977) and Llyod Burton's *The Yellow Mountain* (1978). White writers' version of the liberation struggle is contested in texts on the Second Chimurenga written by black writers. At the beginning of the referred contestation, mainly black male writers participate, and their texts are the "most popular" (Lyons 2004, 26). War representation by black male writers has two interrelated dimensions; war glorification and challenges to such glorifications. Major black male-authored war texts, include Katiyo's *A Son of the Soil* (1976), Mutasa's *The Contact* (1985), Samupindi's *Pawns* (1992), Chinodya's *A Harvest of Thorns* (1989), Kanengoni's *Echoing Silences* (1997), Hove's *Bones* (1988) and Nyamufukudza's *Non-Believer's Journey* (1980). Katiyo and Mutasa's texts are some of the texts that are best described as "glorifications" of the war that contributed to the "official celebrations" of the attainment of independence (Kaarsholm, 1991, as cited in Hochbruck 1996, 168). On the other hand, Samupindi, Chinodya, Kanengoni, and Nyamufukudza's narratives (and others) question the romantic narrative and paint a complex picture of the war. Both male dimensions of the Second Chimurenga are far from giving a complete picture of the struggle, for, the discursive tendencies in these novels are largely masculinist and tend to downplay women's involvement or participation in the liberation war. Black women writers (and some male, for instance, Hove's *Bones* (1988)), give a new dimension to the liberation struggle's history by highlighting the forgotten black woman's experiences of the war. In foregrounding and highlighting the shortcomings of masculine war narratives, feminist texts "broaden and deepen the understanding of the contradictory nature of liberation history in the hope that the insights will count in the construction of a new and liberated society" (Zhuwarara 2001, 139). The response to the biased narration is located in a 'feminist' perspective meant to illuminate the role played by women in the fight for national struggle and the impact of the struggle on women's lives. Such narratives are then directed at "bringing women back in the study of nationalism and national politics" and have since filled in an important gap in Zimbabwean war historiography elsewhere and in literature (Nagel 1998, 243). What is emphasized in such an approach is the importance of gender in understanding war experience.

In this chapter, I intend to revisit the Zimbabwean anti-colonial liberation struggle and to relocate the black woman through an analysis of Nyamubaya's "That Special Place" (2003), Vera's *Without a Name* (1994) and Dangarembga's *Book of Not* (2006) as reflections on the impact of war on the black woman. The selected texts belong to different genres (short story and novel), but are related to each other, thematically, and are chosen because they forcefully represent the Second Chimurenga from a gendered perspective. They take an oppositional stance to nationalist historiography on the liberation struggle, and also notably place emphasis on different aspects of the liberation struggle. Where Nyamubaya's "That Special Place" focuses on the writer's experiences as a freedom fighter, Vera's and Dangarembga's texts selected for this chapter mainly focus on what happens to women who are on the margins of the war (civilian women). Dangarembga's narrative is more complex than the others in that, it goes beyond reflecting on women as victims of war violence to including the often ignored aspect of women as less attractive characters, especially the woman sell out in war discourse.

Freedom Nyamubaya is a black Zimbabwean female poet and short story writer whose texts include *On the Road Again* (1985), *A Dusk of Dawn* (1995) and "That Special Place" (taken from a collection of short stories, *Writing Still,* edited by Irene Staunton and published in 2003). Nyamubaya is one of the writers of the late 1990s who challenge the unqualified glorification of the Zimbabwean liberation war. In almost all her texts, she "revisits the war, to reveal its pains and horrors and to appraise the sacrifices made by the freedom fighters who participated in it . . . *also* poetically *re-inscribing* into Zimbabwean society's memory of history the sordid details of the experiences of the past" (Musvoto 2007, 62, emphasis added). She responds to an official recalling of the contribution of black women to the liberation struggle and shows that their contribution was rather complex.

For the purposes of this chapter, I analyze Nyamubaya's "That Special Place," which has been described as an "autobiographical return to a 'special place' . . . to redeem the true stories of the revolution' (Muchemwa 2007, 14). Nyamubaya's text revisits the Second Chimurenga, in a significant way, because though literary, autobiography is "a form of historical writing" (Forguson 1979/1980, 139). Nyamubaya in "That Special Place", goes back into a personal archive and retells her experience of the war as a woman liberation fighter and highlights how men who fought were not always heroes of the liberation struggle. From that perspective her narrative, thus, can be read as a double challenge to the front and rear war categories.

In traditional discourse, any war has two different sections; the rear and the front. The front-rear dichotomy affords us to see the world "in terms of dualistic and conflicting binary opposites" (Murray 2009, 3). The battle front is constructed as a territory to be occupied by strong men whereas the battle rear is reserved for weak men, children and women. In terms of hierarchy, the battle front is perceived as the most important and the rears are subsidiaries. Such dualization corresponds to "a subtle mechanism of hierarchization which assumes the unique valorisation of the positive masculine pole while perpetuating the inferiority of the negative feminine term" (Murray 2010, 490). Extremes of such hierarchization, especially in Zimbabwe's nationalist discourse, imagined the liberation fighter as male (cf. Hove, 2011). Such a masculine notion on the war was challenged by women who participated in the Zimbabwean liberation struggle as fighters.

In "That Special Place," Nyamubaya reflects on her personal experience as well as those of other soldiers as trainees at Tembwe Training Camp. In the narrative, besides focusing on the woman warrior, Nyamubaya is very consistent in reflecting on the injustice of the liberation struggle with special reference to soldiers' ill-treatment by fellow soldiers, especially those in positions of authority. Upon joining the training camp, they are branded suspects for various reasons. Writing a synopsis of their lives is a requirement for all new recruits. Nyamubaya and other prisoners are held in captivity, because their biographies do not satisfy the Camp Security Commander. The story is a gloomy picture of such captivity, where the suspects are given nothing to eat and drink and are physically tortured. The reality of such a traumatic experience is witnessed in body disfigurement. Nyamubaya relates how the captives "looked ghostly and frightening with their disfigured cheeks, lips, eyes and noses covered in grey dust. One of them had a thick swollen sagging lower lip and a large swollen forehead that seemed to hang over his eyes" (219). Reference to body disfigurement becomes "the loci of both psychic and physical pain" (Murray 2010, 489). Such a narration of gruesome aspects of the war undermines the nationalist narrative that largely glorifies it.

Notable for this discussion is the black woman's experience of war terror. It is common knowledge that for many women, physical appearance is very important. For the narrator, there is a sense of great discomfort, when in captivity, her afro hair turned white, and she had dust on her face and on the java print dress she had once been proud of. She feels utter discomfort when Nyathi (the Security Commander) instructed his men to cut her hair, and destroy any feeling of beauty that the narrator had. Though the precision and force that normally characterize traumatic recall is lost in the narrative, Nyamubaya informs the reader that Nyathi also raped her (Murray 2009, 4). The irony can be located in the sense that the perpetrator is one who has a key post in the liberation struggle, thus the Camp Security Commander's liberating role remains questionable.

The recruits are meant to participate in the liberation struggle which aims to free people from the clutches of colonialism. Ironically, the recruits further lose their own freedom in the process, to fellow soldiers, when they are held in captivity. In captivity, they are removed from the real business of the liberation struggle. Such alienation is captured in the metaphoric reference to the hut they occupied during the captivity which, as Nyamubaya writes "fell a long, long way from the liberation struggle of my dreams" (223). In this regard, Nyamubaya also forces the reader to rethink the concept of freedom.

The overall picture we get from Nyamubaya's reconstruction of the liberation struggle in "That Special Place" is that not everyone who joined the war got a chance to make a meaningful contribution; others like her and the fellow soldiers were victimized and alienated from the real battle. Such aspects of the liberation struggle are never the limelight of the official narration of the liberation war. Nyamubaya refers to the darker side of the war events as the experiences of a "special place: the place that many people in this world will never know" (228). Her text, then, is an alternative text that subverts the official nationalist narrative of the liberation struggle. In *Without A Name,* Vera, just like Nyamubaya, also defines black women victimhood in the Zimbabwean liberation struggle, and the victimiser status that liberation fighters also assumed.

Vera achieves this through a representation of Mazvita's rape by a freedom fighter.

Yvonne Vera was a prolific Zimbabwean black female that died in 2005. She published *Why Don't You Carve Other Animals* (1992), *Under the Tongue* (1996), *Without A Name* (1994), *Butterfly Burning* (1998), *Nehanda* (1993) and *The Stone Virgins* (2002). Most of her texts, explore in various ways, the liberation struggle theme from a feminist stance. The short stories that make up *Why Don't You Carve Other Animals* are female centred and largely set during the liberation struggle. *Under the Tongue* focuses on "the rape of a very young girl by her father, while the liberation war engulfs the whole country" (Gunner and Kortenaar 2007, 6). *Nehanda* (1993) is about the spirit medium, Nehanda and her role in the liberation struggle. By writing the story of Nehanda, Vera "defies the notion that women were simply peripheral to nationalist struggle or that they played back-seat roles," thereby challenging "both the colonial and the male-centred African nationalist erasure of African women's subjectivities and agency" (Desiree 2004, 193).

Without a Name (1994) presents Mazvita's experiences from the rear of the war. She is the protagonist of this novel. At the beginning of Vera's novel, she is on a journey by bus. She carries, metaphorically, "the fragments of her being" on her tongue (3), for "she had suffered so much that her skin threatened to fall pitilessly to the ground" (4). Vera shows that Mazvita's suffering takes place in the context of the liberation struggle; for the story is set in the year 1977 (during the turbulent years of the struggle). She is raped by a liberation fighter, and commits infanticide in an effort to metaphorically "forget" the sexual abuse.

Rape is one of the "issues whose existence may not have been made visible in nationalist discourse" of the Zimbabwean liberation struggle (Lipenga 2012, 271). According to Muchemwa (2005), "patriarchal history and memory gloss over taboo experiences of rape" (197). Through a representation of Mazvita's rape by a liberation fighter, Vera highlights how women's bodies are sites of the liberation struggle. In that context, Vera's focus on the taboo of rape is a radical challenge that has "interrupted traditional relations of speech and authority by uttering the unsaid taboos" (Devault 1999, 183). In *Without a Name*, Vera also emphasizes the fact that Mazvita is not just a victim of rape but also emerges out of the experience as a survivor. She saves herself from the traumatic memory of the rape through infanticide. Vera describes the process of killing the baby as follows: "She rested her fingers shakingly on the child and remembered. The past came to her in rapid waves that made her heave the child forward, away from her, in a deep and uncontrollable motion of rejection" (17). Mazvita's hatred and subsequent rejection of the baby, captured in the above words, is linked to the hatred directed at its father. Faced with the long-term possibility of raising the 'unwanted' child, and being reminded of the sexual violence, Mazvita's response is a realistic way of dealing with the effect of the past rape violence. Her efforts in committing infanticide are directed at erasing any evidence of the violation of the past, as the presence of the child would have testified.

Even though women are excluded from "national community . . . through the violence inflicted on their bodies, they become some sort of unofficial displaced sites of struggle" (Toivanen 2009, 66). Mazvita, as the narrative states, was not an active freedom fighter, but, the violation directed at her body transformed her to an identifiable victim of the war. It is also quite paradoxical that the female body is more often than not violated, yet the nation is conceived in terms of the same female body. This is implicit in "the familiar discourse of the rape between the colonizer and the colonized country" (Kanneh 1995, 347), during the colonial process.

During her rape, Mazvita could not see the rapist's face, yet she needed to see the face to hate the man for the abuse. She then transferred the hate to various elements that seemed complicit in the act of her violation. She hated the land, the dew-covered grass, the call of the strange bird and the mist. The things she hated "contained the loss *and* continued to remind her of her pain" (30) and contributed in various ways to the pain and horror of the moment of violation. She hated the dewy grass "she had felt graze tenderly against her naked elbow in that horrible moment" (30). Mazvita wanted to cry out her pain but an unknown bird "had silenced her when she needed to tell of her suffering . . . to hear her own suffering uttered, acknowledged" (30). Crying would have meant a release of pain for Mazvita. The unknown bird's silencing force relates to the traditional silencing of women. Women are not given an opportunity to articulate their existence—which for the greater part is characterized by pain. However, African women have found ways to articulate their voices in serene ways, although often their voices remain subordinate. A good example of such serene voices can be located in the feminist narratives churned out consistently by African women writers, which, for the greater part, act as representative black women's protest voices. Mazvita also "hated the land that pressed beneath her back as the man moved impatiently above her, into her, past her" (30). She connected the man to the land, because it had "allowed the man to grow from itself into her body" (30). The violence that she experiences in the rape incident is inseparable from the land and other geographical features which become accomplices, thus making it very difficult for Mazvita to have any sense of connection with the land, that which, in the Zimbabwean worldview, gives one an identity.

Psychologically, anger and hatred have significant functions for sexual violence survivors. For Mazvita, anger and hatred function "as some kind of psychic glue . . . *and as alternatives to sexual violation*" (emphasis added).[2] The rage of anger and hatred then "function as a defence against shame that feels unbearable."[3] The unbearable shame, in Mazvita's case, is connected to an emotional feeling as she emerges out of the act of rape "damaged *and* that sense of damage can mean that the self is felt to be in pieces, in danger of collapse" (emphasis added).[4] The three related emotions "hatred, anger and rage serve a defensive and cohesive function."[5] Mazvita's healing process begins with the hatred, which, later culminates in the killing of the product of the sexual violence, the baby.

Nationalist narratives insist on the centrality of land since colonial occupation was understood as "geographical violence." Through decolonization, the oppressed people reclaim their "geographical identity" (Said 1993 as cited in Mangwanda 2003, 141–42). Vera's contribution to the land debate in *Without a Name*, through a reflection of the way black women relate to land in the context of the liberation struggle is significant. She shows that there are notable contradictions in the way colonized people relate to land. Nyenyedzi, Mazvita's lover, is loyal to the land, while on the other hand, Mazvita rejects it. Land, supposedly, gives Mazvita an identity, but to her, land is not just a cultural artefact but rather reminds her of the personal violation that she experienced during the rape incident, an experience that she struggles to forget. Her other reasons are grand; black people have been dispossessed, alienated, and are now labourers who have lost ownership of productive land and what they occupy is quite unproductive and very repulsive. The land has also been "desecrated by commercial cash crop farming" and has become privatized through commercialization and the creation of farms (Samuelson 2012, 94). Mazvita agrees that land is a cultural artefact that black people should guard jealously, but she believes that such an understanding of the significance of land is not the only truth, and is, thus, limited. She asks Nyenyedzi the following question: "What you say about land is true, but does this truth belong equally to all of us?" (33). Her personal experiences have forced her to revisit issues of land and identity, land and loyalty, and land and attachment. The intricate relationship between land and black African people changed for the violated Mazvita. In essence, the position that Mazvita takes in *Without a Name* represents a rebellion against the cultural loyalty to land (Pucherova 2012, 186). Vera writes: "She had loved the land, saw it through passionate and intense moments of freedom, but to her the land had no fixed loyalties" (34).

Mazvita's personal story dramatizes violated women's alienation from the land. At the same time, the story satirizes Nyenyedzi's and, by extension, any uncritical belief in land as a cultural artefact and site of identity. Through a foregrounding of how Mazvita and Nyenyedzi differ in their perception of the land and the freedom fighters, Vera refers to such differences in perception as "heterogeneity of expectations and aspirations" (Musila 2012, 9). The differences are noted where "Nyenyedzi has a firm belief in the freedom fighters" struggle to free the land, while for Mazvita the soldiers are terrorists (34).

Dangarembga's *The Book of Not* is related to Nyamubaya and Vera's texts, but differs from them in that it largely focuses, not on the black women war victims but on the less attractive black women characters. *The Book of Not* (2006) is a sequel to Dangarembga's internationally acclaimed *Nervous Conditions* (1988). The story that begins in *Nervous Conditions* is about Rhodesia and the place and experiences of the colonised from a feminist's point of view. *Nervous Conditions* focuses on the lives of black Zimbabwean women from mid-1960s to 1970s Rhodesia. The *Book of Not*, specifically, focuses on Tambu's experiences at a white majority, Sacred Heart girls high school during the liberation struggle up to the attainment of independence. Tambu's story of unbecoming (as suggested in the book's title) takes place in the context of the Second Chimurenga. Dangarembga's focus on the place of the black woman in the liberation struggle represents a new version, altogether. Her black women in *The Book of Not* are not warriors as demonstrated in the Nehanda myth, and they are not just victims of the war as shown in "That Special Place" and *Without a Name*. Tambudzai is clearly affected by the violence of racism, but the decisions she takes translate her to more of a sell-out than a victim.

Unlike Nyamubaya and Vera, Dangarembga, in *The Book of Not*, greatly emphasizes the racism of colonial oppression. Racism in Rhodesia, like in other colonial spaces, was institutionalized, and the war widened the racial divide as shown through the experiences of the narrator and other black girls at the white majority Sacred Heart. In what Tambu learns on her way to Sacred Heart, there are disparities between white and black workers. The narrative also shows how the school is particularly made an apartheid structure in Rhodesia. Besides the fact that black students belong to the minority group at Sacred Heart (Tambu sees black students as "dots" (63)), the few black students are all crammed in one dormitory named after its inhabitants (African dormitory). They are not provided with incinerators for the proper disposal of their feminine hygiene items, and are thus humiliated when the headmistress announces at the college assembly that girls from the African dormitory clogged the sewerage system with their menstrual pads. Some of the staff members at Sacred Heart are clearly racist. The waitresses serve both European and African students. When serving the former, they "move fluidly, but when they set a jug or a plate before Ntombi or [the narrator], they smack it down with a jut of the chin and spills, as though slapping a hard, crushing thing down on obnoxious crawling objects" (45–46). Tambu gets the best Ordinary Level results, but the honour is bestowed on a white girl, Tracey. No skin contact is permitted between blacks and whites and such contact is dramatized throughout the novel. For instance, the black girls live in fear of accidentally touching the skin of white girls. When Tambu literally gets into contact with Sister Catherine, she feels guilty that she had "soiled" her teacher in some way. As Hlungwane (2009) argues; "black girls at the Young Ladies' College often feel like exotic animals on display. In one uncomfortable episode in the school's cafeteria, a white student named Tracey compares the eyes of Ntombi, a black student, to those of a cow" (451). Tambu is forbidden from taking science lessons at the government-run Umtali Boys High School at a time when her own school suffers shortages of teachers during the fight for liberation. As the war intensifies, the science teacher from Europe does not arrive. The students studying science subjects are bussed to a segregated boys' school from which Tambu is excluded; she is left to study on her own without a teacher (Hlungwane 2009).

The above background helps in our judgement on Tambu's loyalty in the liberation struggle. Though Hlungwane describes Tambu as "a victim of a dehumanized colonial Rhodesia" (452), the narrative confirms that she is a tragic figure who conforms to the role of a sell-out. She is easily labelled a sell-out, because she accepts the status quo, which is white rule. At the beginning of the text, Tambu conceives and describes her sister, Netsai, as a "piece of person" (3) rather than as a whole person after she had stepped on a landmine and lost her leg. So lost is Tambu that she describes the *pungwe* (political night meetings attended by civilians and freedom fighters) as a primitive scene (28), a description which is influenced by African images she gets from films and books. Tambu dismisses Netsai as a "wild and irresponsible girl" and wishes she were not her sister (31). It has always been Tambu's wish to run away from her Africanness. At Sacred Heart, Tambu identifies with white classmates and the white school administration. Her identity as a black Zimbabwean woman is effectively erased by her mother who refers to her as a white person who has metaphorically lost the taste for *mufushwa* (dried vegetables). Tambu dismisses what she describes as an "inferior African syllabus" (117) in the black mission schools like Nyasha's. She displays an ignorance of influential authors like Ngugi wa Thiong'o. Tambu assumes that the book Nyasha reads, Ngugi's *A Grain of Wheat*, is not only "about agriculture" but is, written "by someone like poor Bongo in the Congo, a starving Kenyan author" (117). As Kennedy (2008) argues, Tambu has internalized "a Eurocentric view of her African "inferiority" (89). Her colonised psyche gets to extremes when she decides to contribute to the war from the side of the supposed enemy for blacks and volunteers to weave clothes for Rhodesian fighters. Although Tambu does eventually stop knitting for the Rhodesian army, the fact that she wants to be aligned with a racist Rhodesia rather than a new postcolonial nation speaks volumes about the level of her disorientation (Hlongwane, 456). Knitting helmets and scarves for the Rhodesian army earns her the label of sell-out by her black peers at school.

In the following extract from the *The Book of Not*, Tambu trivialises the liberation war; a position that is normally taken by those who identify with the colony, and subsequently stands to benefit from it.

> I emerged from my studies to a new dispensation. I could never, after all the years at Sacred Heart and Fridays in the town hall, bring myself to believe Rhodesians had died; definitely they had not done so in sufficient quantities to cause a great blimp in the course of history. . . . [C]onvinced it was not the deaths of Rhodesians that had caused Mr. Mugabe and Mr. Smith to talk to each other with some degree of sincerity, I assured myself happily that the phenomenon was due to a bigger and better motive on both sides: a desire to desist away from chopping away lips, ears, noses and genitals from the bodies of people's relatives by the elder siblings; a desire to develop a larger, kinder heart on the part of Europeans. (198)

Despite these thoughts, Tambu is keen on being accepted by people who do not care at all about her. Tambu, who is not at all concerned with the loyalty demanded by the nationalists, the Big Brothers who violently beat her uncle for sending her to a white school during the liberation struggle, comes close to deserving the accusation of collaborator levied at her by her black school mates. She is so insensitive to the realities of others that she makes no effort to understand the black servants, the "nannies, dressed in pink" (45) who, understandably, see all the black girls at the Young Ladies' College as traitors and subsequently regard them with great hostility (Hlungwane 2009, 455). Kennedy explains such "contortion", as that which "stems from colonial racism" (2008, 88). Colonial racism gives the colonized subject "unhealthy, conflictual solution[s]" (Fanon 1967, as cited in Kennedy, 88).

Tambu's mother, known in the novel as Mai, can also, on a different level, be labelled a war sell-out. Mai is hostile to her husband's brother (Babamukuru) and informs the freedom fighters that he is a sell-out. During the *pungwe* , she breathes in "catches of satisfaction" (14), as Babamukuru is beaten by the freedom fighters. The reader tends to sympathise with Babamukuru, who is charged as "not exactly a collaborator, but one whose soul hankered to sell out (5) and condemns Mai's malicious lies; Mai who is described by her daughter , Tambu, as "avaricious and hollow" (9). Through both Tambu and Mai, Dangarembga demonstrates how "the colonized are not unified against the white minority" (Kennedy, 89).

Besides focusing on Tambu and her mother as potential war sell-outs, Dangarembga reflects on the character, Netsai. Her engagement as a freedom fighter in the liberation struggle is notable. However, the writer makes a conscious decision not to make her the centre of the narrative focus. Not much is said about her experience beyond what is said in the text's opening scene; that she lost her leg when she stepped on a landmine set by the Rhodesian forces, thus, she is projected as a victim of the brutality of the Rhodesian forces. There is a possibility that Netsai is sexually abused by one of the Big Brothers. Considering what the community said about her relationship with the Big Brother, Tambu says, "love was never mentioned . . . they said he said, when he drank too much after the war, he was in love with both of them. Netsai was his first war love, picked as she brought *sadza* to this freedom fighter's hideaway (5). Before joining the liberation struggle as a fighter, Nestai, and other girls in the community, supported the freedom fighters as *Chimbwidos* (pliant peasant girls). As suggested in the community rumours, Netsai was picked by the freedom fighter when she was running such errands. This can be taken as an instance of secretive sexual relations (often translating into abuse) between freedom fighters and girls, which were a common feature of the liberation struggle. Besides Nyamubaya and Vera's texts discussed earlier in this chapter, other texts that also represent the secretive sexual relationships between pliant peasant girls and liberation fighters include Stanley Nyamufukudza's Non-Believers' Journey and Alexander Kanengoni's Echoing Silences. Resulting from such moral misconduct by the freedom fighters, civilians described them using a pejorative term, *Magandanga,* "that was used by the Rhodesia media to describe liberation fighters" (Hove 2011, 40).

There are various scenes in the text on war related violence. At the beginning of *The Book of Not,* Tambudzai attends a "pungwe" and witnesses her sister's (Netsai) maiming as well as Babamukuru's (Tambu's uncle and guardian) trial and punishment by the freedom fighters. These two incidents demonstrate that violence which affected the colonised subjects came from both warring parties; Netsai loses one of her legs after stepping on a landmine set by the Rhodesian forces and Babamukuru is brutally beaten by the liberation fighters. Babamukuru's punishment is meted out as a way of consolidating legitimacy by the freedom fighters (Bull-Christiansen 2010, 53). These two incidents persist as metaphors of the war's violence that pervades the novel from beginning to the end.

At assembly, the headmistress of The Sacred Heart announces that the parents of Rhodesian twins at the school were brutally murdered by the "freedom fighters." Newspapers circulated at assembly, showed pictures of the girls' slain father, and announced that the girls' mother died shortly thereafter. The Headmistress condemns the killing as "acts of butchery" (129), and "unspeakable obscene horrors" (130). Later in the text, Ntombi chokes out the horrifying details of the vicious murder of her infant cousin by Rhodesian soldiers, who suspected the girl's mother of feeding the guerrilla fighters (Kennedy 2008, 99). In various ways Dangarembga demonstrates that "the war might have brought us a little nearer to where we think we wanted to be as a people but what did it consist of? It consisted of lies, forced abductions, horrible brutality on both sides, and treachery even within families."[6] "So for *her* the war is definitely a character/and nobody actually has picked up what *Dangarembga thinks* is a very strong anti-war message in the whole novel" (Rooney 2007, 59).

All the three texts discussed in this chapter are written by black Zimbabwean female writers that reimagine the Zimbabwean liberation struggle from a feminist perspective. Texts selected for this chapter re-engage and reconstruct often-ignored aspects of the history of this Zimbabwean liberation war. More emphasis is placed on the different, largely less attractive aspects of the liberation struggle, with regards to black women's experiences. Both Nyamubaya and Vera reflect more on the victim status of black women liberation fighters and civilians, with the male liberation fighters projected more as victimisers. Vera, in *Without a Name,* specifically shows how the black woman's body is reduced to a site of struggle through sexual violation, and the subsequent pregnancy and infanticide. The position that Nyamubaya recreates in "That Special Place" foregrounds the less attractive aspects of the liberation struggle. The setting is a training camp, but what happens contributes little to the real aim of the revolution. Those who intend to join and contribute to the liberation struggle are tortured by freedom fighters in positions of authority. Women participate in the war as soldiers but are sexually abused and humiliated by fellow male soldiers occupying influential positions.

In both *Without a Name* and "That Special Place," not all liberation fighters are constructed as heroes. Some are "rapists" and sell-outs as is the security commander in Nyamubaya's autobiography. Through such representation of male liberation fighters, the narratives largely destabilize the "aura of honour, dignity and veneration" acquired by ex-liberation fighters in Zimbabwean nationalist cultural memory (Hove 2011, 39).

Unlike Nyamubaya and Vera, Dangarembga effected a shift in the depiction of black women in female-authored texts and emphasizes the processes by which a black girl is translated into a sell-out in a racially segregated white majority school. Tambu gives her support to the supposed enemy instead of supporting the nationalist cause. In her narrative, Dangarembga desists from what Washington (1975) elsewhere described as an "attitude of reverence" towards the female characters that is often displayed by women writers (xxxi). She achieves that by presenting the woman, not just as a victim of war's violence, but also as a sell-out like Tambudzai and her mother, the malicious liar, Mai.

Overall, the selected writers significantly reflect more on impediments than successes of the revolutionary struggle. In an attempt to rewrite the nationalist (largely masculinist) narratives of the Zimbabwean Second Chimurenga, more emphasis is placed on the less attractive aspects of the liberation struggle, and the celebratory aspect is glaringly missing. Yet, in reality, there were also heroic acts committed by the liberation fighters (both men and women) during the liberation struggle, which are worth celebrating. Though the main aim, in writing female centred narratives of the Zimbabwean liberation war, was to redeem the untold stories of black women's war experiences, assessed individually, the authors do not pluralise women's subjectivities. In present day Zimbabwe, black women continue to claim space in the political arena, because they fought in the war and celebrate the heroism associated with participating in the war despite some vicissitudes such as rape.

REFERENCES

Bull Christiansen, Lene. 2010. "Zimbabwe's Liberation Struggle Recycled: Remembering the Principles of the Struggle in Political Ways Documenting Liberation Struggles in Southern Africa." In Select papers from the Nordic Africa Documentation Project workshop 26–27, 2009, edited by Chris Saunders. Nordic Africa Institute.

Dangarembga, Tsitsi. 2006. *The Book of Not*. Banbury: Ayebia Clarke.

Desiree, Lewis. 2004. "Revisioning Patriarchal Nationalism: Yvonne Vera's *Nehanda*." *JCAS*: State, Nation and Ethnic Relations. 193–208.

Devault, Majorie L. 1999. *Liberating Method: Feminism and Social Research*. Philadelphia: Temple University Press.

Forguson, Lynd. 1979/1980. "Autobiography as History." *University of Toronto Quarterly* 49(2): 139–55.

Gunner, Liz. and Kortenaar, N. Ten. 2007. "Introduction: Yvonne Vera's Fictions and the Voice of the Possible." *Research in African Literatures* 38(2): 1–8.

Hlungwane, Gugu. 2009. "A piece of person": Fractured selves and colonial education in Tsitsi Dangarembga's *The Book of Not*." *Journal of Postcolonial Writing* 45(4): 449–58.

Hochbruck, Wolfgana. 1996. "Armed Conflict and Cultural Encounters: Zimbabwean War Fiction." In *Fusion of Cultures?*, edited by Peter. O. Stummer and Christopher Balme, 160–74. Amsterdam: Rodopi.

Hove, Muchativugwa Liberty. 2011. "Strugglers and Stragglers: Imagining the 'War Veteran' from the 1890s to the Present in Zimbabwean Literary Discourse." *Journal of Literary Studies* 27(2): 38–57.

Kanneh, Kadiatu. 1995. "Feminism and the Colonial Body." In *Post-Colonial Studies Reader*, edited by Gareth Griffiths and Helen Tiffin, 346–48. London: Routledge.

Kennedy, Rosanne. 2008. "Mortgaged Futures: Trauma, Subjectivity, And The Legacies of Colonialism in Tsitsi Dangarembga's *The Book of Not*." *Studies in the Novel, Postcolonial Trauma Novels*, 40(1/2): 86–107.

Lipenga, Timwa. 2012. "Rewriting the City: Women's Occupation of Urban Space in *Butterfly Burning* and *Under the Tongue*." In *Emerging Perspectives on Yvonne Vera*, edited by Helen. Cousins and Pauline Dogson-Katiyo, 261–78. London: Africa World Press.

Lyons, Tanya. 2004. *Guns and Guerrilla Girls: Women in the Zimbabwean Liberation Struggle*. Asmara: Africa World Press.

Mangwanda, Khombe. 2003. "Re-mapping the Colonial Space: Yvonne Vera's *Nehanda*." In *Sign and Taboo: Perspectives on the Poetic Fiction of Yvonne Vera*, edited by Robert. Muponde and Mandi Taruvinga, 141–54. Harare: Weaver Press.

Muchemwa, Kizito. 2005. "Some Thoughts on Historical Memory and Writing in Zimbabwe." In *Versions of Zimbabwe, New Approaches to Literature and Culture*, edited by Robert Muponde and Ranka Primorac, 195–202. Harare: Weaver Press.

———. 2006. "Why Don't You Tell Children a Story?: Father Figures in the Zimbabwean Short Stories." In *Manning the Nation: Father Figures in Zimbabwean Literature and Society*, edited by Robert Muponde and Kizito Z. Muchemwa, 1–16. Harare: Weaver Press.

Murray, Jessica. 2009. "A Postcolonial Feminist Reading of Selected Testimonies to Trauma in Post-Liberation South Africa and Zimbabwe." *Journal of African Cultural Studies* 21(1): 1–21.

Murray, Jessica. 2010. "The 'Recidivist Tongue': Embracing an Embodied Language of Trauma." *Social Dynamics* 36(3): 488–503.

Musila, A. Grace. 2012. "Beyond the Frame of History: Colonial Modernity, Love, and Freedom in Yvonne Vera's *Without a Name, Butterfly Burning*, and *The Stone Virgins*." In *Emerging Perspectives on Yvonne Vera*, edited by Helen Cousins and Pauline Dogson-Katiyo, 3–22. London: Africa World Press.
Musvoto, Rangarirai. 2007. "Tensions and Conflicts in Zimbabwean Society: Nyamubaya Reminisces." *English Academy Review: Southern African Journal of English Studies* 24(1): 61–70.
Nagel, Joanne. 2008. "Masculinity and Nationalism: Gender and Sexuality in the Making of Nations." *Ethnic and Racial Studies* 21(2): 249–69.
Nyamubaya, Freedom. 1986. *On the Road Again*. Harare: Zimbabwe Publishing House.
———. 1995. *Dusk of Dawn*. Harare: College Press.
———. 2003. "That Special Place." In *Writing Still: New Stories from Zimbabwe*, edited by Irene Staunton, 217 – 228. Harare: Weaver Press.
Primorac, Ranka. 2006. *The Place of Tears: The Novel and Politics in Zimbabwe*. London: Tauris Academia Studies.
Pucherova, Dobrota. 2012. "Desire, Pleasure, and Freedom in Butterfly Burning." In *Emerging Perspectives on Yvonne Vera,* edited by Helen Cousins and Pauline Dogson-Katiyo, 185–202. London: Africa World Press.
Rooney, Caroline. 2007. "Interview with Tsitsi Dangarembga." *Wasafiri* 22(2): 57–62.
Samuelson, Meg. 2012. "Re-membering the Body: Rape and Recovery in *Without a Name* and *Under the Tongue*." In *Sign and Taboo: Perspectives on the Poetic Fiction of Yvonne Vera,* edited by Robert Muponde and Mandi Taruvinga, 93–100. Harare: Weaver Press.
Terdiman, Richard. 1989. *Discourse/Counter-Discourse: The Theory and Practice of Symbolic Resistance in Nineteenth Century France*. New York: Cornell University Press.
Toivanen, Anna. 2009. "Remembering the Nation's Aching Spots: Yvonne Vera's Authorial Position of Witness and Healer," *Postcolonial Text*, 5(4): 1–15.
Washington, Mary. H. 1975. *Black Eyed Susans: Classic Stories by and About Black Women.* New York: Anchor Books.
Zhuwarara, Rino. 2001. *Introduction to Zimbabwean Literature in English*. Harare: College Press.

NOTES

1. The sections on *Without a Name* and "That Special Place" are largely adopted from my unpublished PhD thesis.
2. J. Burgo, "Narcissistic Rage and the Sense of Entitlement," http://www.afterpsychotherapy.com/narcissistic-rage/ (Accessed April 27, 2013).
3. Ibid.
4. Ibid.
5. Ibid.
6. Martin, Valerie. An Interview with Tsitsi Dangarembga, brickmag.com/interview-tsitsi-dangarembga (Accessed May 12, 2015).

THREE

The Female Body as Locus for National Trauma in the Fiction of Yvonne Vera

Melissa R. Root

A country that has been ravaged by armed struggle, such as Zimbabwe, necessarily suffers long-term consequences to its land and its people. Such violence can result in fragmenting of the body and can at the same time corrupt identity. One's concept of body influences one's ideas of identity; thus a disconnection from one becomes a rupture of the other. Life in the post-colony further stresses the rupture, splitting identity between two worldviews. For the female in the post-colony, the gap widens because she must reconcile her femininity to a patriarchal system in addition to reunifying herself from a colonized object into a postcolonial subject. The fiction of Yvonne Vera—particularly *Without a Name, Under the Tongue* (2002), and *The Stone Virgins* (2003)—explores this gap, equating the disruption of colonized life and nation to a rupture in the female body itself. Vera's characters often function as a piece of a much larger whole, women dealing with national trauma in an individual way.

In these novels, Vera visits the trope of the exploitation of the female body and connects it with the exploitation of the land in interesting ways by writing a physical counter-discourse against patriarchal violence in Zimbabwe. The colonial enterprise often equated land with the female body, the idea being that both should be conquered and tamed. As Deborah Willis and Carla Williams (2002) state, "[T]he female body especially bore the metaphorical weight of comparisons between women's fertility and the abundant riches of the conquered lands" (8). The ideology of conquest, domination, and exploitation, thereby, was extended from the land to the women of the land. This equation was further adopted by the postcolonial nation and is a common motif in African literature. Vera addresses a common theme that became integral to the patriarchal discourse of her country.

This chapter theorizes the notion of postcolonial Zimbabwe as a violent place with particular ramifications for women in that nation. In following the theme of colonial and patriarchal deconstructing and reconstructing a new self, physically and mentally, Vera's work examines violence against women, rape being the most predominant. In the three novels under discussion, the female protagonists are raped by a soldier, either upon return from fighting for liberation or during said fight, resulting in a fragmentation of female body and identity. Furthermore, the fragmented narrative threads mirror this fragmentation of self as depicted through character. What is truly remarkable about Vera's work, however, is that the characters are (mostly) able, not only to survive the rape, physically and psychologically, but also to connect parts of their shattered selves and once again find agency—even if that agency can be demonstrated in shocking ways. The situation in the nation is so horrific that the ways in which women reestablish their own identity is sometimes horrific as well.

The nation of Zimbabwe is war-torn even after Chimurenga is over. Although "war-torn" is a common idiom used, one rarely considers what lies behind the expression, or that the destruction of war has led to actual tearing of landscape, of loyalties, of family structures, and of people, particularly women themselves. However grim Vera's narratives are, she posits that redemption is possible. For some of Vera's characters, such as Nonceba, in *The Stone Virgins*, the healing of wounds (psychological and physiological) occurs. Vera, therefore, seems to indicate that a healing of rifts is possible as long as all people learn to communicate with each other in compassionate ways and build a unified—male and female—nation.

The female body can be vulnerable both to physical violence and to a violence of gaze, whether from outside or from an inward view. Becoming disconnected, mentally, from the physical body creates a crisis in identity. Body image plays into the notion of defining self through other's gaze, and subsuming that gaze into one's own view. The concept of disunity between self and body is a useful tool for reading Vera's fiction. Even her book jackets for the U.S. editions promote an image of the African female body that raises speculation. For example, the Zimbabwean edition of *Under the Tongue* depicts a roughly sketched figure, apparently naked and resting in the branches of a tree. The lines of the drawing are simple, unspecific. One cannot even discern easily that the figure is that of a woman; the arms hold onto the knees, the body essentially androgynous. The U.S. edition of the same novel, however, uses quite different cover art. In this edition, the woman on the front of the book is represented photographically, is clearly a woman, and is unquestionably naked. Although her arms are crossed under her chin, covering her breasts, the bottom portion of her body is exposed. This woman displays a tiny waist, a flat stomach, generous hips, and a shaved pubis. It seems the Western ideal of beauty is being promoted on this cover, despite the subject being Zimbabwean woman. This juxtaposition of image echoes the theme of fragmented body and identity in Vera's work, which adds to the discourse of postmodernity as well as postcolonialism. As she has said about her own craft: "I always need to be anchored in such a way that I am inside a character, seeing this fragmented or fractured world, and how—usually a woman—is trying to bring the pieces together in her mind, to choreograph her life." (Bryce 2002, 219). Vera thus attempts to fuse the rupture, in body and in mind, in order to live a life of wholeness with a unified identity. If her characters can accomplish such a feat, the possibility exists that the nation can as well.

Postcolonial theory concerns itself with binaries, margin/center and self/other being a couple of the key ones. In *Black Skin, White Masks*, Frantz Fanon (1967), from the colonial French island of Martinique, talks about his realization that he was "different" when a white person in France identified him as black. Thus, his identity, his conception of self, was constructed through the gaze of privileged other of the center. His concept of his identity was also closely aligned to his physicality, for it was the color of his skin which distinguished him as "other." Black man's identity is rooted in body: "In the white world the man of color encounters difficulties in the development of his bodily schema. Consciousness of the body is solely a negating activity. It is a third-person consciousness" (110). The consequence of such consciousness is a viewing of oneself from the outside, and calling into question one's connection with personal identity.

Whereas Fanon explores the idea of dualities, Homi Bhabha (1994) further splinters the binaries of self/other, margin/center to focus on hybridity—which can lead to a fusion of or dissolution of identity and body. However, Bhabha, like Fanon, positions the beginning of hybridity as the condition of the colonial encounter and promotes the fusion of various aspects of self as a postcolonial necessity. As he states: "What is so graphically enacted in the moment of colonial identification is the splitting of the subject in its historical place of utterance" (1994, 46). Bhabha goes on to say: "Black skin splits under the racist gaze, displaced into signs of bestiality, genitalia, grotesquerie, which reveal the phobic myth of the undifferentiated whole white body" (92). The idea is that the white body and identity are whole, complete, the black body and identity subject to splitting through an outsider's view. Subject/self splits into object/other under the colonial gaze, and the project of the postcolonial person is to become subject once again, but with a difference, for one's identity is forever marred by the colonial influence. Nonetheless, both Fanon and

Bhabha concern themselves with the black *male* body; the female body suffers another layer of objectification, being viewed not only from the colonizing powers but also from the patriarchal culture. This threat, as well as the potential for reconciliation, is the meat of Vera's fiction.

In his article "Symbolisation Compulsions," Ato Quayson (2001) theorizes the notion of postcolonial sites as places of violence and the ramification that these hold for women in the postcolony. Building upon the ideas of Jonathan Boyarin, Quayson notes that "ethnic and nationalist discourse tend to draw on and centralise metaphors of the body, the links between the body and the nation operating at the level of organic metaphors of nationalist ideologies" (192). Vera's fiction clearly falls under this rubric of equating nationalism with the (specifically female) body.

Quayson uses Freudian terminology to examine trauma, specifically, in the postcolonial context, focusing on Freud's ideas of trauma and the uncanny. As he points out, an important aspect of the uncanny is fear of dismemberment (196). In unstable or violent social/political situations, the individual may transfer the fear of fragmented society to the fear of fragmented self (196). For some African writers, such as Zimbabwean Dambudzo Marechera (whom Quayson uses as an example), the uncanny feeling is communicated stylistically as well, "by a variety of fragmenting effects at the level of form" (2001, 199). Furthermore, as society struggles to obtain order, it must pass through a period of violence, which may be visited upon the individual body as well as the body politic: "there is a suggestion that the human body has to undergo a form of violence and dismemberment for the body politic itself to come into being" (200). It is necessary for this to occur on both the individual and national level because of colonialism's legacy that strived to make the colonized less than human:

> Since the colonised's quest for identity cannot be fully expressed without the dismantling of colonialism and since this dismantling, in this particular context, has to be achieved through so much bloodshed and violence, the quest for a language that seeks to shape reality is always undermined by the consciousness of the brutality and violence that attends the colonised's body. (Quayson 2001, 201)

This idea as applied to the female body resonates with Vera's fiction as the dismantling of colonialism under patriarchy has traumatic consequences for the female protagonists.

Quayson's article is also building upon the work of Frantz Fanon. In *The Wretched of the Earth* (1963), Fanon comments upon the colonized body, and colonized neuroses, under the yoke of colonialism. He connects lack of sense of self to lack of sense of nation, asserting that, "[F]or the people, the party is not an authority, but an organism through which they as the people exercise their authority and express their will" (185). In other words, the body politic is a living, changing being. It was in the colonial power's interest to deconstruct the colonized identity, and to deconstruct community along ethnic lines, to rebuild colonized people into imperial subjects with few common interests with their fellow Africans. In order to reconstruct an identity free from the taint of colonialism, the colonized must shatter that colonial identity and self, often violently. As Fanon further notes, "The colonized intellectual who takes up arms to defend his nation's legitimacy and who wants to bring proofs to bear out that legitimacy, who is willing to strip himself naked to study the history of his body, is obliged to dissect the heart of his people" (211). Only through dissecting the heart of community and self, only by disassembling the colonial construct so as to reconstruct a new self, can one become a thinking being capable of making political decisions. Another layer of this dismantling occurs with women, for rejecting patriarchal constructs in addition to colonial ones can produce a further dissection of community and self. The woman, therefore, needs to reconcile these myriad parts in order to become an agent of change.

In following this theme of first colonial and then patriarchal deconstructing and then reconstructing a new self, physically and mentally, Vera's work examines violence against women, rape being the most predominant. Through her attention to female body parts in her work, Vera turns the notion of the fragmented female body as exploitative or imperialistic upside-down. Rather than conflating part with whole, Vera uses part to surpass whole in order to indicate the rift between identity and body. Carolyn Martin Shaw (2004) indicates that, "fragmentation is not the natural state of women in Vera's works, but it is one of the ways that women survive emotional and physical brutality" (242). In other words, Vera's female characters fragment under duress but are able to reconnect due to their own agency discovered through horrific violence. In her works, parts of the body, and even the body itself, have the ability to confine identity, but at the same time, identity has the ability to transcend physicality. Commenting on Vera's writing, Sarah Nuttall (2001) observes thus:

> The boundary between self, consciousness and the world is not clear. The body dissolves, but this is not about decay: the body is—perhaps—not necessary; it is neither assumed nor consecrated: there is something in Vera's creations of the perfect energy of the divine, in which the body gets in the way. But it is also a body reduced to its component parts—only the eye exists, or the arms, or the neck, or a lump on the neck. (397)

Vera's almost cinematic technique of writing focuses on specific bodily parts to evoke female identity as well as threats to that identity. Liberation is possible, but also there is healing, and pleasure, to be found in physicality as well. As Shaw further explains, Vera depicts "women's and girls' struggle for self-definition, against bodily fragmentation, and for individual agency" (2004, 40). By defining and uniting fragments of self, women become subjects in history rather than merely objects.

Vera's canon is well known for its often graphic depiction of violence. *Without a Name,* Vera's second novel, is set during the Second Chimurenga, the war for independence against Ian Smith's government. The protagonist, Mazvita, is so destroyed by the circumstances of her life that she kills her newborn baby of questionable paternity, straps it to her back, and returns it to the site of her rape for burial. Such a horrific act is certainly shocking, but Vera succeeds in making Mazvita all too human and sympathetic. In the background of Mazvita's story is the larger story of a nation's struggle for independence. The novel is set in 1977, at the peak of the independence war, yet the fighting never takes center stage in the action of the novel; it is always in the background. We, as readers, are interested in the effect of war on Mazvita rather than the fighting itself.

Pauline Dodgson (1999) summarizes Mazvita in this way: "It may be possible to see Mazvita as one victim of the war representing other women who are also victims of the war but this is not an interpretation that the reader arrives at easily. If there is a collective history of female suffering and experience . . . then it departs radically" from other texts dealing with this same time period (96). The trauma of the independence struggle is borne by this individual character in ways the history books do not explore for the collective.

The fight for independence depended upon unity among blacks in Zimbabwe, but such unity did not always exist. The Rhodesian Front (Ian Smith's army fighting to maintain his rule of the country) drafted blacks to fight against the insurgency, creating tension even within ethnic identities. Men venturing out to fight in the bush were displaced from home and family and from the land over which they were fighting. Women who wished to join the fighting were misunderstood or shunned outright by the men, in the bush or at home. Shona and Ndebele, the two main cultural identities in Zimbabwe, may have had a different agenda for the direction of an independent nation.

In a variety of ways, Mazvita symbolizes this disconnection felt by a group struggling for nationhood. She has no family. She cannot fully connect with a man in an intimate relationship. Nyenyedzi, her rural lover, wants her to stay with him and work the land, providing some stability for her, but she wants to go to the city. As she tells Nyenyedzi, "[I]t is the perfect place to begin. It is better there than here. Harare. The news about the freedom in that city has reached all the ears in Mubaira. . . . It will be easier in Harare. You can forget anything in the city" (Vera 2002, 30). Whereas Nyenyedzi clings to his rural lifestyle and his roots—responding to Mazvita that "you can forget your own mother"—Mazvita wishes to start anew and forget her past, her connections, and her home (30). When Mazvita arrives in Harare, she lives with Joel through convenience, not love: "There were no greetings, preliminaries, or rituals of courtship. At least none that Mazvita recognized" (56). She does not question the start of the relationship with Joel; she views it as a matter of survival. Having a man to provide for her is a necessity. Yet there is no nurturance or caring or even genuine connection in the relationship; it is merely sexual and economic in nature. Her lack of satisfying personal relationships serves to keep her isolated from her community.

Mazvita lacks other forms of connection as well. Contrary to Vera's other heroines, she no longer feels a connection with the land, relinquishing it to the soldier who raped her, instead. For her, the land represents masculinity and violence, not sustenance. She has no familial connections to bind her to her homeland, her family having been killed during the fighting. When the soldier rapes her, she feels disconnected *from* her own body as well as a disconnection *in* her body: "He removed her legs from her body, and she lay still, not recognizing her legs as her own" (97). The rapist visits the trauma on the lower half of her body, so Mazvita disassociates herself from that part of herself. She mentally fragments herself, physically, in order to keep her identity whole and unharmed.

The way in which the story is told ensures that we do not hold the entire picture of Mazvita's story until the very end, and this only with quite active participation on the part of the reader. The setting shifts from chapter to chapter, leading to a sense of dislocation that echoes Mazvita's own feeling. Quayson views this narrative technique as a fragmenting of chronology: "even past and present are fragmented, with different trajectories of both epochs being woven into a structure of labile images" (2001, 204). The narrative threatens to disintegrate before unity of story, protagonist, and ultimately, nation, succeeds in the end. Quayson further notes that "the deferred circuit of the referential locus is enacted throughout the entire chain of discursive relationships (both symbolic and social) and not just with respect to the personal narrative of an individual's fragmented subjectivity" (206). Through disjointed narrative, the reader ascertains Mazvita's shattered identity as a rural Zimbabwean woman within a community. Uniting the pieces of the story into a cohesive narrative thread demonstrates to the reader how difficult it is for Mazvita to connect the pieces of her own story.

The trauma visited upon the female body in this novel manifests as pregnancy. During the course of the novel, Mazvita, the protagonist, is raped by a soldier and has two lovers, Nyenyedzi (in the countryside) and Joel (in the city). Although most likely the father is Nyenyedzi, Vera leaves paternity mysterious. The significantly female child is distanced from not only her father but also from her mother. Beginning with the pregnancy, Mazvita attempts to deny the child's very existence. Later, she does not bond with the child, does not name her, refers to her even in her thoughts as "the baby" or "the child," not "my baby," thus creating a linguistic distance between mother and child that she does not attempt to bridge. By using definite articles as determiners rather than personal pronouns, Mazvita never claims kinship with the baby. She lacks any agency in her life, as does the child. Ultimately, Mazvita takes the shocking step of breaking the child's neck, disconnecting head from body in an act that both frees and imprisons her. Beyond literal physical disconnection, disconnection from land, disconnection from family, and even disconnection in the mother/daughter relationship predominate in this novel.

Mazvita herself projects the baby's physical trauma onto her own body, showing a fluidity between mother and child, despite the large emotional distance between them. The first chapter of the novel sets the scene in a bus, where she is carrying the dead child on her back. Chapters set on the bus intersperse Mazvita's back story; by the end of the novel, she has reached her destination, her home village, the place where she would like to bury the child. Even though the circumstances of her situation are not clear at the beginning, Vera establishes the theme of disconnection, even on the physical level. Mazvita's thoughts while on the bus are chaotic, sometimes incoherent as the narrator indicates: "Her neck was twisted. A bone at the bottom of her neck told her that her neck had been turned and turned till it could no longer find a resting place. Her neck had been broken. She felt a violent piercing like shattered glass on her tongue, where she carried fragments of her being" (7–8). The physical violence Mazvita imagines she is experiencing threatens her very identity. Her being itself is in danger of fragmentation, and she carries pieces in her mouth, though she is unable to speak of it. As Meg Samuelson (2002) describes, "[T]he baby's dismembered body, and the rupture in time that it represents, replicates the sense of dismemberment that Mazvita experienced in her own body during her rape and its aftermath" (95). Such a reading could indicate that the rapist is, indeed, the father of the child, but on another level the "rupture in time" symbolizes Mazvita's break with her past stimulated by the physical trauma that happened to her there. Additionally, Samuelson asserts that Mazvita's alienation pushes her into breaking her baby's neck (95). She is thus rupturing the baby, physically, to mimic her own ruptured self.

Mazvita's worry that her neck is broken echoes the scene in which she kills the baby. Both her own body, figuratively, and that of the baby, literally, experience fragmentation of a final kind as Vera describes in this scene:

> That pressing [of her hand on the baby's face] granted her an elaborate and fierce energy to free herself from this baby, it drove her into a violent but calculated trance as she moved forward toward the child and picked it up from the bed, picked it up slowly and finally, picked it up in sobs that rendered her body into half, in sobs. She picked up the baby slowly, as though not to waken it. Her desire was to close the baby's eyes finally and truthfully. (107)

Although she makes the choice to end the baby's life, the decision "render[s] her body into half" (107). Mazvita's figurative splitting will soon become reality on the body of the baby as she hangs the baby with a neck tie. Vera captures this scene very intensely:

> She drew the bottom end of the tie across the baby's neck. She pulled at the cloth while the baby remained blinded and trusting. She strained hard and confidently though this pulling choked her and blinded her and broke her back. (109)

Mazvita empathically absorbs the very trauma she is inflicting on her child, and it is in the moment of killing that she finally claims kinship with the child: "She felt the neck break and fall over her wrist. She felt the bone at the bottom of that neck tell her that the child had died. The bone broke softly. . . . The head swung back and fell onto her palm, because she had broken it. She had broken the neck of *her child*" (109, emphasis added). At that moment, she is able to bridge the gap between past and present, between home and city, and with more purpose than she has yet shown, she returns to her ruined home with the only family she has left—a dead baby.

Mazvita decides that a return to her homeland with the dead child is her only course of action. When she boards the bus to return home, strands of herself are not closely conjoined, as reflected in her experience of the other people on the bus. Mazvita sees faces as seemingly separate from bodies: "She watched a soldier standing under the dusty window. He held a gun close to his body, close to his face. His face was scarred. She stared at the scars on the face of the soldier" (89). In a nightmarish scene, she even sees an alter-ego of herself, whom she refers to in the third person. This other self is trying to discover Mazvita's secret, and Mazvita is terrified that the dead baby on her back will be found. Her very identity splits in this crucial moment when the horror at what she has done becomes clear. Vera pinpoints that a woman's psyche cannot withstand such trauma. Yet, Mazvita brings her selves back together:

> Mazvita turned to see that the woman was wiping her face with her scarf, and the wiping made the men laugh. . . . The women laughed with the men. Mazvita laughed with the women and the men. . . . Mazvita rubbed the dust, slowly, from her own eyebrows. (104–5)

In joining the laughter of the men and women, she becomes a part of a community again. This is the first step toward forgiveness. The second step is reconnecting the divergent strands of herself. In order to experience forgiveness, she must reconcile the parts of self and other that have caused a schism in her identity. Returning the dead child to the earth is the final step, an attempt to reconnect her shattered self to the land which had nurtured her earlier in her life. This is her attempt to reconnect the disconnected strands of self that occurred through rape and become whole again. Mazvita returns her baby to her rural homeland, bringing together the various threads of her narrative into a conclusion. She carries the trauma of war in her own body; perhaps, symbolically, the baby represents her ability to purge the trauma from her body and to work toward renewal. If the soldier/rapist is, indeed, the father of the child, his connection to war manifests in the child and is a constant reminder to Mazvita of what she attempted to escape. Even if he is not the father, his act instigates her departure to the city and her disconnection from community. The war had devastating effects on the populace, and through the character of Mazvita, a reader can empathize with these effects in a more personal way.

In *Under the Tongue*, Vera continues her theme of personal trauma as the locus for national trauma. Dealing with a time period just a couple of years after *Without a Name*, *Under the Tongue* takes place in 1979, on the eve of independence. Vera explores both the disruption to family inherent in the war for independence, as well as the powerful connection between women that is still possible. The protagonist, Zhizha, suffers incestual rape at the hands of her father, a soldier returning from warfare. The novel concentrates on her path to healing her physical and psychological wounds, drawing upon the strength of her mother and grandmother. Thus, potential healing comes from connecting within female, familial relationships.

Rather than fully castigating the father, Muroyiwa, for his heinous acts, Vera fragments the narrative thread of the novel, alternating a first-person narration of Zhizha's thoughts and feelings with a third-person account of Muroyiwa's story. At first this method is disconcerting until the reader determines the pattern: a chapter from Zhizha's perspective (which often encompasses that of Grandmother as well), then a chapter from Muroyiwa's perspective, and so on. Vera's style makes an impact through fragmenting perspective, chronology, and language itself. Smith (1999) indicates that "Vera manipulates the English language in staggering metaphors of starkness and brokenness, as she relentlessly drives home the message of the nightmarish effects of misplaced hostilities toward women and children and the search for hope amid hopelessness" (382). Readers naturally intuit Zhizha's trauma, but as the novel unfolds, they also get a sense of the traumatic events surrounding the Grandmother, Runyararo (Mother), and even Muroyiwa as well. The focal point of trauma here is the loss of family and familial structures, a necessary result of a long-fought war.

Zhizha's chapters are marked by a childlike diction and style and frequent repetitions as she tries to make sense of her world and heal. Her very identity is slippery, identifying herself alternately with Mother or Grandmother: "Zhizha's 'I' moves to and fro in endless shiftings and displacements, the boundaries of her 'self' are indistinct and permeable. At the end of the narrative we learn that she had been literally split open by her father" (Kopf 2005, 248). Her permeable boundaries indicate an identity that is not cohesive, and her expression communicates her confusion about herself and her situation. She does not use the language of rape or of violence; one is not clear if she understands what has happened to her. She only knows that she has been scarred: "I see a scar grow farther and farther. I am certain this is the path through which I will be born. The scar widens, peels like bark. I wait" (Vera 2002, 124). Zhizha seeks wholeness through the very pain that fragmented her, for through the cracking of the scar, she can be reborn. Yet, there is a passivity to Zhizha, an inability to take action to bring about this wholeness. If she is patient, wholeness and healing will come to her. As Shaw notes, the rape at the hands of her father has torn Zhizha asunder as her feelings illustrate: "Each part of her body has a separate existence, a life of its own: the ears that heard his insistent whispers, the stomach that broke and rooted her to the ground, the bloodied mouth, the legs smeared with her blood and his semen, the eyes parched and dry, and the tongue that refused sound. Her rape is not a repressed memory—it lives in every part of her body" (2004, 41). Only by reconciling those parts of her body with the traumatic memory can she achieve wholeness.

Zhizha learns that her mother has been imprisoned for killing her father, and the suffering she is experiencing is compounded by being separated from her mother. Although Grandmother's story is woven into the chapters told from Zhizha's perspective, Grandmother is dealing with her own pain, that of losing her baby son many years ago. Zhizha needs her mother's love to keep her body and mind together. Fear of losing all the women in her family threatens her actual physical body: "I watch my toes dissolve. I watch my feet which are no longer my feet. They are large, not quite there, not part of me. It is the same with my arms which have discovered their own ability for silence. Only my shoulders say these are my arms" (Vera 2002, 134). Without an established place in a solid family structure, Zhizha is unsure what parts of her are actually her or hers. Even when Runyararo visits Zhizha (whether in actuality or in fantasy), Zhizha lacks a complete picture, constructing a kaleidoscope of her mother to mirror her own image:

> I move back from her pouring words. I am not complete without possession of her memory and her desires. . . . I find a dim spot where I hide, and watch. Her visit is a fragmented togetherness, a handful of caress like blinding noon dust. (209)

Zhizha attempts to embody her mother and grandmother to find healing, but at the same time she cannot. Runyararo and Grandmother have also had traumatic events in their lives, but they were not visited upon their bodies. They are, therefore, limited in the amount of aid they can offer in putting her back together again.

Indeed, it is unclear whether Zhizha ever recovers psychically from the damage caused her. The novel does not follow a straight chronology. The final chapter, which revisits Zhizha's perspective on the rape scene, emphasizes her brokenness at every level.

> A sudden shove, brutal and repeated. My knee breaks, slides sideways, contracts. My elbows are bruised and broken. He lifts my face, swings my head sideways, my head pressed down, my face cupped in his wide palm. . . . I cannot breathe. My forehead grows with a painful throbbing, grows into his waiting hand, grows into a rounded shell which he breaks and breaks with a clenched fist. (230)

Not only is Zhizha physically broken, but she also, psychically, splits off and disassociates herself into a tortoise to deny what is happening to her. As the narrative voice observes here, "[A] tortoise moves slowly forward, carrying a broken shell. It pulls its head inside, and hides. It pulls its legs in and hides. Its shell is broken and crushed because it has swallowed its own head, swallowed its own legs" (231). She displaces her identity into the tortoise as a way of dealing with her trauma. To return to Quayson's reading of Freudian theory, Zhizha must go through displacement and fragmentation in order to reach healing. However, this schism on the physical, mental, and emotional level manifests itself into an inability to communicate as well. At the end of the above rape scene, Zhizha remarks: "My voice grows from inside me, broken and dry" (231). She is unable to express through language what has occurred, breaking communication even with Mother and Grandmother.

What, perhaps, gives readers hope for Zhizha and the nation in which she lives is the final chapter, which is set in 1980, after victory has been achieved by the freedom fighters. Celebrations are taking place in the streets, and Vera creates the ritual of women breaking mirrors in the street to commemorate the occasion, the mirrors reflecting on the women's external identity. In Lacanian theory, we identify ourselves as separate from other people as soon as we can recognize ourselves in the mirror. Mirrors are integral to identity construction based on our exteriors. Shattering mirrors again indicates the process of fragmenting physically in order to heal mentally: "Breaking glass. Some said this was a ritual the women had invented in order to keep their longing ripe and ready. . . . And when the broken mirrors had become forgotten there was only the hurt lingering underneath coaxing words" (Vera 2002, 233).

The smashing of mirrors is a significant symbol. Slivers of glass have the capacity to cut, to wound. Mirrors reflect our own reflection, an aspect of ourselves. The women are potentially wounding themselves by smashing their reflections, either the ones they have of themselves or those the men perceive. One woman even smashes a life-sized mirror, representing herself. It is a triumphant moment, however: "History was a spectacle, and this woman had found a new dream to make her own waiting real, original to her suffering and her particular endurance of anguish" (233). Women have borne unspoken trauma behind the scenes of war, but they have endured, and one hopes Zhizha does as well, in wholeness.

The complexity of fragmenting and then unifying female body and identity as well as nation culminates in *The Stone Virgins*, Vera's final novel. Here the segmentation of Zimbabwean society between the rival political parties (and cultural identities) of ZANU-PF (mostly Shona, led by Robert Mugabe) and ZIPRA (mostly Ndebele, led by Joshua Nkomo) is epitomized through the literal fragmentation of the two female characters, Thenjiwe and Nonceba. The bodies of Nonceba and Thenjiwe are fragmented, just as the body politic of the new Zimbabwe is fragmented. Their female bodies represent both the land in which they live as well as the other people who live there. Vera extends the metonymy to represent all the people, Shona and Ndebele alike, of Zimbabwe and the struggle to come to terms with their national postwar identity. Further, as Lene Bull Christiansen (2005) explains, "the spiritual narrative of the nation has become blurred, fragmented and broken and, as such, it does not correspond with any nationalist version of the nation's temporality" (212). Nonceba, especially, whose lips are cut off in a violent attack, is a metonymic representation of silent women who were objects of history but who find a voice and become subjects in their own lives.

The major action of the novel focuses on the trauma visited upon these sisters—Thenjiwe's decapitation and Nonceba's rape and dismemberment. As Shaw (2004) points out, "[T]he sisters think of themselves as one, and, because of this, the violence done to them doubled: they are separated and their individual bodies violated, cut apart" (42). These characters, as well as the male characters Cephas (Thenjiwe's lover) and Sibaso (the perpetrator against the sisters), embody the strife of a nation struggling to find its identity after a political and military struggle for majority rule. In *The Stone Virgins*, Vera examines the price paid after victory as well. After the war for liberation ended and Robert Mugabe, along with his ZANU-PF party, assumed power, he sent his 5th Brigade into Matabeleland (in southern Zimbabwe) to massacre ZIPRA dissidents or anyone he considered a threat to his power and regime. Incidents from this period in Zimbabwe's history are brought to life in the novel. Even more significant is Vera's almost sympathetic treatment of the monstrous Sibaso, a supposed dissident who is suffering from the trauma of both fighting in the liberation war and also being an Ndebele in a Shona-ruled country. Sibaso rapes and mutilates the two sisters, and then, he murders one in the presence of the other. Nonceba, however, recovers, and at the end of the novel, she finds potential love with Thenjiwe's former lover, Cephas, who is an archivist in Bulawayo. This new prospective relationship between the two defines *The Stone Virgins* as Vera's most hopeful novel, ending on what could be considered a positive note after all the horror that has come before.

Although the novel is divided clearly into two time periods—before and after independence—and those two parts are chronological, what happens within those spans does not follow sequentially. Readers are left to sort out the complicated relationship between cause and effect, especially when the effect is sometimes related prior to the cause. For instance, Sibaso's perpetration of rape and murder is narrated before glimpses of the causes for his violent actions are revealed. Vera's attitude to the fluidity of time in this novel reflects lived experience rather than remembered experience. Time has the ability to move and shape people, but the past and the present are not her only focus. The future has the power to hurt as much as the past or the present, even though it is yet to happen. In *The Stone Virgins*, chronology is not a fixed entity; what is to happen holds as much power as what has already happened. It is the narrative that makes these non-chronological relationships possible. Vera provides a moment concerning Thenjiwe's future harm, which we are privy to as outside witnesses, but the character herself is not. In this instance, Vera uses the third person to tell us something about the character's future, stating: "She [Thenjiwe] takes the stranger home. She has a lot to forget, so this is all right. She has no idea now, or ever, that some of the harm she has to forget is in the future, not in the past, and that she would not have enough time in the future to forget any of the hurt" (2003, 36). The power of personal relationships can heal or harm; Thenjiwe can take Cephas home to forget past harms, but future harms guarantee that this relationship, though loving, will not be redemptive.

As mentioned above, the novel is broken into two parts to represent pre- and post-independence. The first part covers a larger span of time relatively quickly, whereas the second part settles in for a much shorter time frame (and where readers are within that frame is not always entirely clear) and expands the personal narrative to exemplify historical occurrence. The novel ends in 1986, as already mentioned on a hopeful note, which is particularly interesting given that it was written and published after 2000, when the presidential elections and Land Reapportionment Act caused further strife in an already wounded country.

The beginning of the text establishes one setting of the novel by providing an in-depth description of Bulawayo, the streets, and its people. The time is not during the actual colonial era but rather that of Ian Smith's rule, and segregation is a fact of life. There are different bars for black and white; society is fragmented. Living as separate entities, identity crises results when a large portion of the populace is not valued for its humanity. In the chapter that covers the end of the fight for liberation, Vera establishes the tension that exists between man and woman, which will explode into violence later in the novel. Female fighters are returning from the bush and congregating at Thandabantu Store, formerly the terrain of the men in the village. The tension that exists between the displaced men and the returning female fighters, confident in themselves and their bodies, evokes the misunderstanding between individuals that also marks larger miscommunications among people suddenly identified as "Zimbabweans." Even though the fight for majority rule has ended successfully, fighting in the country is far from over: "Independence is a respite from war" (Vera, 58); it is not an end. War—between individual people and among peoples—still lurks in the hearts and minds of (significantly) men. The narrator observes:

> The men stare and let themselves be enamored by the possibilities of freedom. Who would have thought that . . . they would congregate with women fighters and listen to the soccer score . . . unable to imagine anything at all they hold in common, not even independence or the soccer score. (62)

There is no common ground to be found between women and men at this point. They are no longer united against a common enemy and must find a peace between the sexes in order to move forward as a united country.

With majority rule comes a new set of problems, breaking the patriarchal traditions of the past to ensure freedom for everyone in the new Zimbabwe. Women fought in the war for liberation and would no longer be content with a subservient role in the household and in the country for which they fought. Men may not want to exchange that status quo for a new reality in which they are no longer king of the homestead. Coming to terms with this gender gap is an issue that is played out in violent ways throughout the remainder of the novel. Vera's seems to be showing the human, personal dimension of the consequences and not just the rewards of political independence.

In this novel, there is also a clear separation between rural and urban settings. The depiction of the rape of Nonceba by Sibaso starts with one word: "Kezi." We know we are back in the rural area, no longer in the Bulawayo teeming with people and ideas about fighting. Then, we are led into what could be an intimate experience but is not, at least not in the usual sense of the word: "The man places his hand over her left shoulder. Her thoughts turn blind, ashes stirred by a small wind. He presses his hand down on her limp arm. He turns her body toward himself" (67).

Up to this point, this could be a depiction of lovers. However, the last sentence continues: "looking for something in her he can still break, but there is nothing in her that can still be broken" (67). Now, the reader apprehends the violence in this scene, that this interaction between man and woman is not out of love. Yet, there are gestures of intimacy in Sibaso's treatment of Nonceba. At one point, he says, "Sit here, on my knee" (67). This is not the action or language to expect from a rapist and murderer (of course, we do not realize that he is a murderer yet). He wants her to touch him, to hold him, to look at him. He even asks: "Are you afraid to look at me?" (70), when the answer should be obvious. Sibaso experiences a split in his own mind, being at once violent and in search of intimacy. In this novel, in particular, not just the female characters are fractured, physically as well as mentally; the male characters also experience fragmentation, though only mentally.

The chapter depicting the rape presents the first instance of first-person narration that delineates the fragmentation of perspective. It opens with both characters, unnamed at first, presented from a third person narrative perspective which suddenly changes to Nonceba's viewpoint. "I am waiting. I am alive, now, a companion to his every thought. I am breathing. My temples, beating" (68). The remainder of the paragraph returns to third person: "She closes her eyes and her body listens as his movements pursue each of her thoughts. She breathes. Harm" (68). However, the crucial opening sentences establish Nonceba's will to live, thus providing insight into her character. Interestingly, this becomes our first introduction to her personality, the name having been mentioned earlier by Thenjiwe, tangentially. Vera's shifting perspectives from first to third person, in one paragraph that deals with a single or same character, reflects the ambiguity of identity. This style creates, simultaneously, a closeness to and distance from the reader. Consequently, Nonceba's identity is ambiguous, because she is neither fully the narrative "I" of the first person, nor the "she" of the third person viewpoint. Thus, her identity eludes clarity or recognition. Although privy to her thoughts, readers fail to fully grasp her essence as she experiences harm and moves from internal monologue to external gaze in a matter of sentences.

Time in this scene becomes fluid, evoking a reminiscent fluidity of Thenjiwe's experiences making love to Cephas. This is a disturbing connection, however, for Nonceba is not Sibaso's lover by choice but rather through violence. As she struggles to survive the attack, the thought occurs to her: "Has she lived before this moment of urgency and despair? Is there something whispered before a cataclysmic earthquake, sleep, before a frightful awakening to death? Is life not lived backward in flashes, in spasms of hopeless regret?" (69). The concept of time moving backward, of the future inflicting harm in the present, recurs here with the addition of déja vu. Perhaps the horrific moments in our lives are constantly being relived; if that is the case, can we prevent their harm? If we know anguish awaits us in a future time, can we do anything to avoid it? Or, are we destined to experience suffering as a condition of our humanity? Vera indicates the latter; even if we move backward through time, aware of what the past (or the future) holds for us, we can only undergo "spasms of hopeless regret."

Nonetheless, healing may be possible. Nonceba undergoes reconstructive surgery to repair the damage to her mouth: "With some powder on, she looks almost unharmed. Almost" (70). One could look at the nation of Zimbabwe, ignoring its secret genocide of Ndebele dissidents, and find unity beyond harm. However, the harm is still there. As a review in *The New York Times* states, Nonceba's "struggle to heal reflects, in many ways, this nation's struggle to acknowledge and come to terms with its raw, self-inflicted wounds" (Swarns 2002, E1). A nation must not forget (or deny) its past, or it will not have a future. Notably, Vera also maintains that "[A] new nation needs to restore the past," not hide, deny, or change it, including the blemishes (2003, 184). Commenting on the significance of female agency in Vera's novel, Vambe (2004) acknowledges thus:

> In her [Vera's] novel it is the historical agency of the African women, their memories of anger and pain and their desire for total freedom that is emphasized. The ways through which the war narratives, memories, and contribution of Vera's female characters enter into the novel, becoming *the* text that interrogates the 'official' ZAPU war narrative, reveals the latter as fragmented, fragile and one-sided. (101)

The fragmentation of the female body both represents and subverts the fragmentary narrative of nation-building and the segmentations within society. However, there is hope to be found in the interrogation of the war and nation-building narrative, a hope present in the character of Nonceba.

This essay has attempted to reconcile the notions of mental and emotional identity on one hand, and physicality on the other; it has demonstrated how both are threatened by the violence endemic in a colonial and postcolonial society. Vera's protagonists experience schisms in mind and body, although healing does seem to be possible. The trauma inflicted upon the female body in Vera's fiction represents a larger national trauma. How these characters cope with trauma provides a blueprint (positive or negative) for moving forward as the nation of Zimbabwe.

REFERENCES

Bhabha, Homi. 1994. *The Location of Culture*. London: Routledge.

Bryce, Jane. 2002. "Interview with Yvonne Vera, 1 August 2000, Bulawayo, Zimbabwe: 'Survival Is in the Mouth.'" (Appendix 1). In *Sign and Taboo: Perspectives on the Poetic Fiction of Yvonne Vera*, edited by Robert Muponde and Mandi Taruvinga, 217–26. Harare, Zimbabwe: Weaver Press and Oxford: James Currey.

Christiansen, Lene Bull. 2005. "Yvonne Vera: Rewriting Discourses of History and Identity in Zimbabwe." In *Versions of Zimbabwe: New Approaches to Literature and Culture*, edited by Robert Muponde and Ranka Primorac, 203–15. Harare: Weaver Press.

Dodgson, Pauline. 1999. "Coming in from the Margins: Gender in Contemporary Zimbabwean Writing." In *Post-Colonial Literatures: Expanding the Canon*, edited by Deborah L. Madsen, 88–103. London: Pluto Press.

Fanon, Frantz. 1963. *The Wretched of the Earth*. Translated by Constance Farrington. New York: Grove Press.

———. 1967. *Black Skin, White Masks*. Translated by Charles Lam Markmann. New York: Grove Press.

Kopf, Martina. 2005. "Writing Sexual Violence: Words and Silences in Yvonne Vera's *Under the Tongue*." *Matatu: Journal for African Culture and Society* 29–30(1): 243–53.

Nuttall, Sarah. 2001. "Reading, Recognition, and the Postcolonial." *Interventions: International Journal of Postcolonial Studies* 3(3): 391–404.

Quayson, Ato. 2001. "Symbolisation Compulsions: Freud, African Literature and South Africa's Process of Truth and Reconciliation." *Cambridge Quarterly* 30(3): 191–214.

Samuelson, Meg. 2002. "Re-membering the Body: Rape and Recovery in *Without a Name* and *Under the Tongue*." In *Sign and Taboo: Perspectives on the Poetic Fiction of Yvonne Vera*, edited by Robert Muponde and Mandi Taruvinga, 93–100. Harare: Weaver Press, and Oxford: James Currey.

Shaw, Carolyn Martin. 2004. "Turning Her Back on the Moon: Virginity, Sexuality, and Mothering in the Works of Yvonne Vera." *Africa Today* 51(2): 35–51. https://muse.jhu.edu/login?auth=0&type=summary&url=/journals/africa_today/v051/51.2shaw.html.

Smith, Pamela J. 1999. "Review of *Under the Tongue*." *World Literature Today* 73(2): 382.

Swarns, Rachel L. 2002. "Zimbabwe's Novels of Reckoning: Writers Explore Despair and Violence Under Black Rule." *The New York Times* 7 October. http://www.nytimes.com/2002/10/07/books/zimbabwe-s-novels-reckoning-writers-explore-despair-violence-under-black-rule.html?pagewanted=all.

Vambe, Maurice Taonezvi. 2004. *African Oral Story-Telling Tradition and the Zimbabwean Novel in English*. Pretoria: University of South Africa Press.

Vera, Yvonne. 2002. *Without a Name* and *Under the Tongue*. New York: Farrar, Straus and Giroux.

———. 2003. *The Stone Virgins*. New York: Farrar, Straus and Giroux.

Willis, Deborah, and Carla Williams. 2002. *The Black Female Body: A Photographic History*. Philadelphia: Temple University Press.

FOUR

Fanta Nacro's *Night of Truth*

The Journey to the End of the Night

P. Julie Papaioannou

Since the early years of African cinema, up to the turn of the century, films like *Sambizanga* by Sarah Maldoror (1972) on the war of Angolan independence, *Camp de Thiaroye* by Ousmane Sembène (1987) on the Senegalese *tirailleurs* in the Second World War, Ingrid Sinclair's *Flame* (1996) on the war of Zimbabwean independence, and Issa Serge Coelo's *Daresalam* (2000), a historical fiction based on Chad's war of independence in the 1960s and 1970s, have treated the theme of war in terms of independence and resistance. With the exception, perhaps, of *Camp de Thiaroye* that presented resistance in a conflict between the French African troops and metropolis, the narrative of independence wars addressed the role of women mostly within the frame of national liberation movements. In most recent years, wars of independence shifted to ethnic wars, and films such as Fanta Régina Nacro's *Night of Truth* (*La Nuit de la Vérité*, 2004), Newton Aduaka's *Ezra* (2007), Jean-Stéphane Sauvaire's *Johnny Mad Dog* (2008), Mahamat-Saleh Haroun's *A Screaming Man* (*Un homme qui crie*, 2010), Abderrahmane Sissako's *Timbuktu* (2014), to name the most notable ones in West African filmmaking,[1] focus more clearly on the traumatic effects of civil and ethnic crises. Such crises profoundly affect existing gendered identities, all the more so by constructing new social identities, such as children soldiers, victimized civilians, refugees, survivors, and rehabilitators.

In general, war narratives presuppose clear-cut gender roles in existing gender relations: men go to war, and are in the center of the conflict as militants, whereas women and children stay at the periphery most often as victimized civilians, refugees, and in times of peace, as survivors and rehabilitators. "In "Gendered Violence and the Militarisation of Ethnicity" in *Postcolonial Subjectivities in Africa,* Sharon Hutchinson and Jok Jok discuss gender roles in zones of ethnic conflict in South Sudan, noting Cynthia Enloe's (1995) quote that "[M]ilitarisation . . . simply won't work unless men will accept certain norms of masculinity and women will abide by certain structures of femininity" (Werbner 2002, 84). To that extent, it is of particular interest that early on in African filmmaking, women filmmakers have taken up the challenge to question the historical and sociopolitical climate of their times, and the role of women amidst a national, regional, or political conflict. Maldoror's *Sambizanga* (1972), for example, corroborates the notion of intensified gendered identities during the war, and brings to focus the social position of women in the Angolan war of independence. The wife of an imprisoned militant, Maria, is going from prison to prison to look for her husband who might have faced death by torture. The husband's unknown fate defines Maria's social position as a widow, propels her wandering and search for him, and brings her to the forefront of suffering. In later years, Sinclair's controversial film *Flame* (1996) places the main character Florence (or Flame by her codified pseudonym of a soldier) in the position of fighter next to male comrades amidst an armed conflict. Flame faces a double fight: she must negotiate her femininity in a highly masculinized environment amongst rebel soldiers. When Flame rejects one of her comrade's sexual advances, she is ultimately raped, and impregnated with his child. Like Maldoror, Sinclair focuses on the inequality amongst male and female comrades to highlight that the manifestation of sex and gender is conflated in the context of war. As men hold power over women, "more often than not, processes of militarisation increase women's vulnerabilities to violence and rape, at the hands not only of enemy troops but also of their own male 'protectors'" (Werbner 2002, 85). In war narratives, the women's position according to prescribed gender roles becomes all the more complex when women find themselves in a paradoxical situation as both victims and combatants.

In Nacro's *The Night of Truth* (2004), the intensification of gendered positions brings women and children to the center of the narrative as both victims of war violence, and fighters against their victimhood in their desire to engage with emotional resilience and intensity in political, social, and familial fronts for the sake of future peace. By integrating traditional structures of gender relations in the context of ethnic conflict in an imaginary African country, *The Night of Truth* also raises questions of origin, historical memory, collective consciousness, and subjectivity, themes that are linked to a postcolonial transnational cinema. The film narrative shifts back and forth from the delocalized conflict of two ethnic groups to a fictionalized war narrative on a global scale, and plays out the personal and domestic elements in the public sphere. Recreating the familial story of Nacro's uncle who died in an ethnic war, the narrative of *The Night of Truth* takes the proportions of a universal tragic story, because it critically connects the theme of horror to women's and children's suffering. The film could have equally been "made as a response not only to the Rwandan genocide of 1994, but to ethnic cleansing in the former Yugoslavia" (Dovey 2009, 255). Although *The Night of Truth* is dedicated to the memory of a man, women hold prominent roles in the film that, most notably, enable them to respond to their victimization by the brutalities of war. Nacro comments:

> This film is written in memory of a man. Accused of having fomented a coup d'état, he has been tortured and sent to jail. One night, some people prepared a charcoal fire, attached him over it and made him slowly roast until the morning. This man was my uncle. From this tragic event I wanted to make a film . . . to relate it to the world. What can we do in front of horror? (Diawara 2010, 295).

The familial story of an uncle's torture to death follows the familiar narrative patterns of an ethnic confrontation, patterns that inherently include the notion of crisis, and violence before any resolution takes place. Interestingly, the film reenacts the scene of torture with one of the two women main characters playing the role of both victim and torturer, and ends with her adversary, a woman in the role of both victim and peacemaker. The notion of horror of war links not only with the desire for peace, but also with the question of human culture, gender difference, and women's familial, social, and political position.

More precisely, *The Night of Truth* (2004) takes place in an undisclosed African country where two ethnic groups, the Bonandés and the Nayaks have just terminated their long-standing conflict, and their leaders are at the crucial point of negotiations for reconciliation. The critical moment of either taking the path of peace and forgiveness, or the path of yet another round of atrocities opens up the wounds that an ethnic war has inflicted on both parties. As physical and emotional wounds attest to the brutality of war, feelings of sadness, fear, and uncertainty for the future overshadow the process of peacemaking. The conflict that had taken place between the two ethnic groups that were otherwise culturally, socially, and biologically interrelated by the common practice of intermarriage, had deeply divided and separated their people.

The film opens with a long shot in a rather idyllic scenery. Yet, the soldiers walking in single file next to a river alludes to the process of militarization, and the division of ethnic groups at the outset: the soldiers' reflection in the water both doubles up and splits their image, underscoring that in a civil war the enemy "other" originates from within. This long opening shot cuts to the close up of Edna, the wife of the President and leader of the Nayak fighters, mourning at the tomb of her son, Michel. Surrounded by guards, Edna assumes the position of victimized civilian seeking solace in the phantasm of her dead child, as he appears running and dancing at the cemetery. Notwithstanding Edna's heightened social position as the wife of President Kouka, this scene delineates the space of gendered "other," with the men presented as war fighters, protectors, or leaders, and the women as war victims, mourners, and sufferers. Edna is devastated by Michel's killing as yet another casualty of war, and her impulse to avenge her son's blood so that he would rest in peace, cancels out her husband's rational response to their loss, as well as his effort to appease and comfort her torment.

The subsequent sequences establish forestalling divides and oppositions between the two leaders and their families the day before they meet to make peace. In the Nayak President's house, Edna is lying on the bedroom floor drunk and desperate, unable to fall asleep without recourse to pills. Edna's mourning intensifies her anguish as a preemptive reaction to the night of negotiations. The idea of dining with the killers of her son, makes her to openly admit to her husband that her heart is full of hate, fear, and disgust. By virtue of having experienced the war from the position of an official leader, Kouka appears to be distant, and rather dismissively sympathetic toward his wife's suffering. Like Kouka and Edna, the revolutionary Colonel, Theo and his wife, Soumari, face a similar situation. Colonel Theo is haunted by nightmares of unfathomable brutality; blood flowing in rivers, dismembered, and decapitated bodies lying in murky waters, ravaged villages and destroyed communities summarize ten years of war atrocities in his dreams. Both Edna's suffering and Colonel Theo's torment are inscribed on the walls around the Colonel's courtyard with paintings that symbolically and graphically attest to the cruelty and violence of war. As an act of memory and protest, women paint on walls a series of horrific scenes of executions, rape, decapitations, and severed bodies. The artistic representation of a collective memory of pain seems to be all too familiar to a group of limbless children looking at the paintings, and nonchalantly commenting about the resemblance of men on the wall to people they know. Notably, in times of imminent peace, this act of "writing" on the wall re-inscribes the horror and victimization of women and children, and rearticulates the question of gender roles in the narrative of suffering.

At the Colonel's courtyard where ceremonial preparations for the peace treaty are under way, the setting exemplifies the traditional gender divide: the women gather in the kitchen, and the men prepare themselves for the negotiations in the yard and barracks. This traditional same-sex grouping is typical in male-dominant societies, and "is reinforced by strong gender division of labor . . . and occasionally, is augmented by ideological formulations or social rules. . . . At times, women demanded the separate space or took advantage of it as a refuge from oppressive features of their society" (Berger and White 1999, liii). In *The Night of*

Truth, if the kitchen provides the ultimate space for women's domestication by division of labor, it equally provides a space to express grief, pain, and laughter against any form of oppression. The kitchen is the place where Soumari along with her *domestique*, Awa, gives orders to prepare the peacemaking meal. Also, it provides a safe haven to the victimized Bonandés women and children, who gather to discuss their personal horror and suffering, their loss of limbs and loved ones. The separate feminine quarters are presented in juxtaposition with the courtyard and barracks where Colonel Theo, the commandant, and his soldiers polish their weapons, and ponder potential agreements before they admit the adversaries. In this setting of ceremonial preparations, it is expected that the courtyard between the kitchen and barracks will become the center of negotiations reserved for the male leaders, while their female counterparts will be on the side, mostly confined in their peripheral domesticated roles as wives and mothers. This traditional gender separation appears to intensify when the Nayak President demands to arrive to the celebration for peace with armed men. The Colonel's wife, Soumari, articulates her fear and contempt of this situation in her readiness to leave, along with her children, in order to seek refuge away from a militarized environment that could potentially result to the continuation of warfare. Almost by instinct, she responds that "men make peace, men make war. It's nothing to do with me, nor the children" (*The Night*). The paradox of holding peace negotiations with armed soldiers that, metaphorically speaking, almost drives Soumari and the children "in exile," highlights the critical time of cease fire in a hierarchized and masculinized space, where women and children have no immediate involvement. If, however, Soumari makes the decision to stay and support her husband, it is because Theo confesses his war crimes to her, openly admits his guilt, and asks for help and forgiveness. On the one hand, Soumari's role as a compassionate wife and mother against the Colonel's masculinized suffering intensifies traditional gender divisions in the film; on the other hand, in the given situation of making peace bearing arms, it suggests that her power derives precisely from her position as wife and mother. In other words, if the courtyard becomes the center of official peace talks for the male leaders, the kitchen creates the center for memory and forgiveness that women cater to peace negotiations. The paradox of making peace in the presence of armed men invites multiple transgressions to take place, so that the male-dominated "militarized" story becomes a story of womanhood, suffering and loss, love and hate.

Nacro, as a filmmaker and artist, "assumes [her] right to critique human culture and practice at large, with whatever sources or tools [she feels] are useful" (Dovey 2009, 200), in order to undertake a filmic journey to explore cultural layers of human understanding of horror in a narrative of war and peace on the brink. The canonicity of the narrative through the tragic themes of love, loss, vengeance, and sacrifice, both reinforces and subverts traditional divides, such as center and periphery, male and female. In addition, it opens a space for feminist views to address two important parts of identity in women's lives, motherhood and widowhood, particularly in an ethnic conflict. Edna's loss of son, signifies her loss of motherhood, and Soumari's loss of husband, signifies her widowhood. The two main female characters, inasmuch as they face similar situations of suffering, differ from each other in terms of how they define and fine-tune the question of woman's role in socio-political terms in a war crisis. With regards to class, both Edna and Soumari enjoy a social status at the upper echelons of society in their respective ethnic groups as the wives of leaders. However, the fact that the two women belong to two opposite groups with different and diverse cultural backgrounds, education and understanding of their womanhood, either undercuts or promotes peace negotiations. Peace will ultimately disarm the men; yet, in the process, the women will re-define their gender positions in society despite their loss.

The Night of Truth progresses with the interaction of the two opposing parties in a rather symmetrical way. After the arrival of the President and Edna at the Colonel's quarters at dusk, the discussion between the two leaders leads to the discussion between their wives, followed by an interaction between the President, Kouka and Soumari, and last, Colonel Theo and Edna. The order of these interactions between the two leaders and their wives adds to the climactic effect, and gets to be interrupted by scenes of conviviality in front of a display of their local and ethnic customs. For example, as a welcoming gesture, the two groups drink the water out of the same calabash; they taste each other's "delicacies," and eat what is not customarily acceptable in their own culture, thus internalizing what they loath in the culture of the "other." Traditional ethnic dances summarize the rhythm of the festive atmosphere, and the night is about to conclude with both parties burying the hatchet of war, and planting the tree of reconciliation.

The personal torment of the last two adversaries, Theo and Edna, implicitly creates a strong coupling in the narrative: that of aggressor-victim. Their personal crisis in the form of aggressor-victim both defines, and blurs their gendered boundaries, but also renders them prone to imminently transgressing these boundaries at the critical time of making peace. On the one hand, Colonel Theo's personal crisis comes from the fact that he broke the ethical law of war by slaying an unarmed innocent child—Edna's son, Michel—and allowed himself and his soldiers to act upon an animalistic impulse to rape women, kill fathers in front of their children, and dismember children. On the other hand, blinded by revenge, Edna transgresses the moral code by brutally killing Colonel Theo during the peacemaking process—an act that would easily spin the wheel of war for another ten years. Furthermore, the leader's guilt, and the mother's revenge allow them to experience a reversal of positions at the emotional level. In other words, the Colonel appears to have a feminized side that does not censure his emotions, thus allowing his remorse to surface. Theo's guilt borders Edna's maternal pain and bends his military masculinity and aggressiveness. Edna's strong intransigent attitude of disavowing any act of forgiveness, because it is not a human's work but God's, compels her to commit a killing that, in the particular context of a military pact is reserved for men. Her "hypermasculine" side that calls for sacrificial blood to be shed in the name of her son, sustains her own oppression and suffering to the point that Edna internalizes the dangerous interplay of maternal love with mechanisms of war.

In *Tales of Love*, Kristeva (1987) argues that the maternal body is bound in heterogeneity since "the child's arrival (which extracts woman out of her oneness and gives her the possibility—but not the certainty—of reaching out to the other, the ethical)" (259). This Kristevan idea presupposes that "*one must include the child*" (emphasis author's) for the woman to allow herself "a coded, fundamental, perverse behavior, ultimate guarantee of society, without which society will not reproduce and will not maintain a constancy of standardized household" (260). Thus, the killing of Edna's son has disturbed the mother's desire to sustain the law, because the loss of her only son removed the reward of social pleasure in her life; in other words, Edna is denied access to this feminine side, because Michel's death disrupted the process of motherhood in terms of introducing her child into society and the law. Kristeva explains this notion of motherhood as "feminine perversion" thus:

> Feminine perversion [*père-version*] is coiled up in the desire for law as desire for reproduction and continuity, it promotes feminine masochism to the rank of structure stabilizer (against its deviations); by assuring the mother that she may thus enter into an order that is above humans' will it gives her her reward of pleasure. (260)

The Kristevan notions of "feminine *père-version*," that is motherhood as "feminine masochism" because of the desire to reproduce in order to maintain the Law of the father, is shared by African writers, as well, from a more pragmatic social perspective. Flora Nwapa comments in "Women and Creative Writing in Africa" that what defines a woman in African societies is "the desire to be pregnant, to procreate" (Nnaemeka 1998, 96). This desire can be overpowering in the woman's life, because motherhood betters the woman's social position than barrenness. Nwapa also observes that "[W]omen are what they are because they can give life, they can procreate. So in African societies, when this unique function is denied a woman, she is devastated. But should this be so, all the time, in this day and age? Does this handicap, this childlessness make a woman less woman, less human?" (Nnaemeka, 97). Motherhood, then, in both psychoanalytic and socio-pragmatic approaches, elevates the position of women and ensures them a socioeconomic status and recognition. However, examining more closely the question of sexual and gender identities, "motherhood can be rewarding, but most of all it can also be enslaving" (Nfah-Abbenyi 1997, 51), not particularly in terms of socioeconomic restrictions in the mother's life to raise children, but if it is used to define women by their sexual identity. In *The Night of Truth,* Edna's case of motherhood brings up the same questions; losing her status of mother makes her lose full status in womanhood. After her son's killing, Edna borders a state of madness because of her condition as a non-mother. More specifically, the fact that Edna had a son does not deny her procreative capabilities, nor her status in motherhood; neither is her womanhood defined by her status as a barren mother, per se. Edna's condition of a non-mother is rather circumscribed by an absence, a lack, a void of horror and death. Non-motherhood does not constitute a full social identity; it is a form denied access to an identity suspended in the hyphen. Edna's identity is defined in her state of non-mother, which leaves her deprived of the potential to channel maternal love toward her other, the child, and the possibility to empower herself in society by raising, and educating her son into her culture and society. Clearly, Edna's pain is accentuated all the more by having lost her only son.

In many societies around the world, both African and non-African, a boy in the family is more valued than a girl because of established continuity with a social order, the family's heritage, and the value of labor. Michel's death creates a void for Edna that is difficult to negotiate in the construction of her gender identity as a woman, mother and non-mother, or in her paradoxical position as a childless mother. Edna's prestigious social condition as the wife of the President of the Nayaks in a monogamous but unfulfilling marriage does not put her in an advantageous centralized social position, but on the contrary, it marginalizes her vis-à-vis Soumari, who is respected and loved by the Colonel, has children, and a support network of women in the courtyard. Moreover, Michel's spectral appearances strongly connect Edna with the supernatural and spiritual realms that situate her in a dreamlike reality where, isolated as she is, she finds both comfort and anguish. When Edna shares her loss with Soumari who ends up expressing her sympathy, it is Edna who comforts and consoles Soumari instead, in a peculiar reversal of roles. Edna's gaze is often void, like the gaze of the mother, who was forced to watch the mutilation and eventual death of her son during one of the army raids in her village, and now articulates the horror and despair in the circle of victimized women and children in the Colonel's yard.

Motherhood, for Edna is hypostasized in a prototype of a modern African family consisting of the President/father, mother, and son. However, the disruption of this relationship creates for Edna a state of isolation, void, and madness. In the familial model, "maternal authority is the trustee of that mapping of the self's clean and proper body," that according to Kristeva, "it is distinguished from paternal laws within which, with the phallic phase and acquisition of language, the destiny of man will take shape" (1982, 72). The transgression of this separation plays out in the film narrative once Colonel Theo admits to Edna that he was the one who gave permission to his men to play the drum of cease fire and trap civilians into a carnage in Govinda, a sound that invited all the young boys, including Michel to run out of school to join the festivity. Furthermore, Michel's death by mutilation of his genitals that were stuffed into his mouth, disrupts both the symbolic and semiotic orders, because the literal act of castration coincides with the metaphorical castration of language and meaning. Colonel's confession of this unfathomable act, the entrapment of young children into slaughter under his orders, articulates for Edna the horror where her madness emerges. Her state of madness then, is located in a paradox: the maternal element is denied by her state of non-mother, and the paternal law is void of the process of signification by the act of castration. In addition, the displacement of paternal authority intensifies Edna's isolation, when she admits to Youba, the President's commandant, that Michel was his own son. Edna internalizes the unspeakable horror of war in a treacherous displacement of paternal law, which leads her to convince Youba that the killing of the Colonel is a sacrificial duty to their son. Theo is tortured, slowly roasting above the fire next to the roasting animals, while Edna is marinating him with his own marinade. The literal display of "abjection," the "boundary between nature and culture, between the human and non-human" (Kristeva 1982, 75), is powerfully synchronized with the *filthy* sacrifice of the Colonel, and Edna's delirium. A low angle medium close-up depicts Edna laughing frenetically, in an internalized interplay of political and military power with the maternal element. The President's wife, the Commandant's mistress, and Michel's mother are marinating "the king of marinade" in a horrific reversal of power roles, while in the night sky, the fireworks seal the moment of Edna's madness with the festivities of a peace agreement.

In a historical examination of madness in the classical period in *Madness and Civilization*, Michel Foucault (1988) associates madness to a totality, and delirium with the "complex of the image and the night of the mind" (103). He further explains madness as follows:

> the totality formed by sleep and dreams together: that is, to a complex which includes besides the image—hallucination, memory, or prediction, the great void of sleep, the *night of the senses* . . . it is madness which takes its original nature from the dream and reveals in this kinship that it is a liberation of the image *in the dark night of reality* (103; emphasis added).

Edna's hallucinations at the beginning of *The Night of Truth*, and her subsequent delirium at the climactic point highlight an artistic narrative *mélange* of boundary crossings and transgressions that deepen her individual crisis. The fact that Theo's truth correlates Edna's horror overtly justifies her darkest dreamlike reality about Michel's killing. Theo's confession beats like the drum of war in Govinda and liberates the image of truth in Edna's mind. Considering the notion of truth and madness, as Foucault discusses it in the article on Madness in *Encyclopédie*, there is the "physical truth" as the "accurate relation of our sensations with physical objects" and "moral truth" that "consists in the exactitude of the relations we discern either between moral objects, or between those objects and ourselves" (105). The collapse of boundaries around any notion of truth is the definition of madness as a totality. In other words, "madness deals not so much with truth and the world, as with man and whatever truth about himself he is able to perceive" (27). Edna perceives Theo's horrible truth of her son's killing as a disruption to the symbolic order; unable to sustain the symbolic order as a childless mother, she assumes the phallic position. Her desire for revenge goes unanswered by the President who refuses to "sacrifice" Theo, but is well executed by his commandant Youba, and his men. If *"sacrifice"* is a ritual that purifies, that "solemnizes the vertical dimension of the sign: the one that leads from the thing that is left behind, or killed to the meaning of the word and transcendence" (Kristeva 1982, 72), then Edna must also endure the cathartic sacrificial contract herself and perish because of having committed Theo's "abject" repulsive killing. At the end of the scene, Edna is shot down by the President, so that ultimately the Law prevails, *catharsis* fulfilled, and the symbolic order restored.

In the schema of multiple transgressions that take a rather tragic stance in the narrative, similar dynamics are called in place by two secondary characters during the process of de-militarization: Tomoto, the "fool," naïve character" in the Bonandés group, and Fatou, a young Bonandé woman who was married to a Nayak, and becomes "taboo" once she returns to her village. Center and periphery are trading places, and Tomoto and Fatou as insiders-outsiders mediate the plot with their uncanniness. Both characters negotiate the narrative by their prescribed position of otherness as messengers who communicate news and details about the war and peace. However, we often see Tomoto and Fatou overstepping dividing lines and getting "out of their place." For instance, Tomoto mingles with the women in the kitchen to share myths and stereotypes about the Nayaks. Fatou, who was saved by Theo during an attack on her village, talks to him in private with a tone of familiarity reserved for his wife. Tomoto's ultimate transgression of a prohibition occurs when he oversteps Soumari's orders to all musicians not to play the drum the night of the celebration, because it was the drum that sounded a celebratory beat the day the revolutionaries trapped and executed the Nayak boys in Govinda including Edna's son. The exclusion of drums aims at controlling, and negotiating rhythm and song that "arouse the impure, the other of the mind, the passionate-corporeal-sexual-virile," as well as avoiding the repetition of the "abject," the carnage, "mimed through sound and meaning" (Kristeva 1982, 28). Tomoto the "fool," oblivious to Soumari's prohibition, plays the drum of celebration and ignites the climactic moment leading to the killing of Theo and Edna in the socio-symbolic order.

While Edna perishes for "speaking up," or rather "acting up" her truth of suffering, Soumari's voice and actions create a continuum of battles she decides to fight in the courtyard where the logic of war still reigns with a pending peace treaty. In contrast to Edna who perishes, Soumari becomes the "other" speaking subject by bringing herself to the front of socio-political interactions. Soumari's desire to deal with peace-making, and the reconstruction of community becomes evident in her potential to positively challenge her immediate familial, and social environment. When the President affirms to Soumari that her father's torturer and killer is in prison, she reassures him that she will not request his execution. As a mother, when the children express their fear about the Nayak President visiting the family compound, Soumari convinces them that their father, the Bonandé leader, works for peace. In the kitchen, she calms down the women and children when stories of suffering and pain create an atmosphere of overexcitement and fear. As the Colonel's wife, Soumari challenges the commandant N'Gové, Theo's brother, about the peace agreement. When the commandant dismissively asks Soumari to return to "her kitchen," she contemptuously and calmly replies to his comment, "yes, go to your kitchen" (*The Night*), but she relentlessly returns to the courtyard with the request that the soldiers put down their weapons. After the Nayak men come armed to negotiate peace, and both the Bonandé and Nayak men become jittery, Soumari repeatedly pleads to the Nayak commandant, and the President to disarm the soldiers. Her efforts to harmonize conflicting forces for the sake of peace are apparent in the libations she performs in front of the soldiers to appease the spirits of the dead, because, as they say, the dead cry their unjustified deaths.

Soumari's character seems to exemplify Ama Ata Aidoo's suggestion that "it is high time African women moved onto center stage, with or without anyone's encouragement. Because in our hand lies, perhaps, the last possible hope for ourselves and for everyone else on the continent" (Nnaemeka 1998, 48). In fact, both Soumari's unyielding position, and Edna's intransigence put the two women on center stage to confront and negotiate their injustice and suffering immediately after ceasefire. As Olabisi Aina observes, however, "ironically, there tends to be a paradigm shift back to 'normal' in gender relations *after* the wars, so that the war of gender equally still remains to be fought and won" (Nnaemeka, 83). If Edna's role exposes the patriarchal and hypermasculinized arrangements that lead her into madness, and ultimately death, Soumari's resilience creates a positive model of womanhood. Once the symbolic order and peace are restored by the President's request that the Bonandé and Nayak bury their dead in the same place, the coming together of the two ethnic groups produces a new cultural environment, that of the "Bonandayaks." This emerging hybrid cultural space calls for an understanding of social innovations to preserve peace and cultural prosperity, and as both mother and widow, Soumari answers the call to balance out a multiplicity of identifications and orientations.

Soumari's model of womanhood leads to the assumption at the end of the film that widowhood will not define, nor restrict her gender position. Throughout the film, Soumari's gender roles as a wife and mother are not presented as restrictive or oppressive, but rather as accepted conventions. The film ending extends to the expression of a desire to create "strong bonds and thoughts" (Kristeva 1987, 263) in order to bypass the problematic and restrictive aspect of the law and society that articulate gender divisions and roles. With the socio-symbolic order restored after Theo's and Edna's sacrifices, there is emphasis on progressive social and gender formations that respond, not only to male-female divisions, but also to female-female relationships, with oneself and the other. Edna's and Soumari's positions bring forth the question of womanhood that differs by ethnicity, social status, topography, as well as individual or collective priorities, to underscore that there is no "one size fits all" approach in understanding gender formations. Yet again, both women protagonists make evident the importance of connectedness with each other. By remaining isolated, Edna is in profound pain, whereas Soumari is more conscious of her role in the community, because she is surrounded by a group of women, relatives, aids, compatriots who collectively respond to suffering. When Fatou returns to the village, for example, to seek refuge at her aunt Awa's, a number of women commiserate with her, but insist that she be strong. In *The Night of Truth*, "the journey to the end of the night" investigates "the way in which societies code themselves in order to accompany as far as possible the speaking subject on that journey" (58); it juxtaposes traditional gender models with potential ethical formations, as the women's desire to choose their gendered "conventions of behavior" (Appiah 2005, 69) in the process of identification. Kristeva's (1987) admonition that the new restored order in "its reformulation demands the contribution of women," and the maternal element that gives women the possibility of channeling desire, is a compelling proposition to consider:

> Of women who harbor the desire to reproduce (to have stability). Of women who are available so that our speaking species, which knows it is mortal, might withstand death. Of mothers. For an heretical ethics separated from morality, an *herethics,* is perhaps no more than that which in life makes bonds, thoughts, and therefore the thought of death, bearable: herethics is undeath [*a-mort*], love. (263)

The film proposes a dialogue of a traditional psychoanalytic Western feminism with a feminist pragmatism, which does not appear as a division of theory and praxis, but provides theoretical patterns of understanding women's suffering, as well as their contribution to social and political practices against the violence of war. According to Olabisi Aina, feminism in Africa, "should not stop at mere access to economic independence and social benefits; rather, it should also focus on the psychological development of the total self, whereby women would see themselves as just as capable as men are of changing the world in which they live" (Nnaemeka 1998, 83). Indeed, social and political expectations govern and conform to gender identities, yet the processes that allow the understanding of choice and desire will benefit everyone's lives, and most importantly, the lives of women.

Toward the end of the film, Tomoto's account of peace at the Colonel's grave attests to positive results in an effort for both men, women, and children to develop an understanding of the world after the war: "the men are now considerate toward each other. You know, your death brought them together. The children? They work well, they make us proud. But their mother . . . she's there where she's supposed to be" (*The Night*). The film closes with a distant shot of Tomoto letting animals free, followed by a sequence with Soumari dictating Colonel Theo's speech to her students at school. The metaphor of the last shots clearly suggests the power of education as the path to freedom and choice, but it equally addresses the need for reconciliation with oneself and the other. The speech is called, "The Crossing" (the text is entitled "*Le Grand Jour*" in French; a literal translation in English is "*The Big Day*"), and the repetition of each phrase for the purpose of dictation, stresses out notions of suffering, memory, and belonging: "We're from the same clay, we've lived the same nightmares, endured the same suffering. In truth, I tell you, I won't forget you. Your pain is my pain, because the same memories live within us, and we all belong to the big day" (*The Night*). The Colonel's speech dictated by Soumari has a powerful double effect, if we accept that it addresses not only ethnic differences, but the male-female divisions, and female-female relationships. Nfah-Abbenyi (1997) maintains that "for a true revolution to take place, women must begin from their position as women (who paradoxically seem to have the adequate powers), to confront the mechanisms by which [they become] enmeshed, at times, into collusion with forces that sustain [their] own oppression" (89). The "big day" brings "love" for oneself and the other, "love" as in confrontation of forces that sustain oppression, and "love" that begins with education, and the understanding of one's own place and potential in the world.

The themes of love and loss that assign to the narrative of *The Night of Truth* a universal appeal through the prism of an African ethnic conflict, create a powerful *mélange* of narrative and theoretical elements about gender identity. The narrative of war supports the traditional patriarchal order, as well as biological gender identities, and thus reinforces structures of domination over women. Taking into account the mythical aspect of the narrative with the horrific images of death that have an impact on the sociopolitical, cultural, and economic lives of the two involved communities, the analysis on the psychoanalytical level allows us to understand the conventions of gender identifications. More importantly, the female characters, Edna and Soumari, respond differently to a series of gender pressures under fire, so that their differences are powerfully juxtaposed and scrutinized. If Edna's suffering articulates a psychoanalytic model of understanding gender position, Soumari claims a territory of personal experience to locate her understanding of womanhood and suffering. The filmmaker's own personal story, the horrific death of her uncle because of an ethnic conflict, makes the film narrative all the more compelling, and sheds light on pain that everyone endures in the dark hours of war, particularly women and children. Nacro's advocacy for the power of education as the women's path to freedom invites the viewer to take one more step into thinking about the filmmaker herself in the position of her main character, Soumari.

FILM REFERENCES

Aduaka, Newton. 2007. *Ezra*. 103 min. Austria/Belgium/France/Nigeria, distr. California Newsreel.
Coelo, Issa Serge. 2000. *Daresalam*. 105 min. France/Burkina Faso/Chad, distr. California Newsreel.
Haroun Mahamat-Saleh. 2010. *Un homme qui crie*. 92 min. France/Belgium/Chad, distr. Pyramide Distribution.
Maldoror, Sarah. 1972. *Sambizanga*. 102 min. Angola/France/Republic of Congo.
Nacro, Fanta Régina. 2004. *The Night of Truth* (La Nuit de la vérité). 100 min. Burkina Faso/France, distr. Global Film Initiative, USA, Acrobates Film, France.
Sauvaire, Jean-Stéphane. 2008. *Johnny Mad Dog*. 98 min. France/Belgium/Liberia, distr. Momentum Theatrical.
Sembène, Ousmane. 1987. *Camp de Thiaroye*. 153 min. distr. Metro Pictures.
Sinclair, Ingrid. 1996. *Flame*. 85 min. Zimbabwe, distr. California Newsreel.
Sissako, Abderrahmane. 2014. *Timbuktu*. 100 min. France, Mauritania, distr. Cohen Media Group.

REFERENCES

Aidoo, Ama Ata. 1998. "African Woman Today." In *Sisterhood: Feminisms and Power*, edited by Obioma Nnaemeka, 39–50. Trenton: Africa World Press, Inc.
Aina, Olabisi. 1998. "African Women at the Grassroots." In *Sisterhood: Feminisms and Power*, edited by Obioma Nnaemeka, 65–88. Trenton: Africa World Press, Inc.
Appiah, Anthony Kwame. 2005. *The Ethics of Identity*. Princeton: Princeton University Press.
Berger Iris, and E. Francis White. 1999. *Women in Sub-Saharan Africa: Restoring Women to History*. Bloomington: Indiana University Press.
Diawara, Manthia. 2010. *African Film: New Forms of Aesthetics and Politics*. Berlin: Haus der Kulturen der Welt, Prestel Verlag.

Dovey, Lindiwe. 2009. *African Film and Literature: Adapting Violence to the Screen*. New York: Columbia University Press.
Foucault, Michel. 1965/1988. *Madness and Civilization*. New York: Vintage books.
Hutchinson, Sharon and Jok Madut Jok. 2002. "Gendered Violence and the Militarisation of Ethnicity: A Case Study from South Sudan." In *Postcolonial Subjectivities in Africa*, edited by Richard Werbner, 84–107. New York: Zed Books.
Kristeva, Julia. 1982. *Powers of Horror: An Essay on Abjection*. New York: Columbia University Press.
———. *Tales of Love*. 1987. New York: Columbia University Press.
Nfah-Abbenyi, Juliana Makuchi. 1997. *Gender in African Women's Writing*. Bloomington: Indiana University Press.
Nnaemeka, Obioma, ed. 1998. *Sisterhood, Feminisms and Power in Africa: From Africa to the Diaspora*. Trenton: Africa World Press.
Nwapa, Flora. 1998. "Women and Creative Writing in Africa." In *Sisterhood: Feminisms and Power*, edited by Obioma Nnaemeka, 89–99. Trenton: Africa World Press, Inc.
Palmer, Eustace. 2008. *Of War and Women, Oppression and Optimism*. Trenton: Africa World Press, Inc.
Porter, Elizabeth et al. Edited 2005. *Researching Conflict in Africa*. New York: United Nations University Press
Werbner, Richard. Edited 2002. *Postcolonial Subjectivities in Africa*. London: Zed Books.
Wlordarczyk, Nathalie. 2009. *Magic and Warfare: Appearance and Reality in Contemporary African Conflict and Beyond*. New York: Palgrave Macmillan.

NOTES

1. *Night of Truth* won the prize for best screenplay in Fespaco 2005. *Ezra* won the Grand Prize (Étalon de Yenenga) in Fespaco 2007. *Un homme qui crie* won the Jury Prize at the 2010 Cannes Film Festival. *Timbuktu* was in the main competition section at the 2014 Cannes Film Festival; it won the Prize of the Ecumenical Jury and the François Chalais Prize. It was nominated for the Academy Award for Best Foreign Language Film at the 87th Academy Awards.

FIVE

Resilient Strategies and Emotional Memories in Leonora Miano's Literary Writing

Paul N. Touré

This chapter examines the idea that Léonora Miano's literary writing reveals a philosophy of self-reliance and resilience.[1] To illustrate such claim, three powerful stories are presented here, and they highlight how Miano painstakingly shares critical lessons of life with readers through the emotional memories of her characters. The first story is from *The Season of Shadow* (2013), and the other two are from *African Sequel,* a trilogy of novels. The study suggests that the presence or the absence of resilient attitudes in the characters originates mostly from various disruptive experiences in their respective memories. As such, the analysis of positive and negative emotional patterns in horrible war conditions shows that the author's fictional world demonstrates the paradoxical nature of the human mind. In the search for happiness, some characters display admirable emotions such as optimism, attachment, courage, compassion, empathy, and survival mechanisms that embolden them to better their lives and those of people around them. Others, aiming at the same pursuit of happiness, somehow fail and surrender to negative emotions such as fear, terror, anger. So, what are the recurrent stylistic and semantic patterns that drive the author's creation of resilient strategies? Why do readers feel beneficial emotional feelings when deciphering images created in the texts while others feel embarrassment and anger for the same images? How do characters react when they are completely frightened by death or by extremely difficult conditions of conflict? What does it feel like for a woman to be resolutely fearless when going after her missing son?

A THEORETICAL PERSPECTIVE ON EMOTIONS AND RESILIENCE

In the past decade, Léonora Miano has quickly emerged as one of the most prominent francophone women writers. This literary success is largely due to the way she encodes and represents Africa's past and current social, political and cultural experiences in her work. On the one hand, she argues that the persistent political violence and social unrest in postcolonial Africa are historically rooted in the fact that many Africans disown the continent's responsibilities in the transatlantic slave trade. On the other hand, in the persistent sovereignty's debate in Africa, she shatters the common propensities of those who, backed by dependency theories, still maintain that the political freedom and economic development of the continent ought to come from outside. Moreover, while refuting this self-deprecating argument of dependency, she astutely suggests that Africans ought to acknowledge their own values, regardless of previous and current racist views about them. For Miano, if the descriptions of her novel *Dark Heart of the Night* were wrongly considered as reinforcing negative views of people of sub-Saharan Africa, it is because these people are usually looked down and regarded as mere animals in the economy of human consciousness. She thus writes:

> What I'm interested in, is the African point of view on the topics I work on. I think we've spent too much time hoping for understanding and recognition from people other than ourselves. It's time we focus on our problems and deal with them, no matter how painful it is. I'm confident in our ability to do so. (Miano 2010)[2]

Miano's writing style on the longue durée of economic and political history of Africa in the world is another notable reason for her literary achievement. Indeed, her writing strategies on historical perspectives are quite different from those of her fellow francophone African female writers. Though culturally impactful and socially relevant in postcolonial Africa, the topics these female writers have worked on had short-term historical roots. An author like Mariama Bâ, with her masterpieces (*So Long a Letter* 1979) and (*Scarlet Song* 1981), has made impressive contribution to African literature by virtue of her engagement with social consciousness of African women, polygamy, and interracial issues alike. Nevertheless, the tone and scope of Bâ's work are quite different from Miano's, since the latter's recurrent positions on gender issues set her apart, as will be made evident in this chapter. We could further the comparison with other notable francophone African women writers regarding the romantic love related narratives. From this perpective, writers such as Cameroonian Calixte Beyala, Beninese Colette Sènami Agossou, or Congolese (DRC) Clémentine Faik-Nzuji, come to mind. Because her writing dwells mostly on the violence, sex, misery, the physical, economical, and emotional exploitation of African women, Beyala has been labeled as a radical feminist. Besides her numerous award-wining novels and essays, she has written a bold erotic novel, *Naked Woman Black Women* (2003). The same romantic aesthetic contrast applies to Agossou's The *Dawn on the Cactus* (1981), or Faik-Nzuji's *The Time of Lovers* (1969).

Two main patterns differentiate Miano from the other female writers. The first is that, even though the authors dealt admirably with the core problems of human nature, in general, and the condition of women in postcolonial Africa, specifically, their respective writings did not take Miano's philosophical stand on human suffering and emotional memories, mainly the topics of the Transatlantic slave trade and the African and African Diaspora's place in human consciousness.[3] The second key difference is Miano's originality in addressing Africa's contemporary core challenges related to the philosophical debate on the freedom of choice. This radical philosophy oscillates between two interrelated views. The first aspect of this choice may not actually be very different from the first group aforementioned; it is the motivation of the writers to use the writing process as a way to deal with their own personal psychological issues and life dilemmas. In this sense, Ayané, the protagonist and female character of *Dark Heart of Night* wittingly points out this inner struggle. Her observation could have been said by any character portrayed by the writers mentioned above: "Perhaps that was it, the meaning of life: this battle against one's darker self" (Miano 2010, 111). But such personal choice does not mean a withdrawal from the world because, it is the second aspect of the freedom of choice that ultimately sets Miano apart. This concerns the way Africans appreciate themselves in the economy of global consciousness. Due to the very weight of the history of domination, the role and responsibility of the artist in post-colonial Africa does not solely consist in creating in terms of pure aesthetic criteria, even though this aesthetic experience is crucially central in Miano's work.

Miano's role as writer and as public figure indicates that she is predominantly driven to writing in order to heal and to awaken greatness in her readers insofar as good literature can address issues of public concern. Her literary imagination is a purposeful reflection of two key interconnected components of the human condition: if we are prone to suffer, in one way or another from war or conflictual conditions, we also ought to build resilient capabilities and recover quickly from the difficulties of these conditions. For Bertrand Vergely (2005), the philosophical implication of the concept of resilience demonstrates that after a tragedy, the participation of other people in the recovery process always helps us overcome our sufferings, since "our 'rebounding,' when everything goes wrong and obscure, comes from others" (74). If individual suffering is provoked by humans to whom the sufferer belongs, it is likewise the same that "must heal the wounded humanity" (74). It is this purposeful need for healing that enables Miano to write about suffering and resilient agency in times of tumultuous conditions of conflict in contemporary Africa.

Indeed, theoreticians of the concept of resilience maintain, for example, that individuals are resilient when, despite being victim of abhorrent and violent circumstances, they manage to resist the traumatic situation and achieve sustainable quality of life. The notion of resilience is described as "the human capacity to deal with, overcome, learn from, or even be transformed by the inevitable adversities of life" (Grotberg 2003, 1). But a resilient person uses appropriate coping strategies to successfully "project herself in the future despite destabilizing events, difficult conditions, sometimes severe traumas" (Vanistendael 1996, 9). And yet, the fact that some of Miano's characters possess clever resilient strategies does not mean that they are not vulnerable, since the people who are portrayed as resilient suffer as much as anybody else from the same burdensome conditions. What set the resilient people apart from those who abdicate under the weight of painful experiences is their psychological strength and adequate quality of life they develop afterward.

Nonetheless, the study of literature to uncover resilience in human mind, in relation to psychology, may perhaps lead one to question the inability of literary theory to solely accomplish such task. However, referring to Julia Kristeva and Patrick Colm Hogan's insightful critical discourses validates the very methodological necessity to do so. Kristeva's specific question "How does one speak to literature?" reveals the idea that the implementation of theory and the practice of reading are not two separate activities in the literary field: human experience and the literary experience interfere. In Kristeva's critical discourse, the multiple meanings that are lying dormant in the literary text are able to, overtime, refine and enrich the scientific theoretical framework and analytical perception of the critics. In other words, the immanent nature of such intertextual interpretative approaches does not solely limit the literary critics to only literary theory. For this reason, Kristeva (1980) argues that literature does not need "to reproduce the norms of Sciences" (95) in order to become a "dignified" part of them, since it is actually the "missing link of human sciences" (98). More importantly, the key fulcrum of her methodological argument is that "the science of literature is an always infinite discourse, an always open enunciation of a *search* for the laws of the practice known as literature." In this condition, the purpose of such search, for the critics, is "to make *manifest* the very *procedure* through which this 'science,' its 'object' and their relationship are brought about, rather than to apply empirically such and such a technique to an indifferent object" (95).

Patrick Hogan also acknowledges the centrality of literature in the social sciences by arguing that literature is among the arts that can brilliantly simulate the positive as well as the negative behaviors and ideological attachments of human experiences. His groundbreaking work on the relationship between literature and emotion, indeed reveals that the latter is not simply "part" of human life, but "central" to it. In this sense, Hogan (2011) contends that "[l]iterature points us toward an attempt at actually re-creating the eliciting conditions of the emotions in such a way as to reproduce the emotional effect" (30). When we hear or tell stories, this act does not simply consume our time; it also takes "as much or more of our emotional energy than our primary engagements in real life" (3). In this regard, the aforestated core role logically bestows to literature an "ecological validity in the study of emotion" (3). It becomes obvious, following Hogan's argument, that some literary texts can "alter our spontaneous emotional responses to the world and to ourselves, and to imaginative elaboration of those responses" (8). As a consequence, an immanent reading of Miano's literary writing under the lenses of the notion of abjection and human suffering, the theory of emotion in literature, resilient theories, and other theoretical approaches of the social sciences does not merely reveal the nature of the uncanny, unspeakable, and yet, lingering forces that dwell in the psyche of her literary characters in times of violence; it also helps the critics to bring to light the abilities of the mind to overcome unwanted and severe hardships. The logic of such literary discourse is that the reader learns that the mind is able to nurture strong resilient habits despite dire political and social upheavals.

ON STYLISTIC AND NARRATIVE PATTERNS OF THE NOVELS

Altogether, Miano's imagination on violence, suffering, and emotional memories covers mainly two African historical epochs. The first is set in pre-colonial Africa, during the height of the transatlantic slave trade, and it is covered in *The Season of Shadow* (2013). The novel is a sort of whodunit and is plotted around a shocking mystery of disappearance of people in the small Mulongo clan, located in the interior lands of Africa: after a big fire, twelve men of the clan have mysteriously vanished. The mothers of the missing men are suspected of having devoured their children through practices of witchcraft. In the mist of such emotional turmoil, three separate investigations are conducted, two of them being unofficial. The first and only official investigation is conducted by Mukano, the clan's chief, and after an emergency council, he courageously goes after the missing men with eight of his best elite soldiers and bodyguards. They, unfortunately, perish in a fierce storm, stuck in a swamp in the forest, without solving the mystery of the vanished men. The second person to go after the missing men is Mutango, the chief's half-brother and his main political adversary. He secretly goes alone, because his primary goal is to use the crisis to scheme a political conspiracy against the latter and take the reigning throne that—he is convinced—was supposed to be destined for him. The egocentric nature of his hidden motives ultimately leads to his capture by the soldiers of a nearby kingdom, the Bwele, who eventually enslave him by putting him in the service of a bloodthirsty princess. However, as it will be examined in this chapter, this character eventually redeems himself in a very noble way, by freeing from prison the third character who attempts to find the missing men.

As matter of fact, this third person who goes alone after the missing people is a strong woman, named Eyabe, one of the mothers of the missing boys. Half way in her investigation, she learns how and by whom the ten young adults and their two spiritual leaders were actually captured. The investigation does not stop here. The subsequent events show two other intertwined stories. The first—the small story—begins with the birth and the rapid growth on the coast of a slave trade kingdom, Isedu. This little African kingdom has quickly become strong due to the economic impact of the Transatlantic slave trade, and militarily powerful because of the weaponry provided to them by Europeans, in exchange for slaves. As a result, the Isedu kingdom, to maintain its economic and political domination over weaker kingdoms, puts pressure of waging war on other kingdoms when they refuse to give them more captives (Miano 126). Still in this small story, a weaker neighboring kingdom, the Bwele, partner with both the Mulongo clan and the Isedu kingdom. The people of this kingdom happen to be responsible for the disappearance of the twelve Mulongo men, captured as a self-protective strategy against the military power of the coastal African allies, the Isedu.

However, this story depends on a greater history, the birth and expansion of globalization, with its well-crafted ramifications from the Enlightenment.[4] When the Bwele's slave raiders captured the twelve men, they sold them to their partners on the coast, who, in turn sold them to their partners, the European slave traders that had settled on the coast and known as "the foreigners from Pongo by the ocean" (Miano 184). What was then a shocking mystery for the Mulongo clan becomes clearly explainable: the disappearance of the twelve men from the small village is the result of a larger and stronger system, emerging from the economic globalization of Europe. Miano (2013) craftily unfolds the scenario as follows:

> The Mulongo, like others, had been embroiled in something that was beyond them. The night of the big fire, when the Bwele had cast their nets on the twelve males of the community, they were far from suspecting that their misadventure was just one of the thousand adventures peppering a complex history. How many men, women, children, from how many people, would also be taken away from their loved ones on often unknown routes to end up here at the end of *wase* (earth). (189)

The second historical period developed in Miano's writing is the postcolonial era, particularly in *Dark Heart of the Night* (2005), *Contours of the Coming Day* (2006), *Scarlet Dawns Sankofa Cry* (2011). In these novels, initially conceived as a trilogy, *African Sequel,*[5] the story is set in Mboasu, an imaginary African country, formerly colonized by a European country. The civil war started by a group of dubious rebels in the first novel (2005) ends in the second novel (2006), but the country is in ruins. Its inhabitants live in a permanent desolation, still suffering from dire poverty caused by the war. The same physical and emotional turmoil is depicted in the third novel (2011). The semantic fields of violence and suffering in postcolonial Africa are skillfully connected to a stronger psychological pain—that is the compelling thread of negative emotional memories of the colonial and the Transatlantic slave trade histories. The major themes developed in these well-crafted novels range from the critique of neo-traditionalism of African cultures, the deconstruction of masculinity, to the repeated ambiguous attitude of African intellectuals and political leaders in periods of crisis, the disintegration of the family unit, the representation of child soldiers and warfare, and the lack of basic education for children.

Seemingly, the stylistic features of these three novels take precedence over their semantic features: the "how Miano writes" (the aesthetical aspect) appears to be far more important than the "what is being written," (the semantic patterns) even though these features are intrinsically intertwined. For example, musical forms are ingenuously inscribed in the narrative structure of the novels. Miano herself has conceded that musical genres—Jazz and Blues particularly—have enormously influenced her act of creating. Miano (2012) indicates that *Dark Heart of the Night* is composed according to the classic AABA song form used frequently by jazz composers (18). In this first novel, most actions take place in the small village, Eku. In the narration, the first A is centered on the description of the setting related to the main theme of the novel, which is the self-inflicting suffering of certain Africans, symbolized by the human flesh ceremonial meal. Here, both the emotional disquiet of certain characters and the greatness of others are elegantly depicted. In the second A, the reader witnesses the actual ceremonial meal with the murder of the boy, Eyia. In the B, the fiction moves from the village of Eku to the large city, Sombé, with Ayané, the main protagonist. In the third and last A, the story of the consumption of the ritual meal is retold by Inoni to Ayané when she returns to the village.

The same musical pattern is replicated in the two other novels of the trilogy. The story of *Contours of the Coming Day* (2006) is woven around the inventiveness of the little girl, Musango, to thwart her bitter emotional memories and to recreate a better life for herself. To do this, Miano uses several American Negro Spirituals to imagine Musango's story. The song "Motherless Child" helps to stress on the journey of homelessness and wandering of the girl, since the meaning of the song motivates Miano to gradually build the resilient mindset of her young character to such an extent that the latter doggedly refuses to abdicate to her fears and struggles. If the song "Wade in the Water" was composed with explicit instructions to slaves who were fleeing from their masters in the south of the United States in order to successfully make their way to freedom in the north, its theme of escape from suffering guides Miano to reveal the freedom mindset of her young character. The exuberant, but powerful words of positive change of the songs "Down Here Below" by Abbey Lincoln and "Endangered Species" by Dianne Reeves also contributed in shaping Musango's fundamental character traits. The third novel, *Scarlet Dawns Sankofa Cry* (2011) also uses Jazz musical composition. Miano (2012) admits that the emotional traits of the three main characters (Ayané, Epupa, Epa) are comparable to musical instruments: " The characters appeared to me, as musical instruments, each with its tone, its sensitivity, and its breath: Ayane is a dull bass; Epupa is a drum set; Epa is the solo singer of the group" (19).

If Jazz helps the writer stylistically, the Blues participates in creating, semantically, the narrative sensibility and sullen atmosphere of the texts. As textual strategy, introducing the Blues in her narrative becomes, therefore, semantically relevant due to the advantage of saturating the text with the musical structure of the Blues. Further, the Blues also imparts meaning associated with the genre's unpredictable rhythmic structures, and above all, its surprising birth in times of atrocious physical and emotional suffering. Encoding and representing the paradox of the human mind of her characters through the lenses of this musical genre is advantageous, because it possesses the brilliancy of amplifying the quirky nature of the human experience facing exceptional adversity. Hence, Miano's narratives masterfully bring to light the human flaws and the wisdom of her characters. Considering that we are strangers to each other because of our social, cultural, or political affiliations, the nature of our emotions, however, remains the same. In the same way as the Blues do, people also express, differently, their human emotions around the globe, but these emotions remain universally the same in all cultures. Miano (2012) recognizes as well this common semantic nature of her imagination when she writes: "It is exactly what my novels propose. They accept to acknowledge all realities, including the darkest, because it is precisely the only way to overcome the dark" (22).

RESILIENT STRATEGIES AND MIND POWERS

In his influential book on narrative universals and human emotion, Hogan (2003) argues that there are three universal narrative structures that invariably appear in all or almost all traditions of literature and orature. These semantic features—heroic, romantic, and sacrificial—are generated by simple principles from emotional prototypes (11; 109; 150). A thorough semantic interpretation of Miano's novels leads to the findings that they are explicitly more heroic and sacrificial than romantic love presumably because of the resilience topics she chooses to work on. Even though these themes on human emotions help her characters to develop strong personalities, the author's literary work has constantly been an object of controversy. We feel beneficial emotional effects when we read her novels. But sometimes, we feel embarrassment and anger, because, we—critics and literary reviewers—consider that she adopts an overly pessimistic posture about Africans and Africa due to the gloomy descriptions of Africa in her novels. At first look, these descriptions seem to match the familiar stereotypes about the continent. In the trilogy, *African Sequel*, the writing on themes, such as ethnic wars, hunger, and poverty seems to give the impression to the reader that she uses the same strategies and anthropological Hegelian vision about sub-Saharan Africa. This does not, in and of itself, imply that Miano is thrashing Africa; on the other hand, her defenders appreciate the uncompromising tone of the novels, as she addresses difficult issues that impede Africa's development. Miano herself has been compelled by such controversy to give some details about her style and motivation as a writer. She maintains that her fiction is not directed against Africa or African people. Replying to her accusers, she asserts: "My texts are not an indictment, but the testimony of a demanding love towards sub-Sahara Africa and its peoples. They are calls to understand ourselves, our willingness to accept personal and collective responsibilities, which is the first step toward the achievement of a complete freedom" (Miano 2012, 6). The act of creating strong characters in the midst of difficult conditions seems to be the measure of this practical philosophy of demanding love and acceptance of personal and collective responsibility. Here are three stories that illustrate the resilient mindsets. Let's consider the first universal narrative—heroic—in *The Season of Shadow* (2013).

The publication of this novel on the theme of the transatlantic slave trade is itself an innovation, especially for Francophone African writers in general and for female writers in particular. It has been rightly recognized that "the Francophone literature is full of allusions to slavery, but there is still a certain silence about the slave trade" (Miller 2008, 39). Few of them have actually seriously considered this very topic.[6] As a matter of fact, it is safe to say that *The Season of Shadow* is basically the culmination of Miano's thought on this very topic. Indeed, the negative emotional memory of this theme has always been of a major concern for this writer since the publication of her first novel (2005). She has repeatedly managed to include the theme in her entire literary work in one form or another. For instance, at the end of *Dark Heart of the Night*, the emblematic female seer, Epupa sets the stage on the psychology of guilt and responsibility of Africans regarding the Transatlantic slave trade: "We cannot pretend that millions of our sons have been snatched from us without the slightest collusion on our part. . . . We are claiming that the West should take the blame, but who will our children call to account?" (Miano 2010, 142).

One of the functions of Miano's slave trade narratives is to validate the fortitude of her female characters when they face tragedy. It is the case for Eyabe, the main protagonist of *The Season of Shadow*. David B. Feldman and Lee D. Kravetz (2015) notice that if suffering is real, resilience is also real. Human nature is so strong that when they are stricken by suffering or disaster, "after a period of emotional turmoil, most trauma survivors eventually recover and return to their lives. They bounce back. And in some cases, they do much more. They bounce forward, and in truly remarkable ways" (3). Indeed, what is stunning about Eyabe's resilient stratagems is not simply her poised and obstinate resolution to unveil, singlehandedly, the mystery surrounding the disappearance of the men of the clan, including her own first born son. She goes further by defying the laws that strictly forbid women to leave the village. By doing so, she faces unimaginable dangers and challenges generally uncommon for women. Three key attitudes demonstrate the resilience of this character.

The first element is her self-awareness. She is first portrayed as a woman with unfeminine character traits. Her male-mindedness has always been acknowledged by the villagers not necessarily because she intends to compete with men or with her own husband. Even though she somehow admits the key differences between men and women, in the bedroom, for example, as the narrator notices, Eyabe delights herself in surpassing the husband with her sexual prowess. Such attitude of defiance, carried out by Eyabe, makes a gender related point as she declares with a witty tone to her amused partner: "You need to know that I, too, am a man. When the goddess shaped the human being, she gave it these two energies." (Miano, 2013, 119). She recognizes here the social constructive nature of gender. The second key factor of her resilience is her commitment to action, whatever danger it may entail. Her philosophy of setting and striving relentlessly to achieve the goal of going to "the land of water" emanates from the very idea that mothers' love for their children is so strong that when these children are in danger, "[n]othing and nobody has the power to stop" them, because such "love becomes the star that guides them" (112). Eyabe's motivation to know what happened to the men of her clan eventually becomes more powerful than the subsequent hurdles, fears, and emotional and physical pains she endures during her life-changing journey (114). She knows that she will be extremely exhausted and the journey fraught with danger before she finds the answers to her quest, yet, she remains undeterred and continues her journey, altruistically, as a duty to the community. The third essential factor of her resilience is her ability to remain in a complete state of composure while facing death. Indeed, she almost dies in her perilous adventure when she gets stuck in the same swamp that killed Mukano, the clan's chief and his eight elite soldiers. The narrator indicates that in the midst of such nightmarish situation, "Eyabe tries not to panic," and she even encourages herself to stay confident: "She is tired. She keeps advancing. The mud covers her calves. It makes the fringes of her *manjua*[7] heavier but she keeps advancing" (113). When she is on the verge of losing hope for survival, Eyabe is eventually rescued by some friendly strangers, later identified as the fugitives of Bebayedi, a collection of people who have escaped from the slave raiders.

When Eyabe finally reaches the coast or "the land of water," her resilience is once again immeasurably tested, because she is bewildered by her discoveries. She comes upon a considerable number of slaves refused by European slave traders, either for being unmarketable, or unlikely to survive the crossing of the Atlantic. As she discovers the horrifying fortresses built to hold the captives before their embarkation, the character is more astonished by the vile and submissive attitude of these captives who have freely surrendered to their African masters for fear of death (169). However, three additional critical circumstances narrated with suspense reveal that Eyabe ultimately passes her test of possessing a strong resilient mindset with an unyielding bravery.

The first event occurs when she, surprisingly, finds out "how the imposing notable, Mutango [the chief half-brother who was plotting to get the political power of the village], so feared in his village" has now become a "docile servant of a Bwele princess" (162). This single discovery could have understandably deterred her. Surprisingly, it rather strengthens Eyabe's perilous quest to know the actual fate of the missing men. The second event happens when Eyabe herself is captured by the soldiers of the Prince of the coast, after being eventually denounced by a female slave. Dragged to the slaves' market place, she painfully watches the Isedu dignitaries selling Africans to the European slave merchants, echoing a scene in Ousmane Sembène's movie *Ceddo*.[8] Here again, she courageously witnesses the unspeakable horror of captivity and slave trading: "Eyabe trembles, thinking that the sons of her clan were dragged here by force" (211). At the same slave market, Eyabe also learns that her entire clan has been wiped out by the Bwele, those who captured the twelve men; that the survivors have been scattered in different parts of the Bwele kingdom. The third critical event demonstrates Eyabe's true heroic mindset. Unlike the other slaves who have given away their freedom to save their lives by not daring to flee, she refuses to be enslaved and consequently makes the radical choice of drowning in the sea right before the African and European slave merchants (215). This remarkable ethical choice of dying instead of being enslaved is, however, unsuccessful, because she is saved from the waters by some Isedu soldiers, at the orders of their king. Eventually, she is incarcerated in a fortress and her heroic act is rewarded by Mutango, the once imposing, notable character but now turned captive. He secretly enters into the prison, and to conceal her escape, he exchanges his clothes with Eyabe's and allows her to return in Bebayedi, the fugitives' village.

This village of the refugees, therefore, becomes for Eyabe and the other survivors of slave traders a symbolic place of recovery (226). Imagining and creating such place in her writing is a genuine of celebration of life, a triumph of the oppressed over death. In fact, Boris Cyrulnik rightly demonstrates that displaying such resilient attitude is always beneficial to a larger number of people, particularly when we are able to transfer a mental image of a tragedy into a piece of art or a literary text, because it allows the survivor to give to the tragedy a proper meaning. For Boris Cyrulnik (1999), it is actually this "story" said or written in the aftermath of a major setback that empowers the victim to understand, afterward, the specific process she used to transform the *misfortune* into a *marvel,* since "every wounded person is condemned to a metamorphosis" (10). Bebayedi, the fugitives' village, a place where Eyabe becomes a key leader, represents a powerful image for the creation of a new world; it shows Africans and all people who have suffered war crimes and oppressions that they can use the tragedies to transform their lives. Here, death can no longer be an instrument of infringement of freedom; it is surpassed by more a powerful force, that is, the reinvention of self by a purposeful choice. The survivors can thenceforth envision a new beginning, destined to move them forward, yet, these victims are called not to unconsciously repress or be forgetful of their difficult cultural past. For Miano, indeed, "the ancestors are there, and they are not confinement. They designed a world. This world is their most valuable legacy to us: the obligation to invent to survive "(228).

The second resilient strategy is also a heroic narrative, and it is evidenced by Musango's story. The novel (Miano 2011) begins when a nine year old girl, Musango sorrowfully remembers being cruelly beaten by her mother. A witch has allegedly accused the orphan girl of using the power of witchcraft to kill her father who was the only bread winner of the family. The mother has become cynic and cruel to her daughter because marrying the wealthy man miraculously removed her from a dire condition of poverty. His death has brought her back to the old emotional memories of continual lack that she thought were gone forever. Even though Musango eventually escapes from her cruel progenitor who resolutely tries to burn her alive, she wanders for three years in the ruined country. This traumatic experience sets the tone for the whole narrative and in a series of difficult and twisted adventures, backed by a strong willpower to live, she trails with other unwanted street children, orphans, and shares their daily lives. She is first kidnapped by wicked gangs, oppressed by groups of evangelical leaders, and later finds her way to her grandmother's hut in a particularly dirty slum. The novel is truly a genial construction of several monologues of Musango who is haunted by the memories of the emotional and physical pains she is undergoing and of the sorrowful absence of her mother. However, she is neither vengeful towards her mother, nor to her aggressors, because her primary goal is, surprisingly, to find her mother and forgive her (176). The novel ends with Musango finding the latter totally insane in a cemetery, prostrate at the tomb of her deceased husband.

Like the two other novels of the trilogy set in postcolonial Africa, the characters in this fiction live in a cruel and superstitious environment. Beyond these gloomy representations, the overall tone of the novel refuses any fate of misery. It portrays a new generation of Africans rather motivated by hope for a better future. As matter of fact, as outlined above, the semantic structures of the Blues in the construction of the novel is evident. Richard Wright once recognized the contradictory inflection of the Blues when he declared that despite the tone of "defeat and down-heartedness," the Blues is not "intrinsically pessimistic" because the burden of woe and melancholy is always redeemed by the exultant affirmation of life, love and, hope (Oliver 1961, xv). The semantic structure of the novel remains a powerful tool for the study of the best and worst dimensions of human emotions.

Notably, many of Miano's characters usually display recurrent emotions of fear of death or demonstrate a surprising propensity for uncaring attitudes. Those that are not passive have a startling servile obedience towards wicked leaders. However, Musango's courage, her psychological prowess and her own concept of children as free individuals signify a true case of resilience, particularly when she publicly contributes, during a church service, to unmasking the duplicity of evangelical leaders in their proclivity to exploit ignorant and poor people (Miano 103–5). The girl's contemplative thoughts about violence, her ability to focus on positive emotional memory and hope strengthen her mental attitude to imagine a better future. This method validates her mindfulness in coping with any kind of hopeless situation: "I still cling to the idea of the exception; I want to keep believing in the sudden emergence of meaningful existence" (90). Musango keenly demonstrates her resilience as follows: "I dream, and the seditious nature of this mental act warms and strengthens me. Even being a twelve years old, she dreams of "the end of times" that her oppressors "do not see coming, the day they will know that the singular surpasses the plural, that the second has only a chance if she has allowed the emergence of the first" (90–91). Elodie Carine Tang (2013), in her study of the novel makes a strong point when she considers that this young person is a symbol of the future African mother who will be like the model of ancient mothers. Tang writes: "The ancient mothers persevered and gave a sense of security to the life of their children for having given that life" (Tang and Abomo-Maurin 2013, 134). This second novel of the trilogy can be viewed as a deliberate continual meditation of this little girl whose name "Musango" actually means "peace." Her monologues on the issue of power and its influence on freedom of speech in Africa can hardly be ignored by scholars of Africa's economic and social development. One can speculate that among the protagonists under consideration here, this young character, Musango is probably the most resilient.

The third and last universal narrative to be examined here is the sacrificial leadership. The portrait of the female character, Eyabe, shows, in all likelihood, that she does not simply possess boldness and male character traits, but she also displays sacrificial leadership for her disappeared son and for her community, as well. In fact, in terms of gender perspective, Miano's fiction is built on the contrast between women and men in their ways of expressing emotions. The reader naturally recognizes the female and the male characters in the novels. However, their actual personality often indicates a constant switch of temperaments as they express their femininity or masculinity. With a few exceptions, men are generally portrayed as weak and cowardly. When they express endurance and force, they become brutal and violent. In contrast, women are extremely strong and act honorably. This theme of contrast between the temperament of women and men actually traverses her entire work. Miano acknowledges this very inversion of the gender roles. Echoing Judith Butler's *Undoing Gender* (2004), Miano states that our masculine or feminine nature constitutes a biological category and remains a social and cultural construction. For Miano "the simple fact of being born in a man's body does not make you brave, phlegmatic, and capable of handling abstract concepts. Likewise, owning a woman's body does not translate into possessing the qualities of tenderness, patience, futility or housework capabilities" (31).

In *Dark Heart of the Night,* for instance, when the rebels arrive in the village of Eku, two leaders—the male village's chief and the elder of women, the old Ie—are called to perform their political duties. These leaders, like all the villagers, are in danger of death. How do they react to this similar dreadful situation? In the course of the story, we learn that the heavily armed rebels, who have taken the entire small community hostage for several days, ask the village's chief to provide them eighteen young people (boys and girls) for their political insurgency. The aim is to unify two territories divided by the former European empires. The village's chief humiliates himself to such extent that he exposes his emotional weaknesses. He is quickly overwhelmed by the aggression of the armed men and is even portrayed as a "feeble-minded old man crying" (Miano 2010, 54). Despite his genuine intention to preserve his people, he whines before the conceited rebel chief and, as a consequence, fails to audaciously demonstrate his leadership as the protector of his people, because he speaks with a trembling voice: "The words clashed together and tripped over each other in his fevered brain, losing their force in a feeble, jumbled nonsense" (53). His public death at the village square is even assimilated to "the New Year goat that knows its fate" (63). This absence of resilience is equally observed in the behavior of three other men of the village, Ekwe, Esa, and Ebe. Their powerlessness characterizes them as feeble men waiting for the rebels "to deal with them as they wished" (63). Thus, when these "crumbs of men, inconsequential trifles" (77) are ordered to sacrifice the boy, Eyia, they quiver "so vividly that they looked as though they might fall apart and their bodies be scattered on the wind in a myriad of little shards" (77). The negative emotions of fear and fragility attached to the idea of masculinity here constitutes a keen criticism of male leaders who lack a genuine sense of responsibility in times of crisis.

However, the attitude of the elder woman, the old Ie, is different in the same circumstances of death, because she seems emotionally stronger than the village chief. There are three important qualities of a typical resilient person: the person has some exterior supports, such as family, friends, and role models; she possesses remarkable inner forces, and she respects herself and knows how to take care of others (Grotberg 2003, 3–4). The female character Ie is effective in confronting the rebels' chief and preserving the population of Eku, because she genuinely possesses all aforementioned resilient attributes (52). Remarkably, the first virtuous attribute that emerges from "the most senior woman's" character is that she courageously stands before the rebel chief. She is calm, and "everything about her suggests strength, and awareness of her own importance" (64). She does not simply act with grace and poise, but she is also physically different from other women, since she does not even cover her head with any scarf, and "her hair is cut short" (65). She demonstrates a sound attitude and supremely stands up for her people. Unlike the village chief, her method of negotiation is far from being based on fear. Thus, she is not overwhelmed, whatsoever, by the heavily armed men who have already shown their readiness to kill anyone who opposes them. Her guttural, throaty jazz-like voice is noticed by the narrator, and whilst she addresses the rebel chief, she daringly speaks with a quiet voice without taking her eyes "for a single moment" from the rebel's gaze, resolutely ready to outplay any of his tricky and erratic motives: "We did not want to flee the land our ancestors left us." As if she was prepared to face these armed forces, she boldly adds: "We must therefore endure you. You are our test" (64). The emotions of fearlessness, prowess, and firm resolution that emanate from her eventually attract the admiration of the rebel leader who sullenly acknowledges that she harbors "a soul more masculine than any of the men" assembled at the village square (65). He grudgingly grants her the possibility to preserve some members of the clan from the uncanny human sacrifice. The altruistically driven behavior of this woman leader leads the chief of the rebels to reconsider his positon about her and ultimately start appreciating her because of her courage, thinking of others, and intelligent choices were mostly driven by her love for community. He thus declares that "[s]he had chosen, like a chief. She stood very straight, all tears banished by the sense responsibilities." (Miano 2010, 66–67)

> This paragraph shows that the genuine resilient mindset and self-sacrificing leadership of this female leader prevent the rebels from assaulting her entire community.

Despite strong emotional memories, Miano's aesthetic vision conveys a genuine and passionate interest in African people. Obviously, this claim is debatable, and certain literary critics may find such hopeful interpretation irrelevant. But the conceptual contour given above by Kristeva on the multiple meanings of the literary text should elucidate this conflictual interpretation. Besides, Michael Riffaterre (1983) reminds us that "the literary text is constructed in such a way that it can control its own decoding" (6). The methodological consequence of both critical arguments validates this idea of hopeful interpretation. Despite the fact that certain literary critics may still respond that the "sown decoding" of Miano's texts indicates that its lexical fields dwell presumably in their controversial racist frameworks in the representation of Africa and its people, they may, nonetheless, not be able to overlook its many other obvious constructive paradigms, as demonstrated here. Alternatively, the beauty of a literary text—and the critical discourse that it generates—is that any contestable interpretation, other than our own, found in a text is precisely a sign of its semantic structural richness. Put simply, the plurality of meanings of the text does not irremediably lead its ambiguity nor undermine its didactic clarity; it rather creates several semantic paths that the critics can choose to scrutinize.

Literature can help us to better understand our physical and emotional lives. Hence, Miano's literary writing shows that characters reveal beautifully resilient mindsets even though the writing fails to remain uncontroversial. The characters suffer, or face displacement, or even experience bereavement in conflicts, and yet, the suffering becomes an invigorating experience for them, because they rise above their depressed memories to create new lives for themselves and the people around them. The resilient strategies are intentionally built upon negative emotional memories that ultimately reveal the self-reliant ideas of the author: the quality of our self-reinvention towards life tragedies determines how we, ultimately, gain and maintain a personal awareness to foster better lives. In such philosophy, Africans need less freedom from neocolonialism or powerful economic forces of global corporations than from their own limited view of themselves; or how proactive they are when thinking about their challenges. Miano formulates her ethical philosophy of freedom of choice from this personal awareness.[9] She can be considered as a *rational optimist* in thinking about Africa, because she advocates freedom and hope, not only for Africans, but also the African diaspora, and all human beings per se. Writing is, therefore, a means of breaking down barriers, fostering reconciliation between people, and sharing common human values that promote togetherness.

REFERENCES

Agossou, Houeto Colette Sénami. 1981. *The Dawn on the Cactus*. Porto-Novo: INFRE.
Bâ, Mariama. 1979. *So Long a Letter*. Dakar: Nouvelles éditions africaines.
———. 1981. *Scarlet Song*. Dakar: Nouvelles éditions africaines.
Beyala, Calixthe. 1987. *The Sun Hath Looked Upon Me*. Paris: Librio.
———. 2003. *Naked Woman Black Women*. Paris: Albin Michel.
Butler, Judith. 2004. *Undoing Gender*. New York: Routledge.
Cyrulnik Boris. 1999. *A Marvellous Misfortune*. Paris: Odile Jacob.
Dao, Bernadette. 1992. *Share*. Ouagadougou: Imprimerie nationale.
Dartiguepeyrou Carine. 2012. *The Roads to Resilience*, Paris: L'Harmattan.
Faik-Nzuji, Clémentine. 1969. *The Time for Lovers*. Kinshasa, Mandore.
Feldman, David B. and Lee Daniel Kravetz. 2015. *Supersurvivors: The Surprising Link Between Suffering and Success*, New York: HarperWave. Reprint edition.
Gikandi, Simon. 2011. "Globalization and the Claims of Postcoloniality," in *Literature and Globalization: A Reader*, edited by Liam Connell and Nicky Marsh, 109–120. London: Routledge.
Grotberg, Edith H. 2003. *Resilience for Today: Gaining Strength From Adversity*, Westport, CT: Praeger.
Hogan, Patrick Colm. 2003. *The Mind and Its Stories: Narrative Universals and Human* Cambridge: Cambridge University Press.
———. 2011. *What Literature Teaches Us About Emotion*. New York: Cambridge University Press.
———. 2013. *How Authors' Minds Make Stories*. Cambridge: Cambridge University Press.
Kristeva, Julia. 1980. *Desire in Language: A Semiotic Approach to Literature and Art*. New York: Columbia University Press.
Miano, Léonora. 2010. *Dark Heart of the Night*. Translated by Tamsin Black and forward by Terese Svoboda. Lincoln: University of Nebraska Press.
———. 2006. *Contours of the Coming Day*. Paris: Plon.
———. 2011. *Scarlet Dawns Sankofa Cry*. Paris: Pocket.
———. 2012. *Living in the Border: Conferences*. Paris: Arche.
———. 2013. *The Season of Shadow: A Novel*. Paris: Grasset.
Miller, Christophe L. 2008. *The French Atlantic Triangle: Literature and Culture of the Slave Trade*. Durham: Duke University Press.
Muthu, Sankar. 2003. *Enlightenment Against Empire*. Princeton, NJ: Princeton University Press.
———. 2005. "Globalization during the Enlightenment: Diderot Observer of Global trade and the Imperial Power," in *Slavery, Colonization, and Beyond: France, Unites States, Great Britain*, edited by Patrick Weil and Stéphane Dufoix. Paris: PUF.
Oliver, Paul. 1961. *Blues Fell This Morning: The Meaning of the Blues*. New York: Horizon Press.
Riffaterre, Michael. 1983. *Text Production*. Translated by Terese Lyons. New York: Columbia University Press.
Sembène, Ousmane. 1997. *Ceddo*. New York: New Yorker Films.
Sartre, Jean-Paul. 1985. *What is Literature*. Paris: Gallimard.
Tang, Alice Delphine and Marie-Rose Abomo-Maurin. 2013. *Cameroonian Literature Since the Reunification: 1961–2011: Mutations, Orientions, and Perspectives*. Paris: Harmattan.

Tang, Elodie Carine. 2013. "The Subversive Writing as Imaginary Reproduction of *Social Criticism in Contours of the Coming Day* by Léonora Miano." In *Cameroonian Literature Since the Reunification: 1961–2011: Mutations, Orientations, and Perspectives,* edited by Alice Delphine Tang and Marie-Rose Abomo-Maurin, 133–43. Paris: Harmattan.

Vanistendael, Stefan. 1998. *Key for the Future: Resilience.* Les Vendredis de Chateauvallon. BICE: Bureau international Catholique de l'Enfance, Les Cahiers du BICE, Genève.

Vergely, Bertrand. 2005. Philosophical Approach of Resilience," in *Resilience: The Realism of Hope*. ERES "Fondation pour l'Enfance," 67–86. DOI: 10.3917/eres.fonda.2005.01.0067.

NOTES

1. Leonora Miano was born in Cameroun in 1973 and moved to France in 1991. Even though her literary career began very early when she was eight, it is only in 2005 that she published her first novel. Her literary work can be divided into three parts: (1) the first three novels have Africa as the main setting (*Dark Heart of the Night, Contours of the Coming Day, Scarlet Dawn Sankofa Cry*) and the last novel *The Season of Shadow*; (2) the novels and plays focused on the relationship between Africa, Europe, and the Americas: *Afropean Souland Other Short Stories; Like Faded Stars; Equatorial Soulfood; Blues For Elisa.* Afropean Sequences. Season 1; *These Sorrowful Souls; Writings to be Spoken*); *Red in Blue Trilogy.* (3) A compilation of conferences given in Europe and North America published with the title *Living in the Border.*

2. See the comments of the author in "Léonora Miano: *About the Foreword*" http://www.complete-review.com/reviews/frafrica/mianol.htm. (Accessed May 22, 2015).

3. Her compilation of conferences (2012) gives further insights regarding this aspect of her position on this debate. Her last literary production, *Red in Blue Trilogie* (2015), a play, also deals with this transatlantic tragedy.

4. In his bright analysis on the history of globalization (2003), the political theorist Sankar Muthu considers that the current political debate on this topic tends to overlook the keen early humanistic arguments of some Enlightenment thinkers such as Diderot, Kant, and Herder. In a latter article translated in French—"Globalization during the Enlightenment: Diderot Observer of Global trade and the Imperial Power,"—Muthu argues that Denis Diderot detected very early that even though the commercial and imperial ambitions of Europe could bear some peaceful and stabilizing benefits, the political injustices and the psychological and physical pains of such ambition on Europeans as well as on non-European peoples were of serious concerns (Muthu 2005, 26).

5. *African Sequel (Suite Africaine)* was Miano's proposed title for a single volume. Her editor considered *African Sequel (Suite Africaine)* too voluminous to be published as a single novel. It was eventually published as three separate novels, comprising *Dark Heart of the Night* (2005; 2010 [English edition), *Contours of the Coming Day* (2006), *Scarlet Dawns Sankofa Cry* (2011).

6. Ousmane Sembène is probably the most important Francophone writer and filmmaker to have extensively worked in this topic with a novel *The Black Docker* (1956) as well as with a film *Ceddo* (1976). Another notable movie, *Adanggaman* (2000), was directed by Roger Gnoan M'Bala, from Côte d'Ivoire.

7. In the glossary of the novel, the "Manjua" is defined as a fringed garment, made of fibers of a plant; it looks like a skirt, worn in times of mourning (Miano 2013, 231).

8. In this particular scene set in the very beginning of the movie *Ceddo* (1976), an African slave raider appears on the screen with two captives. They are conducted to a European trader by another African. The latter receives the captives, locked them and, in exchange, gives a gun to the African raider.

9. This particular ethical dimension of the author is fully studied in another article under consideration for publication, see Paul N. Touré, "The Ethics of Resistance in Léonora Miano's African Narrative."

II

Trauma, Reintegration, Healing: Transcending the Aftermath of Wars and Conflicts

SIX

Memoir versus Fiction

Narrating Trauma in Girl Soldier: A Story of Hope for Northern Uganda's Children *and* Thirty Girls

Pauline Ada Uwakweh

NARRATING TRAUMA: THE GENRE EFFECT

War and conflict in Africa have engendered narratives by former child soldiers that bear witness to their traumatic experience. These war-bred testimonials or trauma narratives, exist in a variety of genres, comprising fiction, poetry, songs, films, documentaries, life narratives like memoirs, autobiographies, to mention a few.[1] Topping the list are Ishmael Beah, *A Long Way from Home,* (2008), Uzodimma Iweala, *Beast of No Nation* (2006), Faith J. H. McDonnell and Grace Akallo, *Girl Soldier: A Story of Hope for Northern Uganda's Children* (2007), China Keitetsi (Shena A. Gacu), *Child Soldier: Fighting for my Life* (2005), John Kon Kelei, *The Silent Army* (film, 2008).[2] Significantly, narratives by African females, once child soldiers, are fast becoming part of the African literary landscape. Although the female voice provides a crucial gendered dimension to this category of African literary discourse, much remains uncharted about the psychological impact and consequent trauma experienced by young, female ex-combatants, who also served as "bush wives," and in various other gendered capacities to militant rebels. The following questions are vital to this exploration. How does the choice of genre impact the representation of traumatic experience? What are the manifest evidences of trauma following violent experiences, and how does the experience of violence impact female *victim-survivors* in postwar and conflict, or post-captivity settings?[3] Perhaps, most importantly, how do cultural settings and sociocultural stressors impact traumatic conditions? These questions, underscore the possibility that gendered cultural practices may complicate traumatic conditions, impact female victim survivors, peculiarly, and foreground gender as a critical site of inquiry on traumatic experience.

Two narratives of trauma, *Girl Soldier* by Faith J. H. McDonnell and Grace Akallo and *Thirty Girls* by Susan Minot (2012/2014), are focal texts for this inquiry. The narratives uniquely differ by genre. *Girl Soldier* combines Grace Akallo's memoir of her experience as former girl soldier with her coauthor's historical account on the roots of Uganda's ethnic and political conflicts. In contrast, *Thirty Girls* is a fictional narrative by an American writer whose journalistic reports on the real abduction incident eventually became the source for her story.[4] Unlike Grace Akallo, the victim-survivor and memoirist of *Girl Soldier*, Minot is a non-victim, yet her representation of violence and its traumatic effects on captive girls is rendered more palpably in the fiction than in the memoir. Minot not only tells a story she never *experienced,* but she is also separated by race and culture from the girls whose captive experience she fictionalizes in *Thirty Girls*. Since both accounts share the same source—the 1996 abduction incident of high school girls in Aboke, Uganda—reading *Girl Soldier* as Grace Akallo's memoir and *Thirty Girls* as fictional, "non-victim" narrative is, remarkably, complicated by genre. Authorship of the fiction certainly interrogates Minot's adaptation of her "journalistic material" to capture the social, cultural, and political discourse of trauma in the Ugandan setting she writes about.

Furthermore, the necessary desire of victim-survivors to testify or narrate their experience of trauma is noted in trauma studies. However, crucial questions are evoked here about non-victims who write about violence and trauma that they never experienced, themselves. Is vicarious influence enough to represent trauma, creatively? What distinguishes the *owner* and narrator of the traumatic story and the *writer* of the story, more so when that writer is non-native? These questions address both Susan Minot's position as non-victim author of a traumatic experience in *Thirty Girls* and Grace Akallo's victim-survivor position in her memoir, *Girl Soldier*. Where should the reader look for the "truth" of the Aboke incident and its aftermath—in the memoir or the fiction?

The transmissibility concept of trauma theory postulated by Felman and Laub (1992) poses some implications in this regard, considering the status of Minot as author of a fictional traumatic story. Although the transmissibility concept has further shifted established discussion on trauma, it nevertheless heightens the position of the listener or reader of the traumatic story—a situation encountered by Minot as reporter on the Aboke abduction story. In "Trauma Within the Limits of Literature," Geoffrey Hartmann (2003) indicates that media publicity on traumatic incidents may lead to "secondary traumatization" or "distance suffering"

(258) which might affect all those connected with the event indirectly as readers, therapists, relatives, or witnesses. As such, to experience trauma, vicariously, is to become a "secondary victim." Similarly, Irene Visser (2011) argues that vicarious trauma mimics similar conditions as for those with direct experience of trauma. Conditions such as "nightmares, flashbacks, depression, but also an increased sensitivity to cynicism, depersonalization, and distinct changes in spirituality or worldview" have become part of the experience of the non-victim witness of the traumatic story (272). Conceiving Minot as a secondary victim, perhaps, establishes her right to representing or "telling" the story as much as the victim-survivor.

From an analytical standpoint then, authorship in *Girl Soldier* and *Thirty Girls* complicates inquiry into trauma in these novels, since both the memoir and fiction have Western authors or collaborators. Considering these, it is important that textual analysis be informed by theoretical perspectives grounded on both African and Western perspectives on trauma. Incidentally, postcolonial critics have queried the appropriateness of applying Western-oriented trauma theories on African trauma narratives which further illustrates the complexity of evaluating Western-authored African trauma narratives. In this regard, questions about the effect of traditional, cultural practices on traumatic conditions are evoked, since traumatic stressors are culturally rooted, defined, and embedded in the social fabric. How for instance, might gender and race intersect with the traumatic story, symptoms of trauma, and their representations in literature? The tensions and shifts in framing trauma, its physical and psychological manifestations, especially in literary theory has necessitated what Michelle Balaev in "Literary Trauma Theory Reconsidered" (2014) calls "a set of critical practices that place more focus on the particular social components and cultural contexts of traumatic experience" (3). Scholars must engage these sociocultural angles, especially in defining critical aesthetics for postcolonial trauma theory.

Akallo's memoir and Minot's fictional representations exemplify the implications of using two different genres to portray traumatic experience based on the same incident. Interestingly, the degree to which violence and traumatic effects are represented in both narratives differ, dramatically. For example, while Akallo's memoir focuses on her memory of traumatic event, it scarcely accounts for the post-traumatic effect that usually attends violent experiences. The fiction, on the other hand, goes beyond mere recollections of violence by dramatizing the stark realities of female captivity among the LRA, as well as the ill effects of post-captive trauma. Further, *Thirty Girls* illuminates, more keenly, the social stressors that trigger traumatic memory or recall and subsequently perpetuate the cycle of trauma.

Taking these differences into account, it is evident that in *Thirty Girls*, Minot employs western clinical symptoms of post-traumatic distress to heighten and politicize the effects of violence, rape, abuse, forced motherhood, and abductions on female victim-survivors. Her characters show more intrusive recollections of violence, disorientation, incoherence, identity crisis, that are linked to symptoms characterized as post-traumatic stress or PTSD. Cathy Caruth (1995) describes post-traumatic stress symptoms as "a response, sometimes delayed, to an overwhelming event or events, which takes the form of repeated, intrusive hallucination, dreams, thoughts or behaviors stemming from the event, along with a numbing that may have begun during or after the experience" (4). Caruth's perspective on trauma as wound—the "illness of a wounded psyche that cries out, that addresses us in an attempt to tell us of a reality or truth that is not otherwise available" (4)—is underscored by other contemporary views on literary trauma, such as Anne Whitehead's (2004) *Trauma Fiction* which explores the nuances of trauma in literary representations. Observing the recurring shifts in memory of traumatic experiences, Whitehead calls for more focus on the "how and why" trauma is remembered rather than on memory itself. Also, noting evident tension in representing trauma, Whitehead explains that trauma resists representation through language and is only adequately captured by "mimicking its forms and symptoms, so that temporality and chronology collapse, and narratives are characterized by repetition and indirection" (3). This tension between language and trauma has been revisited by trauma theorists and affirmed as an aid for "working through" and achieving catharsis. According to Hartmann (2003), wounds and silence are given voice through language (259).

Post-traumatic stress is a key, but controversial concept in trauma theory that defies precise definition. As noted by trauma critic, Irene Visser (2011), the physical and psychological manifestations of trauma are grounded in various interdisciplinary theories and are not replicable in all humans (272). Visser expands the concept by acknowledging the import of stressors to the traumatic experience. She asserts that "'trauma' refers not so much to the traumatic event as to the traumatic aftermath, the post-traumatic stage. Trauma, thus, denotes the recurrence or repetition of the stressor event through memory, dreams, narrative and/or various symptoms known under the definition of Post-Traumatic Stress Disorder (PTSD)" (272).

To assess trauma in the two narratives under study, Judith Herman's *Trauma and Recovery: The Aftermath of Violence* (1992) provides value for identifying symptoms of PTSD and recovery of victim-survivors, particularly because it is grounded in the experiences of female survivors. Thus, Herman's gendered perspective supports this study of trauma narratives written by and about women. Visser (2011) also imputes significance to Herman's work in terms of its potential for enabling theorizations of postcolonial trauma theory, preferring Hermann's "ahistorical and culturally specific approach" over Caruth's "homogenizing and dehistoricizing tendencies" (274). Visser further states: "Herman's notion of trauma may hold out a more sustainable perspective for a postcolonial trauma theory, not only because it entails an openness to the structuring of narrativization but also because it allows ahistorically and culturally specific approach to trauma narratives" (274).

In *Trauma and Recovery,* Herman delineates the symptoms that characterize PTSD based on three states of its manifestations. The features include the following: hyper arousal expressed in the persistent expectation of danger; intrusion, expressed in the reliving of painful traumatic experience, and disruption of daily existence by involuntary recall of events; and the states of constriction, expressed in altered consciousness, surrender, numbing of victim by experience (15). She also defines the facilitating agents for recovery and healing, including the presence of safety spaces; reconstructing the traumatic story; and restoring connection between the survivor and the community. These factors, while they monitor PTSD and recovery, may also provide significant ways for assessing representations of characters and levels of traumatic effects in both the memoir and fiction.

The symptoms outlined by Herman, seemingly, inform Minot's fictionalized trauma narrative. This assessment will attempt to identify or locate symptoms in *Thirty Girls* as evidence of the degree to which Minot represents PTSD, on one hand, and recovery and healing on the other hand. These evidences will be compared to the representation of similar traumatic conditions in *Girl Soldier.* The goal of this comparative analysis is to delineate the effect of narrative medium on the portrayal of traumatic conditions.

REPRESENTATIONS OF TRAUMA IN *THIRTY GIRLS* AND *GIRL SOLDIER*

Minot's employment of post-traumatic symptoms to define her female character's condition leads to important questions about the impact of genre on trauma representation in literature. A critical look into the genre effect has enormous value for understanding the memoir, *Girl Soldier,* and the fiction, *Thirty Girls.* Both narratives inform and complement each other to a remarkable degree, and so, should be read together for ample insight on gendered violence and traumatic conditions. This recommendation considers that the authors probe female experiences in captivity and post-captivity to a greater or lesser extent. While Akallo, via memory, *recalls* select incidents surrounding her kidnapping and escape, Minot, fictionalizes Akallo's real experience, capturing along the way, the emotional, traumatic, and psychological anguish of the victims. Thus, she brings to bear on her fiction, more graphic details of the violence that are missing from the memoir. By so doing, she enables her readers' vicarious empathy for the victims, and more importantly, fills the gaps and silences in Akallo's memoir.[5]

In *Girl Soldier*, Grace Akallo, as protagonist /narrator, engages memories of her abduction, life in captivity, final escape, and activist involvement on the international scene. Her ultimate goal is to make the world a safer place for children. As Akallo's symbol of collective outrage against the abuse of children, *Girl Soldier* offers hope for female victim-survivors whose voices may never be heard as loudly as hers. As her symbol of human resilience and transcendence over overwhelming odds, *Girl Soldie*r mirrors a spiritual dimension that inserts Akallo's faith in God's providence into her narrative arc. Published ten years after her freedom from captivity, *Girl Soldier* heightens the significance of memory as a site for recall in narratives of violence and trauma. Joya Uraizee (2014) has argued that the collaborative writing of *Girl Soldier by* Grace Akallo and Faith J. H. McDonnell contests the veracity of Akallo's memoir, due to "inconsistencies in the narrative and the imbalance in the collaboration" (64). Uraizee explains further:

> Akallo tells us her story in the first person, in eleven odd-numbered chapters, while McDonnell contextualizes her story in eleven-even-numbered chapters plus an introduction and a conclusion. Not only is this pattern somewhat awkward, but McDonnell's context dominates the narrative: her sections make up 69 percent of the total pages in the book while Akallo's make up 31 percent. More importantly, McDonnell's historical context is extremely depoliticized and rooted in her evangelical ideological. (64)

This observation calls forth the problems inherent in mediated narratives, especially as they relate to child soldier accounts based on conflicts in Africa.[6] Also, the evangelical context of Akallo's narrative may be implicated in the memoirist's selection and representation of traumatic incidents in her captive experience. Could the necessity to present the protagonist in a particular fashion have hindered the "truth" of memoir? If the overarching purpose of Akallo's memoir is embodied in the narrative medium, the possibility exists that this purpose could have impacted the "truth" of memoir and the representation of violence and trauma by the coauthors.

The fictional tale, *Thirty Girls,* poses a set of different concerns. Published in 2012, sixteen years after the Aboke abductions and five years after the publication of Akallo's memoir, Minot's *Thirty Girls* blazes the trail of *Girl Soldier.* However, unlike Akallo's whose writing was initiated by a charitable and evangelical organization, Susan Minot is a seasoned American writer. She discloses in an interview that it took her seven years "to tell a story that she believes needs to be told" and to explore a "particular historical situation—a horrific one pretty much ignored by the world—of the children kidnapped by Kony's LRA from a more interior perspective" (Causey 2014).

Esther Akello, Minot's fictional protagonist in *Thirty Girls,* is apparently cast as Grace Akallo of the memoir. Both females share similar sounding last names. One can safely say that Minot's characters mimic the experience of their real life prototypes, and that her narrative closely recreates the reality of captivity for the abducted girls. The fictional Esther, constitutes a key part of Minot's alternate perspective through whom the burden of post-traumatic syndrome is fully captured. Esther's traumatized consciousness is juxtaposed, in alternating chapters, with that of another central character, Jane Wood, the American journalist and reporter for *Herpes Magazine*. Minot's chapters shift from the reality of rehabilitation in Uganda, to Esther's experience of violence in captivity, to Jane Woods's quest for the story of the girls at the Kiriyandogo rehabilitation center. In *Thirty Girls,* Esther's psychological brokenness is symbolized in the absence of chronology in the text, in her thought processes, and most evidently, in the persistent intrusions of her violent past. These traumatic manifestations align well with Judith Herman's (1992) observations about post-traumatic syndrome. Herman asserts that "[I]n the aftermath of an experience of overwhelming danger, the two contradictory responses of intrusion and constriction establish an oscillating rhythm. This dialectic of opposing psychological states is perhaps the most characteristic feature of the post-traumatic syndromes" (47). An examination of these traumatic manifestations in the memoir and fiction illuminates the subtle differences and attitudes of the authors to their stories. How they represent trauma and violence speaks volumes about the implications of genre as narrative medium.

For these authors, genre has obvious implications, yet, thought-provoking questions remain about its ability to carry the weight of traumatic experience. Further, the role memory plays in the memoir and fictional story comes into question. What are the implications of narrating a personal life experience of trauma using memoir? When a writer chooses one genre over the other, what determines these choices? What determines the writer's choice of incidents that eventually form the corpus of the final story? Speaking to the importance of the writer's decision, Fiona Simpson (2007) accords that "[W]riting decisions are clearly connected to meaning–making. *We can choose what we record and expose.* Writing, therefore, celebrates and records the writer's agency" (317, emphasis added). In a similar vein, David Rain (2007) emphasizes the significance of narrative choices for writers. As he notes, "[T]o work with genre, the writer must understand not only how a given genre is structured, but what it means—what desires and fears we confront and perhaps allay in contemplating this quest" (64).

Indeed, the distinction between memoir and fiction threads a fine and subtle line, since both are fueled and inspired by human imagination.

Presumably, and through narrative selectivity, memoir orders specific events in the life of the author, while fiction recreates human experiences, imaginatively. However, both genres aim to achieve a compelling purpose, nonetheless. Memoirs prioritize human memory and its capacity for recall. In contrast to fiction, memoir's dependence on recollected events, apparently, invests it with the stamp of truth. Thus, while fiction depends on the imagination's ability to recreate human experiences, the memoirist's use of imaginative recollection complicates the "truth" of the memoir. As a result, and ironically also, memoir, a life writing is highly contested. Sedonie Smith and Julia Watson (2010) acknowledge that the structure of memoir, along with its dependence on the writer's life experiences, makes it a subgenre of autobiography. However, unlike autobiography, memoir deals with a slice of experience rather than life history, and therefore, invokes a different kind of reading (4).[7]

Thirty Girls was conceived from the author's desire to "tell" and publicize the horrors experienced by captive children, especially girls, in the hands of armed, LRA rebel groups. Although both narratives depict the effects of violence and captivity for African girl soldiers, the fictional account appears to engage with post-traumatic effects of captivity on the female victim-survivors in much greater and intimate detail. If Minot's graphic representation of traumatic effects and its clinical manifestations are crucial for appreciating the gendered insights of African trauma narratives, so also are her depictions of the gendered strictures that circumscribe the lives of female captives and ex-soldiers in African wars and conflicts. She dramatizes the fact that girls are, inevitably, the most likely to be branded and made social pariahs due to their association with rebels and/or by their participation in military activities. Their militant engagements are perceived to be outside acceptable norms of social expectations for females.

Evidently, Minot seems to have replicated western clinical models of PTSD in her traumatized victim-survivors, most especially, in their feelings of incoherence and loss of identity. Baring the story's African (Ugandan) cultural context, *Thirty Girls* underlines questions about appropriateness when clinical diagnoses or manifestations of PTSD are applied to settings other than western. *Thirty Girls* projects the unstable, emotional, and psychological state of the traumatized individual. Their state of disorientation is more acutely captured in the fiction than in *Girl Soldier*. Fiction mimics reality and Minot captures this paradox through depictions of characters and setting in *Thirty Girls*. The Rehabilitation Center, for instance, is presented as an illusory space for the recovery of scarred children. Obviously, the "safe space" in *Thirty Girls* is a disruptive space where the potential for healing is limited. Being a space where every child escapee is expected to touch base with a counselor before reintegration, Minot underlines its oppressive structure, while indicting the proliferation of ineffective non-governmental organizations (NGOs). Recovery for inmates seems far from being achieved as there are just three counselors for 10,000 children (229). Minot indicts the absence of proper care for the inmates of the Rehab centers, and raises doubts about the possibility of achieving reintegration for victimized children.

As she delineates the rehabilitation experience of Esther Akello, Minot lays emphasis on the traumatic stressors that circumscribe her protagonist's present reality. Graphic depictions of Esther's intrusive thoughts depicts her life among rebel soldiers, violence and rampant sexual abuse in captivity. However, although Esther has escaped captivity, signs of PTSD are expressed in her utter sense of insecurity at the Rehabilitation center. Her sense of security is missing, weeks after her arrival at the Center. Her intrusive memories of violence is juxtaposed with her present experience of social ostracism, stigmatization, rejection, as well as her sense of suffocation, utter helplessness and dejection. She states: "It is strange to be back. When I was with the rebels I stayed calm inside while there was much suffering around me. Now where it is safe here, I am full of anger. Maybe I will nearly explode. I could even pick up a gun and kill someone, I think" (129). Her past and present are interlinked by the intrusive thoughts which heighten the intensity and effect of her pain. "I have decided not to remember, but pictures appear to me no matter" (44). Esther's "thoughts had cracks in them," and she is expected to draw pictures to remove them from her mind.[8] Her physical and psychological scars are shared by inmates of the Kiryandongo Rehabilitation Center where abductees are required to serve time in reintegration therapy. As the narrator states, "Rehab is not a prison but we are not permitted to leave. A young girl is pregnant. Parents have neither visited nor accept the child" (40). In this setting, husbands reject abducted wives because being a rebel's wife is more tolerable than being raped (230). Evidences of damaged identity are symbolized by recurrent fights among the inmates, and as Barbara, the administrative officer at Kiryyandongo Center aptly observes, "[A]fter trauma, there is difficulty having fun" (45–48).

Certainly, in *Thirty Girls*, post-captivity trauma is severe. Evidences of PTSD are intensely dramatized in the form of daily intrusions of violent memories. The refrain, "*What comes back to me*" becomes the leitmotif that marks recurring intrusions and time shifts. Further, intrusions are unveiled as forms of traumatic stressors, compounded by health issues such as feelings of dizziness and persistent nightmares, as "girls wake up screaming" (158). The drowning suicide of a young female inmate of the Center speaks to the effect that death has become an escape mode, a self-willed act of destruction that arises from family rejection and abandonment.

> Her parents do not come. They tell us her parents are dead. We do not believe it. Carol knew her parents were not taking her back. She did not want to live more. Are we surprised? No. We understand. Some of me

> goes with her now she is dead. I let Carol take that part away, the part that would want to die. Instead I would want to live. (264)

Carol's death demonstrates how ruptures in family ties can be a stressor for victim-survivors of captivity in this patriarchal Ugandan society. For example, Esther's memory of her pregnancy is complicated by the attitude of family members. Despite the fact that her mother died while she was in captivity, when she visits home, her father, does not look her in the face: "I am there, but I do not feel among them. A gray curtain comes down and I am apart with only myself" (212). Herman (1992) indicates that the breakdown of family attachments intensifies traumatic experience and the victim's sense of self and identity. She states:

> Traumatic events breach the attachments of family, friendship, love, and community. They shatter the construction of the self that is formed and sustained in relation to others. They undermine the belief system that gives meaning to human experience. They violate the victim's faith in a natural or divine order and cast the victim into a state of existential crisis. It is a shattering of "basic trust." A sense of alienation, disconnection pervades every relationship. (51)

In such a situation, it is only by reconnecting with family and community that healing process for victims of violence can begin. In *Thirty Girls,* that connection is made possible for Esther and her fellow victims through Jane, her reporting crew, and the video camera. The Camera, is an important character and symbol in Minot's fiction, being part of the implied audience for the trauma narrative. It bears witness to the girls' tales of horror. Esther states: "my words were going in the camera. . . . I told *her* all these things I have told you" (249, emphasis added). The Camera is part witness, memorializing the narrative. As witness to the trauma story, it holds the promise of voicing and catharsis for female victim-survivors.

The photo image of Jane and Esther is another powerful symbol that projects empathy and sisterhood beyond racial binds. It reinforces their common bond of gender-initiated suffering. As Jane experiences Esther's suffering, vicariously, the point of contact is gender, not race. Further, connecting with community is therapeutic as are other healing mechanisms embedded in the narrative. These include forgiveness, reconciliation with captured rebel soldiers, dreams of wedding, music, dancing, and connecting with mothers in the community (237). Also, the iconic dragonfly-shaped necklace, Jane's gift to Esther is a symbol of strength and courage (253). This gift symbolizes the possibility of transformation; hence, at the end of *Thirty Girls,* Minot advises her readers, "Do something" (303). This seems to be the imperative for meaningful social action to end the plight of her gender.

Comparatively, in *Girl Soldier,* Akallo's memoir endows her with a level of control solidified by her Christian ethic and faith in God's providence. Compared to the fictional story where the characters' brutalization are strongly portrayed, there are less detailed depictions of violent captivity experience. Traumatic experience is less graphic, and often times, commented upon in passing. There is also significant absence of the post-traumatic symptoms. It appears that the memoir's humanitarian goal impacts the degree to which violence and trauma are represented. While the memoir may have achieved its overall purpose of sharing a young girl's resilience, survival, and transcendence, it falls short of articulating, fully, the critical gendered dimension. Unlike the female victim-survivors in *Thirty Girls,* the narrator/protagonist in the memoir is a model of human resilience. Essentially, the memoir, *Girl Soldier,* maps transcendence by refashioning the victim-survivor. For instance, Grace Akallo's narrative begins with her memory of being "buried alive" and losing her identity:

> The soil has become my blanket. *This bed is warm and comfortable. Where am I? Maybe home? No, this is not home. It is quiet, only whispers of wind and the morning crickets. My foot hurts. I feel weak. What happened? I smell soil. This is strange.* Slowly the bitter memories flow back to me. I am in Sudan, and I have been buried among the dead. Seven months after my capture, I am no longer myself. . . . I can't really tell who I am anymore. And I don't have any clothes on me. I am just like the day I came from my mother's stomach. (27–28, authors' emphasis)

The narrator's account of her death and revival is symbolic. It begins both her physical journey of survival, her journey of transformation and reintegration into human society, as well as her refashioning into a new identity. Symbolically, her memoir constitutes an essential part of that refashioning. Consequently, while she engages the public domain with her private experience, Akallo also evokes admiration rather than pity from her audience. Furthermore, the memoir, *Girl Soldier* projects, highly, the spaces for transformation and healing. By emphasizing healing, recovery, transcendence over odds, and the narrator's future potential as survivor, the memoir showcases itself as persuasive, and invested with utility beyond the text. *Girl Soldier* a personal story, exhibits a touch of missionary zest; it is futuristic in outlook, as well as in its expectation for change and humanitarian outcome. If violence and trauma are downplayed in *Girl Soldier,* faith in God becomes the sustaining core of Akallo's life changing experience. Her memoir's objective is clarified in this 2013 interview:

> *"I have to use the life that I was given for a purpose* . . . not to mourn over what happened to me," she says. "I was supported—I went to school, and I have a family that supports me and loves me. But what about the girls who are still suffering? They are still being beaten. They are still rejected. They still don't have homes or family support or access to any resources or education or health care. Nothing!" (emphasis added)[9]

In this quote, Akallo defines her future role. Thus, unlike Esther Akello in *Thirty Girls,* Grace presents a resilient spirit hinged on her trust in God's divine guidance, and her desire to engage in activism to help others in similar circumstances.

Faith McDonnell's position as coauthor of *Girl Soldier* is important to Akallo's self-refashioning. Her role compares well with that of Jane, the white American female reporter in *Thirty Girls.* Remarkably, both provide moral support, sisterhood, and platforms for *telling* the story of victimhood and survival. In *Girl Soldier,* McDonnell's historical perspective fills gaps in Akallo's memoir by providing statistical evidence that backs up her memoir. Though criticized for her apolitical rendition of Uganda's history, McDonnell undergirds Akallo's narrative by unveiling the historical and sociological contexts that breed and exacerbate traumatic stressors for victim-survivors in the post-captivity. In so doing, she highlights the factors that hinder full reintegration. McDonnell illustrates how rape, silencing among girls and women, and other forms of stressors in the Acholi cultural setting can derail reintegration goals and perpetuate traumatic distress as follows:

> The stigma of rape in Acholi society makes it very difficult for girls to talk about what has been done to them. Amnesty reported that children who were interviewed found it easier to admit to having killed than to having raped or having been raped. A counsellor told Amnesty International that all the girls deny being raped at first, but eventually they will admit it. For a child, denying the trauma inflicted upon him or her—whether the trauma of being turned into a killer or of sexual abuse—is a kind of self-protection. (135)

Other forms of post-traumatic stressors identified in *Girl Soldier* constitute, primarily, social rejection and ostracism of former captives, name calling, unwanted publicity, dreams and memories of past violence, stigma associated with rape, "rebel's wife," forced motherhood, killer, and the challenge of survival in post-conflict society. High on the list of traumatic social stressors are rejection and ostracism resulting from forced motherhood. In an interview, Akallo corroborates this gendered issue: "Neither boy nor girl child soldiers are really accepted back into society, but for the girl child soldier, it is harder when they have unwanted children" (De Grave 2013).[10]

Ultimately, *Girl Soldier* magnifies recovery of the victim-survivor, and safe spaces are defined by such things as communal acceptance and support, as well as the opportunity to restart educational career. Only within such safe spaces can reconstructing and narrating, and resultant healing be ensured. Imbued with a sense of the mission which survival affords her, Akallo's optimism is strongly reflected in her desire to engage in activism to help other children still held captive. The memoir can, thus, be perceived as Akallo's tangible evidence of recovery and agency that affirms her reclaimed identity. While religion plays no part in the fictionalized account, it is the bedrock of the narrator's self-reclamation in the memoir. Her mission to give voice to suffering captive children becomes the process toward realizing this agency. Akallo's *cri de coeur*, comes with her final statement, "To the whole world, this is my cry: There is no future without healthy children who grow up in a peaceful environment. Do not turn your hatred on the children "(195).

In *Thirty Girls,* the breakdown of "temporality and chronology" signifies the protagonist's traumatic anguish, and insecurity. Narrative viewpoint in *Thirty Girls* is in marked contrast to that of *Girl Soldier* where narrative chronology is sustained and heightens the evidence of the author/narrator's transcendence over traumatic experience. Indeed, in the memoir, the narrator's life is in the process of refashioning, and therefore, she is less focused on violence (past); it is rather her agency (present) through communal engagement and for a compelling goal (future) that is underscored. There is little or no evidence of the post-traumatic effect which is so movingly depicted in *Thirty Girls.* Grace is the survivor whose image and identity, as an exemplary model of God's intervention in human existence is being publicized. To appreciate Akallo's memoir, one should take into account the evangelical underpinnings of its publication. In the foreword, Dan Haseltine remarks that "The story of Grace Akallo is a hard one to read," but it is also one that showcases "*God working out his glorious plan*" (13, emphasis added). Graphic violence in *Girl Soldier* is limited. In contrast to *Thirty Girls* where Esther's life as a rebel's wife and her brief motherhood is vividly dramatized, only once is reference made to "husband" as part of the reality of captive girls in *Girl Soldier* (126). If the account is mediated to present a specific image of Grace, certainly, the rendering of the female condition in captivity pales in comparison to the picture in *Thirty Girls.* This raises the question about the extent to which collaboration might have deflected, or refashioned the "truth "of memoir.

Narrative mediation, relating to testimonials on Africa's wars and conflicts is an emerging area for critical exploration. Mediators may be western, and inevitably, mostly white. This situation is reflected in literary representations and publishing field, just as the two narratives illustrate. In *Thirty Girls*. Susan Minot is a white, American author writing about the African female condition. As white female, Minot is separated culturally and racially from her Ugandan protagonist, so also is her fictional journalist, Jane Wood. Jane is a white journalist with an obsessive desire to capture the story of the girls at the Rehabilitation site in Uganda. She is also escaping from a traumatic experience, a failed marriage that, seemingly, compares less to the experience of the victimized girls. In *Girl Soldier*, the opportunity to write/tell and publish her story was presented to Grace Akallo by outsiders, so also does Jane Wood (an outsider) who offers friendship to Esther Akello and her friends, provide them the outlet (audience and camera) to testify to their traumatic experience of captivity. Notably, in both memoir and fiction, presence of white facilitators seem to perpetuate the stereotype of the westerner as "white savior." Minot's role as writer, must, however, be viewed differently from that of Faith McDonnell's, since she (Minot) gives voice to a story, fictionally. If her success lies in intense dramatization of trauma and its effects, perhaps, her weakness lies in failing to offer her victim-survivors the full capacity for recovery. Recovery remains only a potential that is not wholesomely realized at end of her novel. If the potential for healing, recovery, and new beginning is blurred for the girls in *Thirty Girls*, it is one of the strongest points of Grace Akallo's memoir. Overall, and in view of these critical observations, I proffer that *Thirty Girls* evidences more PTSD in the fictional characters than the memoir; the fiction also presents more acute levels of traumatic recall, and there is more awareness of social stressors among the victim-survivors than in the memoir. Conversely, Akallo's memoir exhibits a heightened level of awareness of future prospects, confidence in narrator's capacity to institute change in the society through her narrative.

This study has shown how genre might impact literary representations of traumatic experience. Undoubtedly, both writers—Minot, McDonnell and Akallo—have been driven by a shared sense of empathy for vulnerable children in war torn and rebel infested parts of Africa. They have been compelled by altruistic goals to unveil evil and bring about change in the lives of suffering children and youth. Further, although both stories articulate traumatic experiences of young captive African females, the fictional account seems to have explored trauma in the aftermath much more intensely than the memoir. In *Thirty Girls*, Esther's pathos contrasts sharply with her counterpart's confident attitude, as shown in the narrative voice of the memoir. Here, Grace Akallo confidently engages her destiny. Her voice is controlled, terse, projecting a personality consumed by a sense of urgency toward the despairing children of Northern Uganda. In both stories, there is a sense of community listening and empathizing. Both narratives offer insight to the challenges of rehabilitation for children, especially young women, in the post-captivity society. The role of foreign media, NGOs, Charity missions predominate in both accounts, and almost perpetuate stereotypes of the "western savior." As coauthor, McDonnell publicizes Akallo's voice, globally, so does Susan Minot, through Jane Woods, proclaim the atrocities in Northern Uganda, while also enabling the voice of the female victims. Indeed, Grace Akallo acknowledges her debt to several people, notably Faith McDonnell for "the idea of writing this book and finding the publisher for it . . . to Peggy Noll, who is most responsible for helping me learn how to write in English and write academically" (18–19). While both accounts end poignantly, Grace Akallo redefines herself in a much positive, cogent, and less empathetic way than her fictional counterpart, Esther Akello. Grace Akallo attains a global status by her sheer activism, on behalf of victimized children. It seems, therefore, that the memoir can rightly be perceived as the metamorphosis of the fictional Esther Akello, the fulfillment of the "sparks of possibility," the imperative for action" hinted at in *Thirty Girls* (303).

The two narratives, fiction and memoir, unveil the sites of trauma, though they differ in the intensity or degree of its clinical manifestations, as well as in the authors' representations of the pathways for recovery, healing, and reintegration. *Girl Soldier* and *Thirty Girls* expose the challenges faced by child soldiers in ill-equipped Rehab centers. They illustrate the psychological and emotional disruptions, social exclusion, family, and community rejection confronting girl soldiers. Remarkably, they also offer interesting perspectives on how genre interrogates the impact of memory and gendered stressors as sites of trauma. These representations notwithstanding, a nagging question persists. Does Minot's fiction over dramatize or sensationalize violence and its traumatic effects? Further, can the memoir be accepted as "truth" in view of the author's narrative privilege and selectivity? The assertion here is that the two stories complement each other's lack and should be read together, since the fictional story, to a large extent, makes up for the silences or gaps that dot the memoirist's narrative. Since both narratives accentuate insight on the experience of young female captives, as well as the sociocultural forces that perpetuate traumatic re-memory, both should then be read together for greater understanding of the traumatic aftermath on female survivors of violence. The two stories highlight the urgency for adequate postwar rehabilitation mechanisms for African children and youth caught in the cross fire of wars and conflicts. This exploration calls for more research on African trauma narratives, cultural and gendered stressors that perpetuate trauma, and for awareness on their impact on women and girls in African societies, as well as globally.

REFERENCES

Balaev, Michelle. 2014. " Literary Trauma Theory Reconsidered." In *Contemporary Approaches in Literary Trauma Theory*. New York: Palgrave MacMillan. 1–14.

Beah, Ishmael. 2008. *A Long Way Gone: Memoirs of a Boy Soldier*. Sarah Crichton Books.

Berger, James. 1997. "Trauma and Literary Theory" *Contemporary Literature*. Fall 38.3: 569–82.

Caruth, Cathy. 1995. *Trauma: Explorations in Memory*. Baltimore: Johns Hopkins

Causey, Michael. 2014. "Interview with Susan Minot." March 6. Accessed, July 11, 2016. http://www.washingtonindependentreviewofbooks.com/features/interview-with-susan-minot.

De Grave, Isabelle. 2012. "Former Girl Soldiers Trade One Nightmare for Another." Inter Press Service. Accessed July 11, 2016. http://www.ipsnews.net/2012/06/former-girl-soldiers-trade-one-nightmare-for-another/.

Felman, Shoshana and Laub, Dori. 1992. *Testimony: Crises of Witnessing in Literature, Psychoanalysis and History*. New York: Routledge.

Hartman, Geoffrey. 2003. "Trauma Within the Limits of Literature" *European Journal of English Studies*. 7.3: 257–74.

Herman, Judith L. 1992. *Trauma and Recovery: The Aftermath of Violence—from Domestic Abuse to Political Terror*. New York: Basic Books.
Iweala, Uzodimma. 2006. *Beast of No Nation*. New York: Harper Perennial.
Keitetsi, China (Shena A. Gacu). 2005. *Child Soldier: Fighting for my Life.* Johannesburg: Jacana Media.
Kelei, John Kon. 2008. *The Silent Army* (film). December 11. http://www.imdb.com/title/tt1189008/.
Leach, Diane. 2015. "'Thirty Girls': What We Learned Later." June 2. Accessed August 20, 2016. http://www.popmatters.com/review/193955-thirty-girls-by-susan-minot/.
McDonnell, Faith J. H. and Grace Akallo. 2007. *Girl Soldier: A Story of Hope for Northern Uganda's Children.* Grand Rapids, MI: Chosen Books.
Minot, Susan. 2014. *Thirty Girls*. New York: Knopf.
Morrison, Toni. 1998. "The Site of Memory." In *Inventing the Truth: The Art and Craft of Memoir*, edited by William Zinsser. New York: Houghton Mifflin. 83–102.
Provencher, Raymonde dir. 2010. *Grace, Milly and Lucy,* documentary film. https://www.nfb.ca/film/grace_milly_lucy_child_soldiers.
Rain, David. 2007. "Literary Genres." In *The Handbook of Creative Writing,* edited by Steven Earnshaw. Edinburgh: Edinburgh University Press. 54–64. Accessed December 27, 2015. http://hfs1.duytan.edu.vn/upload/ebooks/5762.pdf.
Simpson, Fiona. 2007. "Writing as Therapy." In *The Handbook of Creative Writing*, edited by Steven Earnshaw. Edinburgh: Edinburgh University Press. 312–319. Accessed December 27, 2015. http://hfs1.duytan.edu.vn/upload/ebooks/5762.pdf.
Smith, Sedonie and Julia Watson. 2010. *Reading Autobiography: Guide to Interpreting Life Narratives.* University of Minnesota Press.
Uraizee, Joya. 2014. "Migrant African Children Remembering War." In *Engaging the Diaspora: Migration and African Families,* edited by Pauline Ada Uwakweh, Jerono Rotich, and Comfort Okpala. Lanham, MD: Lexington. 59–74.
Visser, Irene. 2011. "Trauma Theory and Postcolonial Literary Studies" *Journal of Postcolonial Writing*, vol. 47.3: 270–82.
Whitehead, Anne. 2004. *Trauma Fiction*. Edinburgh: Edinburgh University Press.

NOTES

1. Smith and Watson (2010) categorize memoir as "life writing," a narrative with the essential aim of positioning a "universalizing life story" (3). See *Reading Autobiography: A Guide to Interpreting Life Narratives.*

2. Apart from prose narratives, films based on child soldier experiences are now prevalent in the film industry. Most are being used for political and humanitarian purposes to raise awareness of this problem in Africa and globally. See for example, Uzodimma Iweala, *Beast of No Nation* (film, 2015), currently released as a major motion picture directed by Cary Joji Fukunaga. Also, African female captivity in war and armed conflict has spawned, not only memoirs and fictional representations of these experiences, but also documentary films, such as *Grace, Milly, Lucy* (2010), directed by Raymonde Provencher, that tells the story of girls forced into armed conflict in Uganda. See link https://www.nfb.ca/film/grace_milly_lucy_child_soldiers film. Incidentally, there seems to be as much mediation in the film industry, as there are in African testimonial narratives.

3. I have borrowed the term "victim-survivors" from Regine Michelle Jean-Charles's (2014) *Conflict Bodies: The Politics of Rape Representation in the Francophone Imaginary*. As Jean-Charles argues in her work, the term accords agency to rape victims and affirms their capacity for transcendence. "They are active subjects ready to 'call it rape,' explicitly naming their experience" (6). Jean-Charles maintains that the female body is rarely acknowledged as a site of conflict that implicates human rights transgression.

4. Susan Minot crafts the fictional story from her journalistic information. According to this source, "author Susan Minot traveled to Uganda, an experience described in the essay 'This We Came to Know Afterward,' which originally appeared in McSweeney's and again later in *The Best American Travel Writing*, 2001. *Thirty Girls* is the culmination of Minot's Ugandan experience, a fictionalized account of the 1996 kidnapping of the St. Mary's College schoolgirls." For details, see Diane Leach, "'Thirty Girls': What We Learned Later," June 2, 2015. http://www.popmatters.com/review/193955-thirty-girls-by-susan-minot/. Also, see link below for the interview, "Harrowing Memories, Intersecting Lives In '*Thirty Girls*'" which offers details on the source of Minot's story. http://www.wbur.org/npr/271085443/harrowing-memories-intersecting-lives-in-thirty-girls?ft=3&f=271085443.

5. Grace Akallo was one of the 139 school girls abducted by armed militant rebels of the Lord Resistance Army (LRA) at an all-girls Catholic High School. Following negotiations led by the Italian principal of the high school, 109 students were released. Thirty girls remained captive. Grace Akallo was one of them. Fifteen years at the time of her abduction, Grace spent seven months with her captors, while serving in multiple capacities as "wife," soldier, domestic, etc. *Girl Soldier: A Story of Hope for Northern Uganda's Children* (2007), coauthored with Faith McDonnell is the "harvest" from Grace Akallo's traumatic experience. Susan Minot's *Thirty Girls* takes its title from the 30 girls that remained captives of the LRA.

6. See Introduction to *African Women Under Fire*, "Exploring African Women and the War Experience—A Critical Update" for the editor's views on mediated trauma narratives based on war and conflict in Africa.

7. Interestingly, in her essay, "The Site of Memory," Toni Morrison (1998) alludes to certain "symbiotic" relationships that memoir shares with fiction (85), although "truth" remains a primary point of contestation between fact and fiction. See link below or William Zinsser (1998) *Inventing the Truth: The Art and Craft of Memoir*. See also link: https://www.ru.ac.za/media/rhodesuniversity/content/english/documents/Morrison_Site-of-Memory.pdf.

8. This assignment questions the appropriateness of western models of therapy for traumatized victims. It is arguable whether "drawing pictures" as therapy for easing traumatic recall or stress is at home in this African setting.

9. "Grace Akallo comes back from the last place on Earth," July 29, 2013, http://www.unicef.org/protection/57929_69985.html.

10. See Interview, Isabelle De Grave, "Former Girl Soldiers Trade One Nightmare for Another." IPS. Jun 14 2012 (IPS). http://www.unicef.org/protection/57929_69985.html.

SEVEN

"I Just Wanted To Forget It All. But It Was Impossible"

Umutesi and the Politics of Testimony in Surviving the Slaughter: The Ordeal of a Rwandan Refugee in Zaire

Emilie Diouf

For African women's literature, testimony has been a speech act that has opened rhetorical spaces from which new forms of African women subjectivities have emerged. Testimony is not only a tool to deal with the vast array of traumas that plague Africa's postcolonial condition, but also a means through which African women interpret and challenge the sociocultural, political, and economic structures that victimize them. In this context, testimonial narratives mediate acts of resistance that track the existence of trauma within multiple and intersecting sites of oppression as well as recognize the agency and humanity of African women.

The dynamism of testimony as it intersects with African women's writings, feminist, and human rights discourse can be seen through the outpouring of life narratives, novels, film, theater, poetry, travel narratives, and memoirs that sought to exorcise the suffering caused by the Rwandan genocide, one of the most traumatic event of postcolonial Africa. Such works such as Scholastique Mukasonga's *Inyenzi ou les cafards* (2006), *Cœur tambour* (2016), Gilbert Gatore's *The Past Ahead* (2008), Beata Umubyeyi Mairesse's *Ejo* (2015), Veronique Tadjo's *The Shadow of Imana* (2005), Fanta Regina Nacro's *The Night of Truth* (2004), Newton Aduaka's movie *Ezra* (2007), among others, capture the complex vectors of what

Carol Boyce Davis and Molara Ogundipe-Leslie (1995) referred to as bearing witness to ourselves to document and give testimonies to our lives (22) These trauma narratives have become the most potent tool for human rights advocacy. They demonstrate that the political dimension of trauma does not exclude the moral, aesthetic, and ethical aspect of culture. Along with Human Rights campaigns, testimonial narratives of African women's traumatic experiences operate as "multidimensional domains that merge and intersect at critical points, unfolding within and enfolding one another in an ethical relationship that is simultaneously productive of claims for social justice and [sometimes] problematic for the furtherance of this goal" (Schaffer and Smith 2004, 2). Such trauma narratives have raised fundamental questions about the possibility of an authoritative "master narrative," challenged official historical narratives, and incorporated African women's perspectives into their work. Speaking the "unspeakable" constitutes a social action on the part of African women and their communities that resonates through multiple cultural contexts and regimes and enables women to speak "truth to power." As a result, they have broadened the scope and range of testimony. Concurrently, debates about the literary and ethical values of trauma testimonies, the ethics and politics of bearing witness to the traumas of postcolonial Africa through literature and cultural criticism have added further complexities to the study of trauma.

This chapter responds to this evolving context by attempting to develop an analytical framework for reading the testimonial narratives of African women within the complex political, social, and cultural specificities in which they are rooted. Testimony is embodied by these specificities, just as it is embodied by individual, collective and generational memory, by representation, and by performance. It specifically suggests a consideration of alterity and the discomfiting challenge certain forms of alterity present to what is already familiar and certain in conceptualizations of testimony. How do the sociocultural and political contexts of reproduction, reception, and circulation of African women's trauma narratives inform the aesthetics of their testimonies of political violence? What are the functions of testimony in such narratives? How do African women's testimonial texts challenge or reinforce current paradigms in trauma theory? More specifically, through a reading of Marie Beatrice Umutesi's memoir *Fuir ou mourir au Zaïre, le vécu d'une refugiée Rwandaise* (2000), translated in English as *Surviving the Slaughter: The Ordeal of a Rwandan Refugee in Zaire* (2004), what does a Hutu woman refugee's testimonial narrative tell us about representing trauma at the intersection of, gender, ethnicity, and displacement? How does the provenance of the testimony enable or constrain its circulation in Africa's human rights discourse? What is the impact of such representation or testimony in the transitional justice of post genocide Rwanda?

This chapter aims at using Umutesi's memoir to interrogate Shoshana Felman and Dori Laub's framing of the restorative properties of testimony in psychoanalytical terms only. In *Testimony: Crises of Witnessing in Literature, Psychoanalysis, and History* (1992) Felman and Laub fall short on examining how the particular context of reception of testimonies influence the ethical call of the trauma story and its appeal for historical redress. They have also overlooked what Sidonie Smith and Kay Schaffer (2004) refer to as the transformation of testimonies "when they become attached to a range of different desires, politics, and interpretations" (7). Smith and Schaffer have rightfully stressed that the shape that trauma stories take is always contingent on specific cultural, historical, and political contexts (7). Guided by these observations about the weight of the sociocultural contexts on the production, reception, and circulation of trauma testimonies, this paper explores how, in the setting of Umutesi's narrative, testimony enables a certain mode of political interpellation and social action.

Published in 2000, six years after the 1994 Genocide of the Tutsis in Rwanda which Patrice Nganang (2007) has labeled the "tragedy of African History" (24), Umutesi's *Surviving the Slaughter* seeks to join the collective act of bearing witness through cultural production in post genocide Rwanda. As survivors of the genocide and (as) those who directly or indirectly witnessed the atrocities of the "extermination of masses of Africans by Africans" (Nganang, 24) felt the urgency to tell their stories, there was an outpouring of oral and written testimonies. They included survivor testimonies as well as additional forms of witnessing, such as scholarly work (mostly by Western academics), data collected by UN rapporteurs, NGO representatives, and advocacy groups that sought to gather facts about human rights violations. Umutesi's personal testimony is embedded in this collective movement of witnessing which seeks to be an affective site of ideological and cultural discourse and action. This Hutu woman's perspective on the genocide raises questions about trauma and ideological manipulation through testimony. Her narrative engages the political and rhetorical possibilities of trauma testimony in the context of post-genocide Rwanda.

Umutesi's memoir takes the concept of trauma testimony beyond its usual association with witnessing and mourning, showing its effectiveness as a rhetorical strategy capable of reading the otherwise untraceable rhetorical and temporal mechanisms of post genocide transition. Her narrative also points to the ways in which trauma testimony may seek to erase ideological difference through the survivor's strategic positioning of her experience as the only possible alternative to history. In this sense, the testimonial approach of *Surviving the Slaughter* redefines trauma theory's notion of crisis in witnessing and the incomprehensibility of the survivor's story as a function of the limited frame of the post genocide archival endeavor itself and its gendered limitations. Rather than Felman and

Laub's argument that testimony depends on the intersubjective dynamic between the survivor and the witness, Umutesi suggests that the possibility of testimony rests upon the cultural, historical, and political interpretative frame of the archive. The use of the term "archive" here enters a realm of abstraction that allows it to hint at an interest in larger debates within post genocide public culture.

The production of narratives about political violence in many African countries tends to follow a pattern of exclusion and inclusion. Focusing specifically on the Great lakes region, historian and anthropologist, René Lemarchand (2002), has demonstrated that war in the Great Lakes region has been dominated by the politics of inclusion and exclusion, where the recurring central pattern: "is one in which ethnic polarization paves the way for political exclusion eventually leading to insurrection, insurrection to repression, and repression to massive flows of refugees and internally displaced persons, which in turn becomes vectors of further instability"(2). Lemarchand has paid particular attention to the ways in which the Rwandan genocide has led to the reordering of collective identities by pointing out how new Rwandan narratives about reconciliation, justice, nation building, and genocide have been defined according to prescriptive notions, where people may be defined as perpetrators, killers, bystanders, victims, saviors, etc. In this process, individual memories become obliterated and are replaced by institutional narratives that may favor the current regime's position on human rights, justice, democracy, and the memorialization of the genocide.

Lemarchand suggests that this is problematic in the way that war and genocide are remembered according to the ethnic lens through which they are narrated, because they are widely different ways in which individual members of a given ethnicity will perceive history based on their individual experiences. The danger of remembering the genocide based on an ethnic lens is that the intertwining of gender, ethnicity, socioeconomic class, political position, or affiliation in individual experiences of its horrendous violence is often overlooked. Furthermore, ignoring the disparities between individual experiences of political violence may result in the manipulation of the memorialization project for political purposes. In this context, a victimology framework might serve the purpose of exonerating those who have been responsible for the political violence, hence the multiple contestations and contradictions surrounding the reception of Umutesi's memoir.

While she is not a survivor of the genocide perpetuated against the Tutsis of Rwanda, she is determined to show that she is a victim of the Great Lakes turmoil triggered by the genocide. In *Surviving the Slaughter,* Umutesi, a Rwandan Hutu woman and a refugee in the Democratic Republic of Congo (DRC), formerly called Zaire, positions her choice to witness about her traumatic experience as a corrective political act. She seeks to rewrite the history of the Rwandan genocide by including what she refers to as "the slaughter" of over 700,000 Rwandan Hutu refugees who fled the civil war in their country and the Rwandan Patriotic Front (RPF), accompanied, and to some extent, controlled by those responsible for the Rwandan Genocide.[1] Further, she feels "historically appointed"—by the magnitude of her ordeal that started with the Rwandan war in 1990 and culminated in the genocide four years later—to tell the story and bear witness to what she depicts as the horrendous violence that she and other Rwandan refugees seeking refuge in neighboring DRC have suffered.

Umutesi's testimony is, thus, located within the complex cultural context of the production of personal testimonies that seek to center the narration of genocide on issues of historical agency and responsibility. Zoe Norridge (2013) has observed that in Rwanda, "the way in which the suffering of [Rwandan refugees who fled to (now) DRC] is viewed is intrinsically bound up with ideas of moral virtue and responsibility" (141). As a result, Umutesi's account presents a chronology that gives many more details on the plight of Hutu refugees. She reproaches the Rwandan Patriotic Front (RFP) and the international community for her traumatic experience. With regard to the political context of her trauma (the horrific conditions in the camps that were illegally set up by the United Nations in Zaire within shelling distance of the Rwandan border and further down the road in Tingi Tingi, and by the attacks of Paul Kagame's RPF, UN bounty hunters and Kabila's troops), arguing over the representation of historical events is crucial to her description of trauma. She perceives her traumatic experience in a strongly colored, ideological light. Such testimony, in Umutesi's sense, mediates the minefield of a politically determined representation of trauma through a personal telling of pain. While committed to portraying historically accurate events, Umutesi specifically privileges her own experiences and what she considers the suppressed story of the death of nearly quarter million Hutu refugees from Rwanda. She thinks that the death of these Hutu was met with indifference by the silence of the international community who denied help to the Rwandan refugees under the premises that they were the perpetrators of the genocide. As such, she positions her testimony as an act of defiance toward the new government of the victorious Rwanda Patriotic Front (RPF) and the international community's dismissal of the sufferings of the Hutu refugees (45, 62). During an interview with Felix Holmgren (2010), Umutesi explained her motivation, when asked whether it was hard to make the decision to write her memoir:

> When I left the jungle I just wanted to forget it all. But it was impossible. I was very angry and frustrated, and I thought that the international community had betrayed first the Tutsis during the genocide, and then us, as we fled through the Congo. I had lost friends in the jungle, and several children I had travelled with. I didn't want them to be forgotten. Writing was my way of honoring their memory.

> When I asked people how they could leave us to die in the jungle, they said: "We didn't know. The papers didn't write about it." I thought that if I write a book nobody could say they don't know. (5)[2]

Umutesi shows ownership of her trauma and insists on the political purpose of her testimony to impart knowledge about the often forgotten victimization of innocent Hutus. She points out the fact that many non-Rwandan Commentators (journalists, academics, human rights activists, African artists and writers) view the conflict that led to the genocide dichotomously, as between Hutu and Tutsi, as a reversion to tribalism, and she is determined to illustrate that the conflict was far more complicated. Though she appeals to the readers' empathy, Umutesi is more concerned with asking them to be critically conscious of their own role in what she describes as the ongoing conspiracy of silence regarding Hutu refugees. Therefore, readers of Umutesi's memoir are addressed, not as innocent witnesses, but as bystanders and potential collaborators. Rather than inviting readers to become innocent victims of the trauma as Dori Laub suggests, Umutesi confronts them and denounces the indifference of the privileged, empowered international community to the suffering of the racial, ethnic, and cultural other (166).

Umutesi challenges dominant narratives about gender and war that overlook women's role as perpetrators. These narratives not only circulate in international media but also in feminist theorizations of the effects of conflict on African women. Scholars, like Georgina Holmes (2014), have pointed out that examining Rwandan and Congolese women in conflict via analysis of political testimonial discourse can open a space to assess how they, as political actors, attempt to influence internationally mediatized representations of the genocide and the war in DRC (9–10). Umutesi's testimony participates, as Holmes notes, in "gendered international politics of revisionism" (5) through which actors attempt to influence trauma narratives for political gain. Within this framework, Umutesi makes several competing claims about African women's agency, the representations of gendered trauma as "constituting genocide by attrition" (Holmes 2014, 4). Not only does she highlight the place of the Hutu refugees in Rwanda's archive, but she also, specifically, points to the role of women in historicizing the genocide from the particular ways in which they were affected by it. Therefore, her testimonial narrative interrogates another concept of crucial concern to trauma testimony in the African context: the archive and its relationship to women.

According to the International Center for Transitional Justice, African women's experiences of political violence are often neglected in transitional justice processes. Far too often, judicial opinions, policy proposals for reparations and reform have been written, interpreted, and implemented with little regard for the distinct and complex injuries women have suffered. In fact, women's groups have often criticized the failure of transitional justice to fully appreciate the significant and specifically gendered effects of political violence on various groups of African women. Even though truth and reconciliation commissions in countries such as South Africa and Sierra Leone have attempted to explicitly incorporate sexual violence as critical avenues for investigation, the experiences of women tend to be marginalized against the institutional work of memory that truth commissions seek to accomplish. For example, in the case of South Africa's Truth and Reconciliation Commission (TRC), Antjie Krog, Nosisi Mpolweni, and Kapano Ratele (2009) suggest that, although the TRC paid particular attention to gender, its misunderstanding of one of the Gugulethu Seven mothers' testimony, namely that of Mrs Notrose Nobomvu Konile, indicated that the TRC excluded any narrative by women that did not fit into, as Goeffrey Bennington observes, "the narration at the center of the nation: stories of national origins, myths of founding fathers, genealogies of heroes" (qtd. in Krog, Mpolweni, Ratele, 2009: 86).

The task of explaining why it is important to understand women's interpretation of the sociopolitical and cultural conditions that led to the genocide is clearly the raison d'être for Umutesi's testimonial project. For example, she describes a moment when she was hiding in a cowshed with a young Tutsi woman, and they were arguing over who was responsible for their suffering:

> We were two terrified young women, both of whom had abandoned all our belongings to hide in a cowshed that stank of cow dung, and yet we couldn't agree on who was responsible for this war. She fled the militias. I fled the rebels. She based her ideas on massacres of the Tutsi in 1959, 1963, 1973, at Kibilira in 1991, and at Bugesera in 1992. My thoughts were influenced by the massacres of the Hutu in Byumba, Ruhengeri, and Gisenyi since 1990, and especially by the massacre of members of my family in February 1993. (52–53)

Umutesi is adamant about showing what women went through living in crowded refugee camps in Zaire and trying to survive war. In its preoccupation with radical inclusivity of the suffering of Hutu refugees, especially women, her testimony challenges the Rwandan archive to be more hospitable to gender dynamics and to be open to those who do not fit into categories of ethnic polarization. Viewed this way, Umutesi's endeavor to invite new, previously hidden trauma stories into the archival memory of the genocide becomes for her a matter of justice, dependent on a more complex understanding of the notion of historical truth. Umutesi suggests that it is only through a more complex approach to truth that the archive of the genocide can welcome multiple and contested trauma experiences without necessarily having to answer the evidentiary requirement of legalistic and forensic truths.

Catharine Newbury's foreword to *Surviving the Slaughter: The Ordeal of a Rwandan Refugee in Zaire* introduces us to Umutesi's revisionist conceptualization of the archive by emphasizing, "not all Hutu were *génocidaires*" (xi). She proceeds to tell us that even though some readers "may be tempted to characterize this testimony as emanating from someone who was implicated in the genocide of the Tutsis because the author is Hutu," we should keep in mind that "many people—irrespective of ethnic category—were caught up in the maelstrom" (xi). So the concept of archive here could be read as one which bears a much larger political project, one that has at its root, the remaking of history and public life in Rwanda. The writing of testimony then carries a gendered national and political frame.

Umutesi makes the generation of post-genocide Rwandan archive not just a matter of accumulating more material and new voices by opening it to the voices of Hutu women refugees; by interjecting her testimony, she seeks to make the archive more democratic in its orientation. For her, transforming the archive is also a matter of reexamining the strategies for telling testimonies that neither the archival frame of Kagame's government, nor the polarized international human rights discourse has allowed. Her testimony challenges simplistic interpretation of the genocide. It calls attention to the fact that the Rwanda tragedy is emblematic of the entire Great Lakes region and is far more tragic and complex than the international media and other commentators of the genocide have been willing to acknowledge, even with all the requisite information at hand. In short, as Umutesi puts it, "The Rwandan tragedy is complex. There are not simply victims on one side (Tutsi) and guilty (Hutu) on the other as we have been led to believe" (73). As such, Umutesi's testimonial account of the Hutu exodus from Rwanda seeks to stimulate further conceptualization of collective or cultural memory beyond the framework of the imagined community of the nation-state. In this light, it echoes Elie Wiesel's (1977) claim, that "[A]ny survivor has more to say than all the historians combined about what happened" (147). It also resonates with George Yúdice's (1996) characterization of Latin American *testimonio* as:

> an authentic narrative, told by a witness who is moved to narrate by the urgency of a situation (e.g., war, oppression, revolution, etc.). Emphasizing popular, oral discourse, the witness portrays his or her own experience as an agent (rather than a representative) of a collective memory and identity. Truth is summoned in the cause of denouncing a present situation of exploitation and oppression or in exorcising and setting aright-official history. (44)

Through *Surviving the Slaughter*, readers perceive gender based violence among Rwandan refugee women in camp settings as part of a broader continuum of violence that existed prior to the conflict and that worsened with displacement. Nevertheless, violence has been exacerbated in the camp settings with new dynamics, such as changes in family settings, physical spaces, cultural changes, security, and humanitarian interventions in the process. The fear of sexual violence in the insecurity of armed conflicts and in displacement restricts women's mobility and power to control their lives in terms of livelihood and choices. Therefore, Umutesi sees her own personal trauma as belonging to the collective suffering of women across the political spectrum. For her, this pain is characterized by the permanent loss of everything familiar: "In my work with the women in the camp, I dealt with misery every day . . . the most painful to see were those of middle-aged people who for years had worked hard to take care of themselves . . . whom stupidity now obliged to live like pariahs" (150).

Umutesi is a sociologist who, before the genocide, worked to develop assistance programs for Rwandan women in rural areas, and lived in South Kivu for two years before the Congolese civil war began. As the conflict worsened, the Rwandan Patriotic Army led by Paul Kagame intervened by directly invading the country and aiding Laurent Desiré Kabila's *Alliance des Forces Democratiques pour la Libèration du Congo* (AFDL) forces. Uganda and Burundi also sent forces into eastern Zaire to help topple Mobutu. When the war began, Umutesi and her fellow refugees fled across Zaire from one camp or village to another, each time departing an area just before a group of soldiers or militia caught up with them. She portrays the ways in which being unwelcome in Zaire caused the Rwandan Hutu refugees, including herself to live in fear of attack, not only by RPA and AFDL forces, but also former *interahamwe*, ex-FAR soldiers, and a myriad of various rebel militias.

Umutesi presents her testimony as both a personal and collective act of resistance. She draws us into her testimony as witnesses to the trauma of the Hutu refugees, especially that of women and children. She decided to start writing about her "lived experience" while taking care of a baby boy, Muhawe, whose mother had died in childbirth and who was dying himself of malnutrition in one of the many refugee camps in eastern DRC. Her mind deluged by questions without viable answers, she took up a pen and began to write, stating: "I made a habit of writing so that people would know and break their silence, but also to stop my own pain . . . I often wept while I wrote, but when I had finished, I felt comforted" (78). Her testimonial narrative encompasses both the clinical aspect of trauma through the use of the writing cure, as well as the political implication of her testimony and the ethical dimension of resistance, which proceeds from, and is inscribed within the text. She positions her text as an archival intervention from below that attempts to explore the political dimension of her trauma. Her narrative strategies demonstrate how historical narratives have been used countless times in Rwanda to justify the claims of those in power, and she warns readers that current efforts to account for the 1994 genocide continue to be framed by appeals to absolutist accounts of the past.

Umutesi's testimony might suggest that the capacity to write a testimonial narrative not only embodies some remedy and already belongs to the healing process, but the presence of a woman survivor as a key witness also tells us that what is witnessed is her personal historicization of the events that traumatized her. Akilo Songolo (2005) remarks that Umutesi's "original subtitle in French, *le vécu,* (lived experiences) anticipates possible counter opinions and grounds the authority of her narrative in her personal traumatic experience as opposed to the political or historical official narrative" (108). Umutesi warns us by writing that she "[has] been through Hell, have known horror and now that I have escaped, I want to testify in the name of all the men and women who did not have my luck and who died in Hell. My point of view is neither that of the historian nor of the politician. I give testimony to what I have seen and to what I have lived" (5). She dramatizes her motive for writing her memoir as a predicament imposed on her by her companion who died in the rainforests of DRC. In the prologue, the reader learns that the book is formally dedicated to little Zuzu as a symbol of all the others, particularly the children. Here, then, testimony is an act of personal defiance against death; it also serves to give voice to a collective defiance against those who would seek to erase the memory of the Hutu victims.

However, her position as a Hutu woman whose influential status as NGO worker has often been associated with those who used their position to spread the anti-Tutsi propaganda that led to the genocide, has led some to question the motives of her testimony. Moreover, the contradiction surrounding her own interpretation of ethnicity may have caused some readers to question the veracity and politics of her mediation of the events chronicled in her story. There are ambiguities, gaps, and silences in Umutesi's mediation of her traumatic experience. Her testimonial language unveils an ethnic discourse that is contradictory. She affirms the problems associated with ethnic identities, but at the same time seems to deny them. She informs the reader that she discovered her ethnic identity when she was four years old "The first time I heard talk of Tutsi refugees was in 1963. I was four years old" (6). At this time, during a false alarm about Tutsi rebels attacking her village, Umutesi became aware of her ethnic identity as Hutu. And she depicts this awareness and her embrace of it as a mechanism of defense against the violent climate caused by "Tutsi rebels." Yet, she will later try to affirm the existence of a commonly shared Rwandan identity and will come to interpret ethnic difference as a given, thereby effacing its historical construct and turning it into a neutral category that is a natural component of Rwandan society. This ambivalence toward ethnicity may cause the reader to question whether the true politics of her testimony are not centered on a revisionist history that attempts to deny the genocide.

Therefore, one can safely infer that Umutesi's *Surviving the Slaughter* presents an alternative view of testimony that unsettles the familiar frameworks of Holocaust testimony in trauma theory. Her memoir presents a mode of ideological interpellation that has been eclipsed by a previous theoretical drifting that equates testimony with the basic structure of subjectivity. The overlap between testimony and subjectivity is most explicitly articulated by Agamben's claim in *Remnants of Auschwitz: the Witness and the Archive* (1999) that the subject is always already a witness to the loss of a unique corporeality that the appropriation of language entails and that, consequently, to be a subject and to be a witness means one and the same thing (158). In fact, drawing from Primo Levi's (1947) idea of the Muselmann, Agamben depicts the Holocaust survivor as a split subject for whom, "testimony appears here as a process that involves at least two subjects: the first, the survivor, who can speak but has nothing interesting to say; and the second, who 'has seen the Gorgon,' who 'has touched bottom,' and therefore has much to say but cannot speak" (Agamben, 120).

The appropriation of the notion of testimony as an analytical framework but also as a heuristic tool designed to put forward a theory of subjectivity grounded on the notion of fallen language, which underlay the work of Felman and Laub, blurs the political economy of testimony. As such, it is necessary to first take a detour through some post structural theoretical constructions of Holocaust testimony as they heavily influence Felman and Laub's conception of witnessing and testimony.

TESTIMONY AT THE INTERSECTION OF POSTSTRUCTURALISM AND PSYCHOANALYSIS

Heavily inspired by the psychoanalytic notion of trauma and its related symptoms (loss, lapse in memory, compulsion) as well as poststructuralists notions of testimony as evidence of the limits of representation, justice, and knowledge, Felman and Laub's approach is focused upon a tension between the impossibility of witnessing and the necessity to bear witness to trauma. The latter echoes Jean François Lyotard's (1988) notion of "*differend*" in terms of thinking about testimony as an event in which one is unable to fully express oneself because traumatic memories that the witness tries to express prevent her or him from doing so. While poststructuralists like Lyotard have attempted to erase the temporal gap that is usually assumed to separate testimony from the traumatic event, Felman and Laub, like Agamben, have set the stage for testimony to be a crisis of witnessing that marks the distinctive feature of genocide and other atrocities. For Felman and Laub, testimony discloses the attack on the human capacity to comprehend, to render meaningful, and to share experience. The loss of this unique perspective put forward by survivors' accounts is the crux of the catastrophe and its most destructive weapon. Testimony is, therefore, a material trace of the disaster—a "performative speech act" (5) that brings buried memories into being and represents forgotten or mute victims as such. It is a residue of the psychic and social destruction wrought by violence and oppression, rather than a mere depiction of their horrors.

Felman and Laub start their attempt at theorizing testimony with the observation that the Holocaust is "'an event without a witness'—an event eliminating its own witness" (xvii) because, on the one hand, the Nazis distorted the survivors' sense of their traumatic experience by attempting to destroy evidence of the genocide. On the other hand, the suffering that was inflicted on them exceeded language, because Jewish survivors did not have a worldview through which they could coherently represent the horror they had experienced. Testimony is, therefore, the moral reaction to the never-ending character of a political violence that strives to obliterate its own traces. A private, even intimate gesture of memory, it is, nevertheless, construed as the primary form of struggle against the always-imminent re-emergence of murderous political projects.

Testimonies and eyewitness accounts do not necessarily overlap. Testimonies are not to be authenticated on the basis of actual presence, unhindered observation, and comprehensive reporting. Instead, the validity of testimony and the authority of the witness stem, in the words of Agamben, from the "capacity to speak solely in the name of an incapacity to speak" (168). As such, according to Felman and Laub, testimony takes place as a speech act characterized by a crisis. The latter is due to:

> The risks and vicissitudes of listening: of listening to human suffering and to traumatic narratives. Even when the listener is . . . trained by discipline and by profession to treat trauma and be its witness, the experience of the witnessing—of the listening to extreme limit experiences—entails its hazards and might equally, like reading . . . suddenly—without a warning—shake up one's whole grip on one's experience and one's life. (xvi–xvii)

The crisis of witnessing with which Felman and Laub are concerned about originates from a crisis in one of Felman's courses at Yale on "Literature and Testimony: Literature, Psychoanalysis, and History," when the students reacted to a video testimony of a woman survivor of the Holocaust by estrangement from each other and emotional disorientation. Felman interpreted this as a crisis of witnessing: the students' sense of reality was inadequate to grasp what they had seen. The authors suggest that the greatest originality of their theory of testimony lies in showing how art and culture, like psychoanalysis, may be performative by calling into being something not yet known and perhaps not knowable in conventional ways. The aim of testimonial narratives for Felman and Laub is not to transmit judgments but, primarily, to generate transference of unsettling experiences. In becoming witnesses, the listeners, spectators, and readers of testimony are to relive the disintegration and the recovery of the voice of the victims whose testimonies first appear as a visceral, contaminating effect (47–52). Elevated from a private and discrete act to a social configuration, and regarded as the foundation of a new pedagogy, testimony, from Felman and Laub's perspective is conceived to be operating both as an arena of witnessing and as its medium.

In this theoretical construction, the function of testimony is to give voice to a certain lacuna of representation generated by the moral and political order that reigned in the concentration camps. For Agamben, this lacuna carried the name of the Muselmann, a human being who was stripped of his capacities of speech and comprehension and led a deplorable existence of "bare life"; his conjuring now stood for the mission and raison d'être of testimony. By bringing this burden of silence to the forefront, testimony is supposed to capture the witness's transgression to language. The witness's testimony transcends the silence of those who have lost, not only the will to live, but also the ability to speak of their suffering or the brutality of their captors. Bearing witness to catastrophe is, at the same time, a recalling of the boundaries of discursive genres (Lyotard 1988), of the false promise of universality and absolute truth (Lyotard 1988; Felman and Laub 1992), and of the fragile intimacy between the speaking subject and the living being (Agamben 2000). The theory of testimony that Felman, Laub, Caruth, and others advance is the need for trauma to be spoken in its actuality of suffering, terror, disorder, and violation of all normal conscious processes to someone who listens. For this reason, testimony can be construed as an action that conjoins the memory of past atrocities to the anticipation of future ones—as a therapeutic device that is inescapably also "a critical activity" (Felman and Laub, 206).

Since Felman and Laub's conception of testimony takes the Holocaust as its point of reference from which the relationship of traumatic memory to historical redress is theorized, testimonies by direct witnesses and secondhand ones alike can, in principle, preserve a trace of the traumatic event.[3] Both are taken to exemplify the way in which "[t]he witness, confronted with the sublime object [i.e. the horrible reality of oppression or violence] is rendered . . . speechless and is nonetheless compelled to speak" (LaCapra 2009, 64). Thus, from a poststructuralist and psychoanalytic framework, Felman and Laub constructed witnessing and testimony as imperatives that drew their force from an intimate encounter with the survivor. More radically still, they cast these as the sole remnants (in Agamben's words) of ethics. Therefore, testimony is the resurrection of unfathomable wrongs; the right and the obligation to bear witness fall equally on eyewitnesses and indirect ones.

In Agamben's view, witnessing and testimony marked the shattering of traditional ethical doctrines by the radical moral ambiguity that characterized the world of the concentration camps, whose emblem was the grey zone described by Primo Levi. Confronted by a political space in which the human and inhuman, innocence and guilt had become indistinguishable, normative ethics, premised on a clear distinction between good and evil and on an essentialist qualification of the human, was irrecoverably invalidated. For Agamben (as, in a different theoretical register, for Lyotard), the morally adequate response to the impotence of ethics after Auschwitz was to bear witness to its failure of ethics. This was to be done by shifting the weight of ethics to acts of testimony, a "new ethical territory" guided solely by concern for the victims (13).

While this theoretical paradigm should be credited for bringing the ethical and the political closer together, it has largely left out some of the most crucial aspects of contemporary politics of trauma testimony in the African context. For the most part, poststructuralist critics of trauma like Felman and Caruth ignored the procedures, stakes, and dilemmas of witnessing in less consensual context and, more particularly, the political economy of witnessing in postcolonial settings, where testimony might support certain revisionist agendas that attempt to wipe away responsibilities for murderous political projects, such as the 1994 genocide of the Tutsis in Rwanda. While with the Holocaust there is a sense of who was evil, who was innocent, in Rwanda for example, this may not always be the case. Unlike the testimonies of Holocaust survivors from which much of the theorization of testimony is built, testimonial narratives from Rwanda, such as Umutesi's *Surviving the Slaughter* does not only seek identification and empathy with the reader, but also work diligently to make the reader suspicious of the archive and to question the Tutsi victim versus Hutu perpetuator paradigm. As a result, in this case, the stakes placed on the accuracy of trauma narratives are at a much higher level than theories of testimony are willing to acknowledge.

Since Felman and Laub have suggested that testimony is only possible when there is an empathic listener "who is the blank screen on which the event comes to be inscribed" (7), are there any alterations and complications of this intersubjective relationship between witness and listener when the survivor is somewhat a privileged Hutu woman like Umutesi? The narrator's positionality in *Surviving the Slaughter* is a reversal of the nature of the witness/survivor relationship as theorized in Holocaust testimonies. Whereas in the latter, the witness is the Jewish survivor of the Holocaust who is a victim of Nazi atrocities and whose trauma is denied by the silencing of her experience, in Umutesi's narrative the witness is a member of the Hutu ethnic group responsible for the genocide of the Tutsi. As a result, Umutesi's ethnic identity complicates Felman and Laub's notion of testimony. In this instance, can one talk about a crisis in witnessing? Are there any listeners for this testimony? If there are listeners, do they impede the testimony by interrupting the witness?

Reading Umutesi's testimonial narrative and trying to find the most ethical way to witness and write about the pain and suffering that is being addressed to me by a fellow African woman, I found myself interfering with her testimony by scrutinizing her motive for writing and being skeptical about her reasons for fleeing from Rwanda after the genocide. In such a circumstance, I resorted to chapter two of *Testimony* where Dori Laub lays out the ethics of listening to trauma testimony. In what follow, I build on Laub's notion of bearing witness and its relation to ethical listening to show that for trauma theory's conception of testimony to work in the narrative context of the Rwandese genocide, a shift in its conceptualization from a solitary individual and corporeal level to the psychosocial realm is necessary. Testimony takes place in language and language itself is social. Since relations of power are produced through and reflected in language, then, trauma testimony itself is social and cultural.

ALTERITY AND THE CRISIS OF A THEORY: LAUB, UMUTESI, AND THE OBSTRUCTIVE LISTENER

In the second chapter of *Testimony,* Dori Laub describes a videotaped archive of a Holocaust survivor recounting a Jewish rebellion at Auschwitz. "She was," Laub writes, "relating her memories as an eyewitness of the Auschwitz uprising; a sudden intensity, passion and color were infused into the narrative. She was fully there" (59). In the tape, which Laub presents to an interdisciplinary conference, the woman remembers four chimneys exploding. After the conference screening, the historians in the audience protest the accuracy of her testimony because, in fact, only one chimney had been destroyed. For Laub, this factual discrepancy does not discredit the testimony. The historians' judgment failed to recognize the emotional and psychological dimensions of testimony. The event had happened in several ways simultaneously and the survivor's perspective offered insight into the magnitude of the event in the lives and memories of the individuals most intimately affected by it.

Laub's anecdote raises crucial questions about the relationship between subjective expressions of trauma, the social context of witnessing, and the creation of testimony. The traumatic experience becomes accessible, not only through the presence of a listener, but because it is, also, tied to a system of representation to language. Thus, it is necessary to understand the role that the signifier plays in trauma testimony, since the performative act of testifying is not only encoded in the corporeal reflection of the other (listener or reader) but also through a shared, accepted ideology or institutional structure that is temporally able to make the pain communicated through testimony meaningful (57).

Testimony, therefore, depends on a relationship and a process between the survivor and the witness, as the testimonial narrative emerges to restore a voice severed by trauma. Therefore, the fractured pieces of the survivor's memory come together in the reflection of the listener, and traumatic memory comes into meaning through this social transaction that is heavily influenced by the social and cultural context. Laub asserts, "the absence of an addressable other, an other who can hear the anguish of one's memories and thus affirm and recognize their realness, annihilates the story" (68). The listener becomes an integral part of this awareness and the process of creating meaning from the chaos of trauma.

Testimony exposes the vulnerability of listeners as well. They must face their limitations, their mortality, through the story of another's trauma. Laub states:

> The listener . . . has to be at the same time a witness to the trauma and a witness to himself. It is only in this way, through his simultaneous awareness of the continuous flow of those inner hazards both in the trauma witness and in himself, that he can become the enabler of testimony—the one who triggers its initiation, as well as the guardian of its process and of its momentum. (58)

The testimonial encounter not only happens when the listener comprehends the body's response accompanying the struggle for a language to express the chaos of trauma, but also the social and political signifiers within which survivors and listeners are both situated.

In his understandable concern to define the ethical domain of testimony with respect to the responsibility of the listener, Laub appears to have neglected to some degree the ethical implications of his theory of testimony. Only after having stripped the trauma survivor from any power of enunciation by making the latter's discourse only possible with the presence of a competent listener, did Laub begin to reflect on the consequences that the idiosyncratic voice of the witness and the visceral character of testimony implied for the trauma survivor. The outcome of Laub's conception of testimony may limit the survivor to fitting into a process of normalization and medicalization. As such, the aim of testimony in Laub's case is recovery and the reinsertion of the survivor into power structures. In such examples as when Laub reads the body of the Holocaust survivor while she tells her story, the role of the survivor is constricted to victimhood. In her case, she can only resist the unspeakable aspect of trauma with the presence of a listener who can help her narrate what has happened to her so that she can again trust the social order that betrayed her by being the source of her suffering. Stef Craps has observed that Felman and Laub have turned a blind eye to the political economy with which testimony itself is permeated (41–42). Solely emphasizing on testimony as an autobiographical exception to knowledge, power, and the archive may obscure some of the most crucial consequences of testimony's politicization in our times: its status as a contested concept, a multifarious practice, but also as an increasingly regulated gesture.

In this sense, even though I kept in mind Laub's warning that by asking questions, listeners and readers of testimony can suppress the survivor's message when they hear everything the latter has to say in light of what they already know about the traumatic event, I kept questioning Umutesi's account of the 1996–1997 hunting and massacre of Hutu refugees in Zaire by Kagame's regime and its Tutsi allies in Zaire as another genocide ignored by the international community.

Despite researching and reading scholarship on Paul Kagame's Rwandan Patriotic Army attempts at cleansing refugee camps in South and North Kivu from former interahamwe which involved killings of innocent civilians, blocking access to refugees or relocating them out of humanitarian assistance, extermination of Hutu men suspected to be *genocidaire*, and control of media, I realized that I could not prevent myself from objecting Umutesi's positioning of herself as someone who is as equally victimized as the Tutsis. As a result, my struggle to identify with Umutesi's testimonial voice compels me to question her intersubjective triad among survivor, text, and reader. Regarding testimony as, in Felman's words, "the uniqueness of the performance of a story which . . . cannot be carried out by anybody else" (206), routinizes testimony as a practice whose meaning is immediately transparent to its producers and audience. Even though Felman and Laub have striven to rescue a moral singularity, not only from the rule of normative ethics, but also from the regulation of discursive structures—as illustrated, notably, in Felman's argument that testimony cannot be authentic without crisis, which has to break and to transvaluate previous categories and previous frames of reference (54)—they have failed to account for the prominence of the socio cultural context as it influences the making and remaking of the crisis in witnessing in our "post traumatic age" (54). Although Felman and Laub rightfully point out that testimony is a genre that is estranging, and it is almost impossible to define or delineate its theoretical boundaries, their conception of it as always intersubjective in nature seems to fix its definition.

Therefore, Umutesi has challenged Felman, Laub, and me to consider accommodating what may not feed into the victim versus perpetuator scheme dear to many western governments, organizations, journalists, and scholars who according to Filip Reyntjens "fully banked on the pretence that [Kagame's people] were a victim of genocide, [therefore] the RPF were the good guys" (100). Despite Felman and Laub's warning that testimony is always the occurrence of a crisis, mine was a different one characterized by my inability to intimately encounter Umutesi in her narrative. While I was unsettled by the atrocities Umutesi described, I had a hard time getting into what Felman refers to as the "intensity and intimacy of the testimonial encounter" (48) that affected Felman's students in the aftermath of the screening of the first Holocaust videotape.

Umutesi's testimony suggests a re-evaluation of Laub's notions about how to absorb the content of testimony, evaluate its truth claims, and determine its implications. It also pushes one to wonder whether the critical activity of analyzing text was limiting the ability to engage into what Henke (1998) calls a "scriptotherapy" (3) with Umutesi, or was it because I am a Senegalese woman from Thiès who has not experienced the sociocultural and political conditions under which Umutesi has suffered trauma. So, I had to ask myself, if I had failed to bear witness to Umutesi's trauma. While fixated on Laub's notion of an intersubjective dynamic as a precondition to witnessing, I forgot that the meaning of Felman and Laub's theory of testimony could shift when placed in different articulations and contexts such as the genocide in Rwanda. I came to the resolution that for me to feel Umutesi's "victories, defeats and silences [and] know them from within so that we can assume the form of testimony" (Felman and Laub, 58), I had to shift my own understanding of who I was and try to place myself into the social order that betrayed her through the traumatic event of the genocide. In Lyotard's (1983) terms, I was faced with a "*differend,*" because the notions of testimony developed in trauma theory are not always commensurate with the complex social and political context of the Rwandese Genocide.

Testimony, according to the framing of Umutesi's trauma story depends on culturally sensitive rendering rather than mere expression of trauma. A reading of Umutesi's testimony within the political, social, cultural and historical context of the Rwandan genocide, the issue of Hutu refugees, the 1990s war in Zaire, and the construction of collective memory in post genocide Rwanda, has enabled me point to failures of Felman and Laub's theory of testimony to understand the politics of Umutesi's testimony. Failures such as the limited, individual-centered framing of their notion of testimony are highlighted by Umutesi's story. It is important to point out that my analysis does not present a definitive model for attuning psychoanalytical readings of trauma to the socio cultural and political conditions within which the trauma story emerges, but instead, invites trauma theorists to listen in on a conversation among African women testifiers who offer their voices and vocabularies of trauma to those who advocate for human rights and social change. Though the conversation may not resolve the difficulty of understanding trauma, what may become clear is the fluidity of testimonial politics.

REFERENCES

Agamben, Giorgio. 1999. *Remnants of Auschwitz: The Witness and the Archive*. Homo Sacer III. New York: Zone Books.

Bennett, Jill, and Rosanne Kennedy. 2003. Introduction to *World Memory: Personal Trajectories in Global Time,* edited by Jill Bennett and Rosanne Kennedy, 1–5. Houndmills: Palgrave Macmillan.

Boyce, Carol Davies, and Molara Ogundipe-Leslie. 1995. *Moving Beyond Boundaries: International Dimensions of Black Women's Writing.* New York: New York University Press.

Craps, Stef. 2014. "Beyond Eurocentrism: Trauma Theory in the Global Age." In *The Future of Trauma Theory: Contemporary Literary and Cultural Criticism,* edited by Gert Buelens, Samuel Durrant, and Robert Eaglestone, 45–62. New York: Routledge.

Donals, Michael Bernard. 2001. "Beyond the Question of Authenticity: Witness and Testimony in the Fragments Controversy," *PMLA* 116 (October): 1302–15.

Edkins, Jenny. 2003. *Trauma and the Memory of Politics.* Cambridge, UK: Cambridge University Press.

Felman, Shoshana and Dori Laub. 1992. *Testimony: Crises of Witnessing in Literature, Psychoanalysis, and History.* New York: Routledge.

Gatore, Gilbert. 2012. *The Past Ahead: A Novel.* Translated from French by Marjolijn de Jager. Bloomington: Indiana University Press.

Henke, Suzette A. 1998. *Shattered Subjects: Trauma and Testimony in Women's Life-Writing.* New York: St. Martin's Press.

Holmes, Geogina. 2014. *Women and War in Rwanda: Gender, Media, and the Representation of Genocide.* New York: I.B. Tauris & Co.

LaCapra, Dominick. 2009. *History and Its Limits: Human, Animal, Violence.* Ithaca: Cornell University Press.

Levi, Primo. 1987. *If This is a Man and The Truce.* London: Abacus.

Krog, Antje, Nosisi Mpwolweni, Kopano Ratele. 2009. *There Was this Goat: Investigating the Truth Commission Testimony of Notrose Nobomvu Konile.* KwaZulu-Natal: University of KwaZulu-Natal Press.

Lemarchand, René. 2002. "Disconnecting the Threads: Rwanda and the Holocaust Reconsidered." *Idea Journal* 7.1(29): 3–32.

Lyotard, Jean François. 1988. *The Differend: Phases in Dispute.* Translated by George Van Den Abbeele. Minneapolis: University of Minnesota Press.

Mukasonga, Scholastique. 2016. *Inyenzi, Ou, Les Cafards.* Paris: Gallimard, 2006.

———. *Coeur Tambour.* Paris: Gallimard.

Nacro, Fanta Regina. 2004. *The Night of Truth.* London: British Film Institute.

Nganang, Alain P. 2007. *Manifeste D'une Nouvelle Litterature Africaine: Pour Une Écriture Préemptive.* Paris: Homnisphères,

Norridge, Zoe. 2013. *Perceiving Pain in African Literature.* New York: Palgrave MacMillan.

Reyntjens, Filip. 2009. *The Great African War: Congo and Regional Geopolitics, 1996–2006.* Cambridge: Cambridge University Press.

Schaffer, Kay and Sidonie Smith. 2004. *Human Rights and Narrated Lives: The Ethics of Recognition.* New York: Palgrave Macmillan.

Songolo, Akilo. 2005. "Marie Béatrice Umutesi's Truth: The Other Rwanda Genocide." *African Studies Review* 48:107–19.

Tadjo, Véronique. 2002. *The Shadow of Imana: Travels in the Heart of Rwanda.* 100 mn. Oxford: Heinemann.

Umubyeyi, Mairesse B. 2015. *Ejo: Nouvelles.* Ciboure: La Cheminante.

Umutesi, Marie Beatrice. 2004. *Surviving the Slaughter: The Ordeal of a Rwandan Refugee in Zaire.* Translated by Julia Emerson. Madison: University of Wisconsin Press.

Umutesi, Marie Beatrice. 2010. "The Forgotten Slaughter: An Interview with Marie Beatrice Umutesi." Interview by Felix Holmgren. *Eurozine.* Arena, Jan. 15.

Wiesel, Elie. 1977. "The Holocaust as Literary Inspiration." In *Dimensions of the Holocaust,* edited by Elliot Lefkovitz, 5–19. Evanston: Northwestern University Press.

Yúdice, George. 1996. "Testimonio and Postmodernism." In *The Real Thing: Testimonial Discourse and Latin America,* edited by Georg M. Gugelberger, 42–57 Durham: Duke University Press.

NOTES

1. Reyntjens, Filip (2009), *The Great African War: Congo and Regional Geopolitics, 1996–2006*. Cambridge: Cambridge University Press.
2. Umutesi, Marie Beatrice, and Felix Holmgren (2010), "The Forgotten Slaughter: An Interview with Marie Beatrice Umutesi." *Eurozine*. Arena, 15 Jan.
3. See Michael Bernard Donals (2001), "Beyond the Question of Authenticity: Witness and Testimony in the Fragments Controversy," *PMLA* 116 (October): 1302–15.

EIGHT

Victims' Narratives versus Perpetrators' Testimonies

Understanding Violence against Women in Armed Conflicts in Africa

Moussa Issifou

While historically the use of sexual violence in armed conflicts has been abundantly documented, the magnitude of the current indiscriminate sexual violence deployed against women by combatants in African conflicts must trouble the human conscience. Indeed, the civil wars that ravaged Liberia (1989–1997), Sierra Leone (1991–2002), Rwanda (1994), Sudan (1983–2005), the Democratic Republic of the Congo (1996 to present), and the Central African Republic (2012 to present) have shed light on a systematic and elaborate use of sexual violence against women of the enemy forces. In these conflicts, of all forms of sexual violence, rape has been the most preferred, because it has for long been accepted as part of warfare violence, as Eve Ayiera (2010), of Urgent Action Fund, based in Nairobi explains:

> Women and girls have been the predominant victims of sexual violence, and there has been a measure of acceptance that rape goes hand in hand with the violence of warfare. In addition to looting and pillaging, rape of women and girls of the opposing sides was among the spoils of war. Although recognized as a social vice, it was treated as a reward for war weary warriors who were otherwise engaging in securing the interests of the side for which they took up arms. As such, reprimanding a soldier for sexual assault during combat was the proverbial "storm in a teacup." (7)

James Coomarasamy of the BBC World Service explains that "sexual violence and rape are as old as war itself, but until now, these issues have been rendered invisible or incidental because they were dismissed as private acts, the "aberrational practices of errant soldiers" (as cited in Giles and Hyndman 310). The attitude described above rather complicates the laborious quest for the real motives behind sexual violence against women in conflict zones. One could argue that to think that sexual violence against women in conflict zone is just a collateral damage of war, and therefore, it is not a crime, is to tacitly condone such behavior. This chapter draws on three theories, namely, feminist, strategic rape, and psychoanalytical approaches, to analyze victims' and perpetrators' testimonies in order to understand what motivates perpetrators of sexual violence in conflict zones.

Feminist scholars hold that sexual violence against women is an extension of the political and economic domination of women by men. Susan Brownmiller (1975) captures this view very well. She explains:

> A world without rapists would be a world in which women moved freely without fear of men. That some men rape provides a sufficient threat to keep all women in a constant state of intimidation, forever conscious of the knowledge that the biological tool must be held in awe, for it may turn to weapon with sudden swiftness born of harmful intent. . . . Rather than society's aberrant or "spoilers of purity," men who commit rape have served in effect as front-line masculine shock troops, terrorist guerrillas in the longest sustained battle the world has ever known. (37)

Brownmiller's claim suggests a conscious and sustained war of the sexes where men do not spare any means in their quest for triumph and domination over women. However, on their part, Lee Madigan and Nancy Gamble (1991) have opined that, "rape is a reenactment of social dominance, no matter who the victim or perpetrator is. Its motive is the subjugation of another person and demonstrates contempt and objectification of another. It is the acting out of power role" (17). Both of these viewpoints share one thing in common: power. However, given that these theories seem to discuss sexual violence in normal time, particularly rape, where the perpetrators and the victims are living their ordinary lives, could the same claims be made about rape in armed conflicts, where different parameters are involved?

An interesting corroboration of the perspectives above has been added by A. Nichols Groth and H. Jean Birnbaum (1979), who have rejected "the popular notions that the rapist is a lusty male who is the victim of a provocative and vindictive woman, or he is seen as a sexually frustrated man reacting under the pressure of his pent-up needs, or he is thought to be a demented sex-fiend harboring insatiable and perverted desires" (2). According to them, rape is a sexual expression of power and anger, and forcible sexual assault is motivated more by retaliatory and compensatory motives than the sexual ones. In the words of Nichols Groth and Jean Birnbaum (1979), rape is a pseudosexual act, complex and multi determined, but addressing issues of hostility (anger) and control (power) more than passion (sexuality)." (2) Prima facie, it is easy to agree with the explanation that anger and power motivate perpetrators of sexual violence during armed conflicts, simply because these two catalysts are integral part of armed conflicts. Frustration from having to fight an endless war, the will to force the enemy's camp to surrender at all costs, among other desires, are enough to justify the kind of sexual violence the perpetrators commit on women during armed conflicts. However, anger and power alone do not motivate men to attack women, for there exist other more cruel motives behind the behavior observed in wars today.

On their part, some African feminists argue that the causes of sexual violence against women in conflict zones can be traced back to the history of African military complex. For instance, Yaliwe Clarke (2008) of the African Gender Institute, contributor to *Feminist Africa* echoes these views as follows:

> Being a soldier is purposefully linked to being a "real man." The military attempts to mold all men in uniform guise of masculinity. This is done through an organizational culture that encourages ideal assets of soldiery such as physical ability, endurance, self-control, professionalism, sociability, heterosexuality—these traits tap on masculine performance by contrasting them with images of "otherness" such as femininity, homosexuality, etc. Soldiers are drilled to conform to virile heterosexuality where women are viewed as either sex object that needs to be abused or loved ones that need to be protected. Femininity is equated with weakness, vulnerability and feebleness. (52)

Clarke's argument finds its evidence in the recruitment process and training of new recruits in African armies. Growing up in a military town, I always watched new recruits exercise in the streets with songs that contained derogatory language towards women. Every song degraded women and objectified them. These new recruits also used language that drew contrasts between men and women with regard to their physique, ethics, and trustworthiness. Having forged such a mindset about women in peace time, going after women during conflicts would be justifiable in the eyes of soldiers who perpetrate sexual violence against women. The objectification of women during conflict is depicted in Chimamanda Ngozi Adichie's *Half of Yellow Sun*, a novel that tells the story of the Biafran War during which women experienced sexual violence from those who were supposed to protect them. As Adichie (2006) carefully depicts it, women were referred to as "food," and soldiers who raped women were celebrated by their peers:

> On the floor, the girl was still. Ugwu pulled his trousers down, surprised at the swiftness of his erection. She was dry and tense when he entered her. He did not look at her face, or at the man pinning her down, or anything at all as he moved quickly and felt his own climax, the rush of fluids to the tips of himself: a self-loathing release. He zipped up his trousers while some soldiers clapped. Finally, he looked at the girl. She stared back at him with calm and hate. (458)

The transformation of this outrageous behavior into a spectacle says much about how soldiers view women. In this instance, the female victim is not even from the enemy camp. Both the victim and the perpetrator are from Biafra, the very region these soldiers claim to fight for.

The behavior described above is not surprising, because masculinity thrives on its ability to constantly reaffirm itself. Sjoberg and Via (2010) argue that "not surprisingly, most men attempt to comply, often at high personal cost. Because the edifice of masculinity is a mythic construction, the pressure to 'prove' one's manhood is relentless" (27).

Other African feminists view sexual violence in conflict as part of a continuum of gender relations during peace time. Thus, the theory rejects the notion that violence against women during conflict is an isolated social problem born to the chaos of war. According to Ayiera (17), sexual violence during armed conflict is not a unique phenomenon, even though it is often widespread. It is a manifestation of problematic gender relations that are defined in terms of binaries. Within these rigidly defined brackets, sexual violence is, in fact, the result of a power dynamic that normalizes heterosexual masculinity as the collective "objective" and *others* all other experiences, including female, homosexual, and transgender.

For Ayiera, the pre-conflict gender struggle makes sexual violence against women normal. She does not view sexual violence in conflict as a behavior that emerged from a vacuum. Her argument suggests that sexual violence against women during conflict lays bare the sexual inequality, which, according to Firestone (1970), is "an oppression that goes back beyond recorded history to the animal kingdom itself" (2). Therefore, it can be argued that sexual violence against women in conflict is a logical consequence of unbalanced power structure that has always characterized human society. The immutability of this power structure has, presumably, sealed the fate of women in our diverse cultural milieus. For instance, in patriarchal African societies, women are traditionally expected to conform to roles appropriate to their gender. In other words, they must assume the role that the male-dominated society has ascribed to them. They are expected to be housewives, child bearers, and to be submissive; they are also perceived as sexual objects.

What does it mean to be born a woman in traditional African societies? Feminists like Nawal El Saadawi (2007), have depicted the challenges of being female in patriarchy through the literary medium. In *Woman at Point Zero*, and through her narrator, Fridaus, El Saadawi delineates the female condition in her Egyptian setting, where the treatment of a female infant is a forecast of her status in the society. Fridaus reveals this about her father: "When one of his female children died, my father would eat his supper, my mother would wash his legs, and then he would go to sleep, just as he did every night. When the child that died was a boy, he would beat my mother, and then have his supper and lie down to sleep" (17).

In this quotation, Saadawi exposes the intrinsic problem of gender inequalities that predisposes women to all forms of mistreatments in her strongly patriarchal Egyptian setting. Because of her gender, the life of a female child is deemed less valuable than that of her male siblings. Fridaus' father does not care about the death of his female children, because they are female, and are, therefore, unworthy of his love. In this sociocultural context, the boy grows up knowing that he is favored over his sister and that he is more human than her on the basis of gender difference. For such a boy, the message is crystal clear: his sister's and by extension any girl's life matters little. A boy who reaches adulthood with this mindset may have problems developing sudden respect for women; further, it might be difficult for such a male to accept the fact that women have as much intrinsic dignity as himself. Without this recognition, it is likely that men have found a justification for whatever ill-treatment (including sexual violence) they deploy against women.

A growing number of critics have suggested that sexual violence against women is an elaborate strategy that warring factions use as weapon of war. Maria Olujic (1998) theorizes that "the use of sexual violence in conflict is an effective war strategy because of pre-existing sociocultural dynamics that attach concepts of honor, shame and sexuality to women's bodies in peacetime" (31–32). According to this theory, sexual violence against women in wartime is committed for the purpose of undermining the morale of the enemy. The perpetrators are usually combatants from the enemy's camp, who are very well aware of the status of women in the cultures they assault. All this is part of an elaborate scheme that aims to disable the entire social structure of the enemy through the destabilization of families. In the Democratic Republic of Congo, as well as Rwanda, for instance, the perpetrators are well aware of the negative consequences of sexual violence on the victims and their families. Indeed, these consequences are what they expected. Merger (2010) points out that in the Congolese society, in which women are generally perceived as the sustaining core of the community, being caregivers, child-bearers, nurturers, and workers for the community, sexual violence has a double impact. It is both a physical and symbolic attack on that community, which becomes polluted through violation of sexual integrity of women and girls. Merger also observes that once the husband of the woman who has been raped is confronted with the failure to protect his wife, he either blames himself and abandons the household out of shame or blames his wife and repudiates her (as cited in Maciejczak 2013). These survivors' accounts are cases in point. Diana Zeyneb Alhindawi (2014) reports as follows:

> On a November evening in 2012, around 8 p.m., Congolese government soldiers knocked on her door. Her five children scattered and hid in the bedroom. Her husband was already gone. He fled when he heard bullets fired earlier. When the soldiers entered the house, two of them threw her on the ground and began to rape her. The others began to pillage her home, carrying off the goods that her family had just received from an aid organization—sacks of rice and corn cans of cooking oil. Her husband returned in the morning. When he learned she had been raped, he left. He never returned.

Another reporter, Diane Taylor (2009) of *The Guardian*, reported that Mirindi Euprazi was at home with her family when the rebels attacked. They broke into her home and took all her possessions, before torturing her, her husband and their teenage children. Then the horror began for Euprazi as she describes: "They forced my son to have sex with me, and when he'd finished they killed him. Then they raped me in front of my husband and then they killed him too. Then they took away my three daughters." Taylor notes that Euprazi hasn't heard of the three girls, thirteen, fourteen, and seventeen, since then. A small woman, Euprazi speaks softly and without visible emotion, but as she describes being left naked while her house burned, she raises a hand to cover her face. Taylor further comments:

> Euprazi, 50, lives in the village of Ninja, in the Walungu region of the Democratic Republic of the Congo, close to Rwanda's western border. Today, Ninja is a village almost exclusively of women and children. Most of the husbands have been killed, either by Interahamwe—the Hutu militias responsible for the 1994 Rwandan genocide who then fled over the border into the forests of eastern Congo—or by Tutsi rebels led by General Laurent Nkunda. Almost every woman here has been raped, some countless times. Some have been so badly injured by repeated rapes by different militias that they are barely able to stand. Many of their children were conceived through rape. (*The Guardian* 2009)

Aljazeera's Fredrik Brogelan Laache (2015) reported the following from Goma, Democratic Republic of Congo:

> Inside a small wooden house overlooking the massive Virunga National Park, Bakazi Ndazimo, 70, relives the worst day of her life—the day she stopped feeling human; the day she was beaten and raped. "The only reason I am able to talk about this is because of my age, and the fact that I am not going to remarry,"

According to the reporter Fredrik Laache, Ndazimo told *Al Jazeera* that the attack happened in late November 2012, just after the M23 militia took control over Sake, Ndazimo's hometown, situated twenty-seven kilometers west of Goma in the eastern province of North Kivu.

> She was cooking a meal for her grandchildren when a group of rebels stormed the house, grabbed her, and violently dragged her to another neighborhood.
>
> There, in the shadow of some tall bushes, she was raped by two soldiers. "I was screaming at the top of my lungs when they ripped my clothes off, but the neighbours quietly went back to their houses and closed the curtains. For them it was just another rape," Ndazimo said.

Three weeks later, Ndazimo's family was targeted again. This time, a group of rebel soldiers came for her daughter, who was raped so viciously that she later died from her injuries.

As Diana Zeyneb Alhindawi observes, those assembled in the military court in Minova heard versions of that story over and over again. Such is the fate of the survivors of sexual violence from war torn regions in Africa. The victims whose voices are heard in the above accounts seem helpless, hopeless, and are forced to go from humiliation to despondency. In the first account, the victim, having been violated and humiliated by her assailants, was further humiliated by her husband who did not stay to defend the family honor; rather, he chose to abandon his wife and children when the assailants arrived. Since perpetrators expect a husband to abandon his violated wife, it is important to note that they claim part of their victory through knowledge of this cultural stigma associated with rape.

More alarming is the attitude of the whole community, which largely supports men to ostracize wives and other women who have been victims of rape. This is what Madigan and Gamble (1991) referred to as the "Second Rape," which they define as: "the act of violation, alienation, and disparagement a survivor receives when she turns to others for help and support" (5–6). In this context, the perpetrator's incentive is the vision and extent of damage rape can inflict on victims and their society. Indeed, sexual warfare has far reaching negative consequences. It breaks down the family core and plants the seed of chaos in the entire population. In most African cultures where the survival of households depends on women, degradation of women through sexual violence inflicts more damage on the enemy than the actual warfare on the battlefield does. For military strategists, this cheaper way of winning the war (because combatants don't have to risk their lives fighting the enemies to achieve victory) serves as a motive to orchestrate and condone sexual violence against women of the enemy camp. As Enloe (2000) explained, the systematic use of sexual violence in armed conflict, should not surprise anyone.

> If military strategists (and their civilian allies and superiors) imagine that women provide the backbone of the enemy's culture, if they define women chiefly as breeders, if they define women as men's property

> and as the symbols of men's honor, if they imagine that residential communities rely on women's work—if any or all of these beliefs about society's proper gender division of labor are held by war-waging policy-makers—they will be tempted to devise an overall military operation that includes their male soldiers' sexual assault of women. (134)

Again, it is the motives of those strategists that should be emphasized here; given that the factions in Africa's wars are usually from the same regions and share the same cultural beliefs vis-à-vis women, it goes without saying that it is not a coincidence if they choose to attack each other's symbol of continuity. Each camp does so, because it wants to inflict the ultimate damage to the enemy, for sexual violence, and especially rape has far reaching consequences than most violent crimes, as Kelly D. Askin (2003) reminds us:

> Rape is a potent weapon for a number of reasons. The destructive stereotypes and harmful cultural and religious attitudes associated with female chastity or notions of so-called "purity" make sex crimes useful tools for destroying lives. Prevailing attitudes and beliefs often create an erroneous impression that a woman is "spoiled goods" if she has sex, whether voluntarily or involuntarily, outside a marital context, a stereotype rarely imposed upon victims of non-sexual crimes. Rape crime survivors (and those who do not survive) are not the only victims of sexual violence. The impact and the harm often extend to families, local communities, and society at large. (298)

Of course, the magnitude of the devastation of sexual assault on women makes it the preferred choice when it comes to extending war to the enemy's civilian population. Given the effect of this devastation, sexual violence could be considered as a scorched earth war. The perpetrators' behavior described by the victims speaks volumes. Thus, we are led to believe that the intention of the perpetrators is to harm the enemy's camp, once and for all.

Furthermore, Alexis Arieff (2010) attests that sexual violence against women in conflict settings may be employed as a "benefit" for victorious troops and commanders; a means of initiation and social bonding between combatants; a punishment meted out to civilians associated with opposing groups; a means of humiliating male opponents who were not able to protect "their" women; a method of destroying communities and cultures associated with conflict opponents; and a means of ethnic cleansing by impregnating women or forcing their displacement. In such cases, sexual violence is often portrayed as a "weapon" or "tool of war" (7). During the Rwandan genocide, this pattern was observed in the behavior of Hutus militias, who targeted only Tutsi women for rape and other forms of sexual violence. In some instances, even pastors were enlisted to help identify Tutsi women and convince them to submit to the demands of their assailants. Given that such acts were committed without concern for the safety of the victims, and despite the proliferation of HIV, the situation suggests a concerted effort to commit genocide through destruction of the symbol of continuity. The behavior of Hutu armed forces and militias was later characterized by the International Criminal tribunal of Rwanda as "a step in the process of deconstruction of the Tutsi group."

The enabler of these atrocities was anger at the Tutsi women, whom Hutu men viewed as dangerous and treacherous.[1] However, the ultimate motivation is obvious—to wipe out the opposing camp's population from the face of the earth. With regard to the genocide in Rwanda, this intent was betrayed by the systematic use of rape, which made the U.N. Special Rapporteur on Rwanda conclude that "rape was the rule and its absence the exception," adding that many of these rapes resulted in pregnancy. According to Human Rights Watch (1996), during the 1994 genocide, Rwandan women were subjected to sexual violence on a massive scale, perpetrated by members of the infamous Hutu militia groups known as the Interahamwe, by other civilians, and by soldiers of the Rwandan Armed Forces (Forces Armées Rwandaises, FAR), including the Presidential Guard. Administrative, military and political leaders at the national and local levels, as well as heads of militia, directed or encouraged both the killings and sexual violence to further their political goal: the destruction of the Tutsi as a group. They, therefore, bear responsibility for these abuses (2).

However, can we still sustain the thesis that sexual violence in wartime is a strategic weapon that aims to destroy the enemy when we have learned through victims' testimonies that rapes were not solely committed on the enemy's camp but on the perpetrators' own population? The question then becomes, what motivates soldiers and militia groups to attack the very populations they should be protecting? To answer these questions, we turn to psychoanalysis for help.

Contrary to the notion that sexual violence against women in conflict zones occurs because of sexual desire, psychoanalysts have used Freud's theory of Oedipus complex to argue that sexual violence against women in wartime is motivated by man's insatiate quest for masculinity, as well as his desire to destroy women, who constantly bring back memories of the threat of castration, which he dreads. Indeed, the psychoanalytical perspective, which forms the basis for my argument, suggests that men who commit rape are psychologically disturbed, and as a result, they act with hatred and aggression toward women (Morash 2006, 14). This perspective draws on Sigmund Freud's Oedipal complex theory that seeks to trace adult problems to their childhood, as Freud (1989) writes:

> The young boy, entering into the Oedipal stage begins to manipulate his penis and simultaneously has fantasies of carrying out some sort of activities with it in relation to his mother, till, owing to a combined

> effect of a threat of castration and the sight of the absence of a penis in females, he experiences the greatest trauma of his life and introduces the period of latency with all of its consequences. (25–26)

For Freud, the boy's relation with the female parent (mother) ends as soon as he finds out that the latter does not have a penis, which is the reason for his identification with her. The thought that the mother's lack of penis is a result of castration, which the boy fears may also happen to him, does not make things better. The boy's fear comes from his realization that, his dad with whom he competes for the love of his mother has more power than him and that if caught in his incestuous desire for his mother, he would be castrated. The boy's fear of castration is caused by his mother who threatens to betray him to his father, which will forever haunt him. Thus, to protect himself, the boy simply withdraws the love for his mother. For Freud, this abrupt separation may plant the seeds for a boy's contempt for females in his adult life. This contempt comes from his anxiety about losing his masculinity. In fact, the extent of the damage caused by his separation from his mother determines how obsessed he is about his masculinity and how far he is willing to go to affirm it. It appears that the more damage he sustained during the separation, the more violent he would be in his adult life. In light of this explanation, it could be inferred that masculinity has something to do with violence against women. The question then becomes: is sexual violence against women, in general, and sexual violence against women in wartime, in particular, perpetrated in order to affirm masculinity? Or are there other motives underlying such behavior? Maybe the testimonies below reported by Chiara Rimella and Kitty Knowles in *The Independent* (2014) will help answer this question:

> It is true that we raped here. We found women because they can't escape. You see her, you catch her, you take her away and you have your way with her. Sometimes you kill her. When you finish raping then you kill her child. When we rape, we feel free. (1)

> Nzgira was one of the victims on that night of November 2012, when the mass rape took place. Three men attacked her at once, two of them from the front. She says: "The other said he wouldn't go where the others left their dirt. So the third took me from the back. I thought I was going to die." (2)

> Masika, the founder of a rescue Centre for rape survivors testified thus: "Since I have been doing this work, I have been raped three times." When he finished, he spat on me. That's when I thought about killing myself. I am constantly haunted by this." (3)

These unspeakable atrocities hardly hide an expression of frustration and anxiety about the threat of being emasculated. The soldiers claim that they feel free after raping women, because they have just removed any doubt concerning their manhood, which has nothing to do with their sexual potency; instead, it has more to do with their sociocultural position. These soldiers believe that the long war has interfered with the traditional role of men in their male dominated social culture. The notion of man as provider, protector, and symbol of family stability has been challenged by their precarious situation which prevents them from fulfilling these duties. The following interview responses from DR Congo soldiers recorded by Maria Erikson Baaz and Maria Stern (2009), offer important insight into their psyche:

> Soldier #1: If you look at the Bible, it says "man, love your wife" and "wife be submissive to your husband." . . . Here, a lot of people do not know conjugal life well. You will not ask for submission [from the wife] if there is no love. You impose obligations but there are no rights. That is not good. If you do not give your wife money, she has not eaten, also the children have not eaten, can you then come home in the evening and ask her: did you wash the clothes? Here [in the Congo] the man looks for money and gives to the wife. But many times they give her nothing but still ask her to do a hard job. That is not how it was supposed to be. (507)

> Soldier #2: [A good soldier] is someone who knows discipline. But how can we do a good job when we are hungry, when you haven't eaten something for a whole day, when our children are hungry and don't go to school and when you could not leave any money to your wife in the morning so she can cook for the children? What is she to do? [my wife] She is unhappy. When I come home and want to be with her she is upset and says: "don't touch me" [azosepela te, azoyebisa ngai: simba ngai te] What should I do? If it continues, after three days and I have no money to give for food she will get tired and when I am at work she will give her body to another man just to get a little something to feed the children [akopesa nzoto na ye mobali mususu po azwa mua quelque chose po aleisa bana]. What else should she do? But women are also weak [faible]. You cannot trust them [po ozala na confiance na bango—ezali mua pasi]. (507)

The testimonies above corroborate my argument that at the core of the combatants' behavior toward women is frustration for failing to play their assigned role in the society, as well as the recognition of their incapacity to be the sole proprietors of their wives' bodies. The soldiers are angry at themselves for being reduced to simulacra of heads of family; they also show anger toward their wives, because their love is transactional, that is they are ready to exchange it with whatever they need. Here the Oedipus complex is galloping back into the discussion. The betrayal of the mother is likened to the betrayal of the wife. Therefore, we are compelled to, once again, blame man's insatiable quest for masculinity throughout his life. In this dialectic, the woman is the eternal enemy, who always threatens masculinity; therefore, she must be destroyed. She must not only be destroyed because she is the wife of the enemy; but she must also be destroyed because she is a woman.

The soldier's concern that in his absence, and because of his inability to economically play his role, his wife may give her body to another man to get money to buy food for her children shed another light on the kind of frustration that leads to the atrocities armed groups are accused of. In a culture where people believe that the man is the provider, the role that puts him above the household, the soldier sees the risk of losing his position of power to his wife who has become the provider by default, and therefore, the man of the house. As in the Hegelian master-slave dialectic, where the dynamics of power can shift at any time, if the soldier's wife is de facto a man, the soldier becomes de facto woman. This is what the soldier dreads; in every woman, he sees his wife who usurped his role. For this reason, all the women must pay; the prime organ of their femininity must be destroyed to make them less desirable, as it can be seen in the following testimony: "The men were speaking Kinyarwanda and they took turns. Her husband protested, and they shot him, the blood spurting on her and the rapist. She cried out and they told her to be quiet. She kept crying so they shot her through both legs, multiple times" (Enough Team 2011).[2] In this case, as in many other cases, the perpetrators chose to destroy the principal feminine attribute of the victim. Once again, whatever animus these attackers might have against the women should not justify their behavior. Instead, it is the manifestation of the Oedipus complex in them.

However, theorists' rejection of the Oedipus complex in the African context complicates our psychoanalytic reading of sexual violence against women in African conflicts. For instance, Fanon (1952) argues that the Oedipus complex as presented by Freud is far from being a black complex. Using his Antilles as example, Fanon contends that in French Antilles, 97 percent of families are incapable of producing a single Oedipal neurosis. For him, the fact that Freudian neurosis results from the individual and the family disqualifies Freud's theory of Oedipus complex in the African context. Instead, Fanon locates the causes of black man's alienation in the social and economic context (80).

However, Fanon does offer a possible path to understanding sexual violence against women. In his essay "The Man of Color and the White Woman,"[3] Fanon offers a psychoanalytic reading of the desire of the black man for the white woman. Fanon argues that this desire is caused by the oppressive colonial conditions that alienated him from his culture as well as denied his subjectivity. Having lost all this, the black man thinks his salvation resides in his ability to access the white man's world. Fanon (1952) writes: "Out of the blackest part of my soul, through the zone of hachures, surges up this desire to be suddenly white. I want to be recognized not as black, but as white. Who better than a white woman to bring this about? By loving me, she proves to me that I am worthy of a white love" (45).

For Fanon, the black man desires the white woman because the social conditions of colonialism have denied him the opportunity to access her as white men do, thereby casting doubt on his existence as a human being and as a man. Therefore, using Fanon's framework, and based on the testimonies below, some explanations will be offered for the violence against women during the Rwandan genocide.

In the report titled *Shattered Lives*, Human Rights Watch (1996) published the following Rwandan genocide survivors' testimonies. Since the militias were working in groups, Tutsi women who were taken from their homes, or found hiding, were frequently subjected to gang-rape. Often, women were raped multiple times. Many survived one rape or gang-rape, only to be discovered by another group of Interahamwe[4] who would rape them again. Frequently, women were killed immediately following the rape. The following accounts are from survivors who were raped, because they were Tutsi women. Maria Erikson Baaz and Maria Stern (2009) also recorded the following victims' testimonies:

Victim #1: Bernadette was thirty-three years old and living in Taba commune, Gitarama prefecture, when the fighting began. She recalled that she, her husband and seven children hid in nearby coffee bushes when the Interahamwe first came to their area on April 12, 1994. They hid, listening to the militia killing, destroying and looting all the houses. In the evening, they were discovered by a group of about fifty militia armed with machetes, knives, and hoes. They took Bernadette and her family to the Nyabarongo River. She said:

> The next day, they killed all the men and boys. I was left with my baby and the three girls. At the riverside, I was raped by a group of six Interahamwe one after another. I knew all of them. Some were killed by the RPF and the others are now in Gitarama prison. They said that they were raping me to see if Tutsi women were like Hutu women. After they finished raping me, they threw me in the river to die along with my children. My children all drowned, but the river threw me back. I floated back to the riverside. One of the Interahamwe said, "Those Tutsi people won't die—we raped her and she survived. We threw her in the river and she still survived." They let me go and I tried to go toward Runda commune (the next commune). On the way, I was found by another group of Interahamwe who took me with them back to Taba. They also raped me. I can't remember how many. After the war, I found out that I was pregnant. But I had an abortion . . . no, not really an abortion. The baby just came out dead.

Victim #2: Perpetue was twenty years old and living in Runda commune, Gitarama prefecture, with her husband and child and her sister when the violence began. She hid in neighboring Taba commune until the militia groups from Taba and Runda communes began working together to find out who they had missed in the area. Perpetue was soon discovered by the militia and survived a horrific three months in which she was raped multiple times and her vagina was mutilated. She said:

> On April 9, 1994, they found me. I was taken to the Nyabarongo River by a group of Interahamwe. When I got there, one Interahamwe said to me that he knew the best method to check that Tutsi women were like Hutu women. For two days, myself and eight other young women were held and raped by Interahamwe, one after another. Perhaps as many as twenty of them. I knew three of them. Some Interahamwe watched over us while others went to eat and sleep. All the young women killed at that river were raped before being thrown in. I didn't know any of the other women. On the third day, one Interahamwe saw that I was not able to walk anymore. He told me that I had already died and could go. I tried to leave, but I could barely walk. There was blood everywhere and my stomach hurt. I walked towards Kamonyi and found refuge in an old church there. When I was going there, I saw that the Interahamwe had been burning people to death. I saw at least ten burnt bodies. I was in the church building when the Interahamwe came there on May 15 and told us that it was our turn to be burnt. They took a lot of people outside to kill them. One Interahamwe chose me, but told me that he would protect me so that I would not be burnt to death. He took me to another building near the church and raped me there. Before he raped me; he said that he wanted to check if Tutsi women were like other women before he took me back to the church to be burnt. There were other women being raped there at the same time, maybe ten women and seven young girls. (25–26)

Because of Rwandan colonial history, the behavior of the Hutus described in these testimonies, indeed, merit a Fanon's reading, because the sociocultural conditions responsible for the black man's desire for the white woman are comparable. In fact, as historians have argued, the colonial administration in Rwanda created two classes on the basis of their ethnicities. This resulted in the elevation of the Tutsis to the privileged position under the pretense that the Hutus were incompetent, incapable of governing, and coarse. (Rittner, Roth, and Whitworth 2004, 53). Similar to the dynamics at play between white colonizers and black colonized described by Fanon, the Tutsis were granted all the privileges at the expense of the Hutus; Rittner, Roth, and Whitworth (2004) add that from 1925 to 1955, excessive privileges were given to the Tutsi elite. They were considered the only group capable of offering substantial help in the work of Christianization and colonization (52). Explaining the colonial responsibility in the Rwandan genocide, Kroslak (2008) observed that the Belgians, like the Germans before them, saw the Tutsis as the superior race because of European like features found among them, and this prejudice became deeply rooted in their administrative structures and policies. It justified depriving the Hutus of all political and economic power by the mid-1930s, as a result of centralization. To make things worse, the Belgians initiated a program aimed at reorganizing the hierarchy in favor of the Tutsis.

The consequence of this reorganization was the dominance of chiefly functions by the Tutsi. Thus, by the end of Belgian presence in Rwanda in 1959, forty-three chiefs out of forty five were Tutsis as well as 549 subchiefs out of 559 (21). This was a turning point in the history of Rwanda. The majority group Hutu found itself under the dictatorship of the minority Tutsi group. Another Rwandan specialist, Michael Barnett (2002, 51) argues that although Rwanda was no Rousseauean democracy, there is no evidence that the long-standing ethnic divisions degenerated into ethnic violence. According to him, it is colonialism's introduction of myths of superior race coming from north to conquer an inferior native population, which led to feeling of entitlement and superiority among the Tutsis and massive inferiority complex among the majority Hutu.

In light of the historical background above, one could argue that the perpetrators of sexual violence described in the testimonies share a lot in common with the neurotic patient Fanon referred to in "the Man of Color and the White Woman" (1952, 45). The Hutu militiamen's obsession for Tutsi women is the consequence of the psychological trauma they developed as a result of their socially induced inferiority complex. Hutu men target Tutsi women for rape, because the latter were inaccessible to them. Using Fanon's theoretical framework, one would say that Hutu men desire Tutsi women, because they want to access the same privileges as the Tutsi as well as affirm their manhood. The inaccessibility of the Tutsi woman turns her into the target of various propaganda stereotypes, portraying her as different, other, and sexual temptress. Human Rights Watch (1996) reports that Tutsi women were targeted on the basis of the genocide propaganda which had portrayed them as calculated seductress-spies bent on dominating and undermining the Hutu. Tutsi women were also targeted because of the gender stereotype which portrayed them as beautiful and desirable, but inaccessible to Hutu men whom they allegedly looked down upon and were "too good" for. Rape served to shatter these images by humiliating, degrading, and ultimately destroying the Tutsi woman (13).

This chapter will not be complete without mentioning the effect of long persisting negative views many societies, worldwide, hold about women. The so-called "original sin" was attributed to woman. In the Christian Bible, Genesis 3:12 states: "And the man said, the woman whom thou gavest to be with me, she gave me of the tree, and I did eat." (*New American Standard Bible* 1995). Arguably, the burden of original sin attributed to the female seems to have had a profound influence on the way some societies have, culturally, treated women. In some cultures, females are generally suspected of witchcraft because of their gender. For example, in his study of witchcraft in colonial South Africa, Sean Redding (2006) reports that many rural Africans believed that their wives, as strangers within their husbands' households, often brought with them their ancestors, who had the potential for harming their husbands' family (148). Further, the late seventeenth century witch trials in Salem, Massachusetts, provide overabundant examples of how women were perceived in this colonial society. Reis (1997) observes that the witch-hunting episodes of the seventeenth century, when women were accused and convicted far more than men, and when women actually confessed to being in the devil's snare, display the sense of women's inherent wickedness which the community—women and men—endorsed (2). It would be tedious to list all the accusations leveled against women simply because of their gender.

Whatever theoretical framework one considers, one thing is undeniable; the perpetrators of sexual violence against women in wartime are motivated by their will to destroy their victims. This awareness made the United Nations Special Representative on Sexual Violence in Conflict, Ms. Zainab Hawa Bangura (2012) to declare that, "Sexual violence in conflict needs to be treated as the war crime that it is; it can no longer be treated as an unfortunate collateral damage of war" (as cited in "Outreach Program in Rwanda Genocide and the United Nations," 1). It could be argued that sexual violence on women during armed conflicts is motivated by intent to completely destroy them. Commenting on the atrocities in the Democratic Republic of Congo, Dr. Mukwege, who works in South Kivu Province, the epicenter of Congo's rape epidemic, said, "We don't know why these rapes are happening, but one thing is clear. . . . They are done to destroy women" (as cited in Gettleman 2007, 1). The perpetrators want to destroy women. The fact that even the soldiers from the Democratic Republic of Congo didn't spare their daughters, sisters, and mothers, weakens the argument that the aim of the perpetrators of sexual violence against women is to destroy the enemy; rather, it strengthens the psychoanalytical theory of sexual violence. However, as is demonstrated earlier, and like all the other theories, the psychoanalytical theory of sexual violence does not meet sine qua non conditions to address the various facets of sexual violence in conflict situations. It is, therefore, certain that more work needs to be done, if the motives behind sexual violence in armed conflicts are to be satisfactorily explained.

REFERENCES

Adichie, Chimamanda N. 2006. *Half of a Yellow Sun*. New York: Knopf/Anchor.

Alhindawi, Diana Z. 2014. "They will be heard: The Rape Survivors of Minova. Aljazeera. http://america.aljazeera.com/multimedia/2014/3/they-will-be-heardtherape-survivorsofminova.html, 6 June, 2015.

Arieff, Alexis. 2010. "Sexual Violence in African Conflicts." Congressional Research Service. (2015). www.crs.gov, 12 December, 2015.

Askin, Kelly D. 2003. "Prosecuting Wartime Rape and Other Gender-Related Crimes under International Law: Extraordinary Advances, Enduring Obstacles" *Berkeley Journal of International Law* 21. http://scholarship.law.berkeley.edu/bjil/vol 21/2/4, 28 July, 2015.

Ayiera, Eva. 2010. *Sexual Violence in Conflict: A Problematic International Discourse*. Ed: Jane Bennett. African Gender Institute, University of Cape Town.

Baaz, Maria E. and Stern, Maria. 2009. "Why Do Soldiers Rape? Masculinity, Violence, and Sexuality in Armed Forces in the Congo (DRC)." *International Studies Quarterly*, vol. 53 (2): 495–518. http:// www. Jstor.org/stable/27735106, July 23, 2015.

Bangura H., Zainab. 2012. "Outreach Program in Rwanda Genocide and the United Nations" (March) www.un.org/preventgenocide/rwanda, 12 June, 2015.

Barnett, Michael. 2002. Eye Witness to a Genocide. Ithaca: Cornell University Press.

Brownmiller, Susan. 1975. *Against Our Will: Men Women and Rape.* New York: Simon and Schuster.

Clarke, Yaliwe. 2008. "Security Sector Reform in Africa: A Lost Opportunity to Deconstruct Militarized Masculinities?" *Feminist Africa* 10, 49–66.

Degni-Ségui, René. "United Nations, Report on the Situation of Human Rights in Rwanda." In *Special Rapporteur of the Commission on Human Rights*, under Paragraph. 20 of resolution S-3/1 of 25 May 1994, (E/CN.4/1996/68), (January 1996): para. 16. UN Special Rapporteur).

El Saadawi, Nawal. 2007. *Woman at Point Zero.* New York: Zed Books Ltd.

Ellis, Lee. 1989. *Theories of Rape: Inquiries into the Causes of Sexual Aggression*, edited by Carolyn Ormes and Karla Phillip. Washington, DC: Hemisphere Publishing Corporation.

Enloe, Cynthia. 1938. *Maneuvers: The International Politics of Militarizing Women's Lives.* Berkeley: University of California Press.

The Enough Team. 2011. "Congolese Rape Survivor Shares Her Story: Tell Them We Need Peace." The Enough Team. 2011. http://www.enoughproject.org/blogs/congolese-rape-survivor-shares-her-story-%E2%80%9Ctell-them-we-need-peace%E2%80%9D, 6 June, 2016.

Fanon, Frantz. 1952. *Black Skin, White Masks.* New York: Grove Press.

Firestone, Shulamith. 1970. *The Dialectic of Sex: The Case for Feminist Revolution.* New York: William Morrow and Company, Inc.

Freud, Sigmund. 1989. *An Outline of Psycho-Analysis, 25–26,* translated by James Strachey. New York: W.W. Norton.

Gettleman, Jeffrey. 2017. "Rape Epidemic Raises Trauma of Congo War." (October) http://www.nytimes.com/2007/10/07/world/africa/07congo.html?r=0&pagewanted=print June 6, 2015.

Goldstone, Richard J. and Dehon, Estelle A. 2003. "Engendering Accountability: Gender Crimes Under International Criminal Law." In *New England Journal of Public Policy*, vol. 19: 1. Article 8. http://scholarworks.umb.edu/nejpp/vol19/iss1/8 .

Groth, Nicholas A. and Birnbaum, Jean H. 1979. *Men Who Rape: The Psychology of the Offender.* New York: Plenum Press.

Human Rights Watch. 1996. *Shattered Lives: Sexual Violence during the Rwandan Genocide and its Aftermath*. www.hrw.org/reports/1996/Rwand.htm, December 12, 2015.

Justyna Maciejczak, Justyna. 2013. "Sexual Violence as Weapon of War. E-International Relations Students." (October). www.e-ir.info/2013/10/09/sexual-violence-as-a-weapon-of-war, 8 February, 2016.

Kroslak, Daniela. 2008. *The French Betrayal of Rwanda.* Bloomington: Indiana University Press.

Laache, Fredrik B. 2015. "Scars of Rape in DR Congo." (September) http://www.aljazeera.com/indepth/features/2015/09/scars-rape-dr-congo-150913101349553.html.

Madigan, Lee and Gamble, Nancy. 1991. *The Second Rape: Society's Continued Betrayal of the Victim*. New York: Lexington Books.

Merger, Sara. 2010. "Rape of the Congo: Understanding Sexual Violence in the Conflict in the Democratic Republic." *Journal of Contemporary African Studies* 28 (2): 119–35.

Morash, Merry. 2006. *Understanding Gender, Crime, and Justice*. Thousand Oaks, CA: Sage Publications, Inc.

New American Standard Bible. 1995. La Habra: The Lockman Foundation. http://www.lockman.org, 25 October, 2015.

Nolen, Stephanie. 2005. "'Not Women Anymore . . .':The Congo's Rape Survivors Face Pain, Shame and AIDS." (Spring). http://www.msmagazine.com/spring2005/congo.asp, 25 October, 2015.

Ohambe, Omanyondo, Muhigwa, Bahananga, and Wa Mamba, Mulyumba. 2005. *Women's Bodies as Battleground: Sexual Violence Against Women*. London: International Alert.

Olujic, Maria B. 1998. "Embodiment of terror: gendered violence in peacetime and wartime in Croatia and Bosnia-Herzegovina," *Medical Anthropology Quarterly*, vol. 12 (1): 31–50.

Redding, Sean. 2006. *Sorcery and Sovereignty: Taxation, Power, and Rebellion in South Africa, 1880–1963*. Athens: Ohio University Press.

Reis, Elizabeth. 1997. *Damned Women: Sinners and Witches in Puritan New England*. Ithaca: Cornell University Press.

Rimella, Chiara and Knowles, Kitty. 2014. "Raping Makes Us Feel Free": DR Congo's Soldiers Reveal Astonishing Stories." *The Independent*.

Rittner, Carol, Roth, John K and Whitworth. 2004. *Genocide in Rwanda: Complicity of the Churches?* St Paul, MN: Paragon House.

Simkin, Stevie. 2014. *Cultural Construction of the Femme Fatale: From Pandora's Box to Amanda Knox*. New York: Palgrave Macmillan.

Sjoberg, Laura and Via Sandra. 2010. *Gender, War, and Militarism: Feminist Perspectives*. Santa Barbara: Praeger.

Taylor, Diana. 2009. "Aged One to 90, the Victims of Hidden War against Women." *The Guardian*. https://www.theguardian.com/world/2008/dec/05/congo-rape-testimonies-walungu, 11 July, 2015.

NOTES

1. In 1994, Rwanda's population of seven million was composed of three ethnic groups: Hutu (approximately 85 percent), Tutsi (14 percent) and Twa (1 percent). In the early 1990s, Hutu extremists within Rwanda's political elite blamed the entire Tutsi minority population for the country's increasing social, economic, and political pressures. Tutsi civilians were also accused of supporting a Tutsi-dominated rebel group, the Rwandan Patriotic Front (RPF). Through the use of propaganda and constant political maneuvering, Habyarimana, who was the president at the time, and his group increased divisions between Hutu and Tutsi by the end of 1992. The Hutu remembered past years of oppressive Tutsi rule, and many of them not only resented but also feared the minority.

2. The Enough Project seeks to build leverage for peace and justice in Africa by helping to create real consequences for the perpetrators and facilitators of genocide and other mass atrocities. Enough aims to counter rights-abusing armed groups and violent kleptocratic regimes that are fueled by grand corruption, transnational crime and terror, and the pillaging and trafficking of minerals, ivory, diamonds, and other natural resources. Enough conducts field research in conflict zones, develops and advocates for policy recommendations, supports social movements in affected countries, and mobilizes public campaigns.

3. "The Man of Color and the White Woman": This is chapter three of *Black Skin, White Masks*. In this chapter Fanon does a psychoanalysis reading of black man's conditions in the Colonial regime. He argues that, the black man's alienation from his culture and self makes him see himself through the white man's eyes. Therefore, he desires the white woman for the purpose of winning white man's recognition as equally white.

4. The Interahamwe is a Hutu paramilitary organization. The militia enjoyed the backing of the Hutu-led government leading up to and during the Rwandan Genocide.

NINE

Testimony as Text

"Performative Vulnerability" and the Limits of Legalistic Approaches to Refugee Protection

H. Nanjala Nyabola

Who deserves protection? It is a question we implicitly ask ourselves every time we make determinations on admissibility for migrants of many stripes—refugees and displaced persons, economic migrants. When we admit refugees or asylum seekers into a specific territory, we declare that the individual's struggles and circumstances merit the kind of protection that only another state can provide. Indeed, the concept of protection is at the heart of the relationship between a civilian and the contemporary state. John Locke in his *Second Treatise on Government* (1689) tells us that individuals come together in states as a way of ensuring collective protection from mutual destruction; we leave the state of war or chaos to enter civil society and endow the state with its political powers as a means of protecting ourselves (21). As such, a refugee or an asylum seeker is someone who has forfeited or been denied the protective function of their home state and is seeking this function in another state. Membership of a state in this context is not a neutral thing, but rather a host of privileges relative to the disadvantaged status of the refugee (Goodwin-Gill, 8–23). The receiving state has all the power and the refugee remains at the mercy of whatever framework the state in question has in place to confer these protections of refugee status.

When the idea of an international system of refugee status determination was conceived following the First World War, it was heavily implied that the freedom to seek asylum was a fundamental right that should not be denied under any circumstances. In the 1920's, Nansen passports were created primarily with Russian refugees in mind, to "improve their legal situation, especially in relation to employment, coordinate relief and assistance, and arrange repatriation or 'allocation' to other countries" (Goodwin-Gill, 11). Nansen passports conceptualised protection as diplomatic protection in the face of widespread denationalisation procedures and not necessarily human rights protection, which a person can only receive by virtue of citizenship (11). This agnostic approach, coupled with the meagre provisions that states made for their own citizens at the time arguably facilitated the widespread acceptance of the Nansen system, permitting almost 800,000 Russian refugees to seek and find protection in Europe and North America.

In contrast, the refugee protection regime that developed between WWII and the fall of the Berlin Wall tried to place various interpretations of the human rights of refugees at the core of its framework. Partly, this was a response to the atrocities of the conflict; partly it was an ideological contest between the West and the East. Russia wanted a refugee system that focused on repatriation while Western governments preferred a system that welcomed dissenters and defectors (14). For instance the UN, then dominated by Western governments, in 1946 passed a resolution prohibiting the return of individuals who, in full knowledge of all the facts, refused to return to their countries of origin (15).[1] This is the proto *non-refoulement* provision, a provision that introduced a tension between state and individual rights into the refugee protection system that persists today.

The 1951 Convention on the Status of Refugees, the 1967 Protocol to the Convention and the 1950 creation of the Office of the United Nations High Commissioner for Refugees was a consensus on many contentious issues that had emerged in the shadow of the war, contained a slew of social and political rights and entitlements that the refugee was to benefit from. The idea of United Nations High Commissioner for Refugees (UNHCR) as an independent, permanent international organisation was to be a neutral arbiter of the political dimensions of the convention—the thorny issues that remained unaddressed beneath the compromise (Goodwin-Gill 2008, 18). However, it did not result in the institutionalisation of any processes for refugee status determination (UNCHR Handbook and Guidelines 2011, 37). These processes are left to the state in question "in regard to its particular constitutional and administrative structure" (37). Some countries have ceded this authority to UNHCR based on their specialised expertise, but for the most part, UNHCR simply urges the state to bear in mind the unique and challenging circumstances facing refugees and to request the humane treatment of those seeking status (37).

In the midst of these unresolved contentions, UNHCR produced its own rubric on status determination. Individual determinations are preferred from group status determination, even though the latter is increasingly common as widespread humanitarian catastrophes become increasingly prevalent. As in a legal proceeding, UNHCR becomes the fact-finder, charged with assessing the "validity of the evidence and the credibility of the applicant's statements" (38). In the absence of a global consensus, the UNHCR rubric has accommodated the political exigencies of given situations, resulting in wildly varying standards of protection for different classes of refugees. When the collapse of the Cold War robbed the system of its supra-political principle, refugees are today at the mercy of the political situation in the country to which they flee (Goodwin-Gill, 21).

In particular, the once central principle distinguishing a refugee from a migrant has come under assault. Before 1989, migration did not carry the stigma it does today and refugees were considered a separate, particularly vulnerable sub-class of migrants, even if economic migrants were fleeing particularly harsh circumstances themselves. It must be recalled that the international refugee protection system was principally designed for the protection of European migrants. When Africans began fleeing wars of liberation, UNHCR faced a dilemma on what to do given that the countries that were fighting those wars were its principal benefactors. Treating them as refugees fleeing persecution would constitute a moral judgement on those who caused the war, treating them otherwise would deprive them of many of the specific rights and protections they were entitled to (Goodwin-Gill 20). In the case of Algeria, UNHCR equivocated, treating those fleeing as part of the "good offices" contained in the UNHCR mandate, which recognised their vulnerability but denied them the full rights and privileges of refugee status (20). UNHCR was, therefore, able to continue some of its work with Algerian and Moroccan refugees, but the first cohort of second-class refugees was born.

Since then, refugee identity has been subsumed in broader migration discourse, and international practice on refugee protection has veered towards exclusion before inclusion—increasing the number of hurdles over which those seeking protection must jump before their status of refugee is accepted. For instance, the concept of "asylum seeker" was created by European countries to lengthen the timeframe between landing and acceptance as a refugee, in some cases up to three years. Status determination has become a legalistic determination—many of those who do determinations for UNHCR are actually lawyers—and the list of qualities that a refugee must have before they can be admitted has grown.

Similarly, the discourse of the law has seeped into status determination practice. The UNHCR handbook on refugee status determination makes reference to "the burden of proof," stating that it remains with the person seeking status, but recalls that it is the unusual putative refugee who has access to "evidence of all of his statements" (UNHCR Handbook

2011, 38). Refugees have cases and case files, and "case-by-case determinations" of their status are undertaken. The handbook makes special reference to *evidentiary submissions* (39), language that suggests that the refugee status determination hearing is taking on the normative baggage of belief and truth of legal hearings in other contexts.

Refugees are, therefore, no longer victims who have been denied their objective right to protection from a state, making a demand for surrogate protection from a second state. Regardless of the horrifying circumstances they are fleeing from, refugees today are instead viewed as suspicious and near-criminal, often subjected to complex legal proceedings before they can access some of their basic human rights. At the extreme, European countries have criminalised refugee status to the extent that they hold asylum seekers in prison-like conditions, complete with guards and wardens, before giving them a chance to argue their case before a hearing officer. In Africa, the situation is mixed, with dire conditions facing millions of refugees held in camps like Daadab in Kenya—subject to indefinite detention, major restrictions on their movement amongst other limitations—and full, if not legally sanctioned, integration in host communities (e.g., in the DRC).

Still, today, refugees hoping for the full rights the status promises must prove that they are worthy of the name, and the majority are not making the grade. This is particularly true where encampment is used by the receiving state, and only those who pass the test are able to leave. Those who exist outside the restrictive frameworks of worthiness are often referred to as "illegal," as if their mere existence contravenes laws. Indeed, the discourse of worthiness creates particular vulnerabilities for those who are unable to present the circumstances of their flight in a manner that conforms to what the fact finder believes to be credible. Like any witness in a legal proceeding, refugees, not only have to provide a story that rises to the threshold required by the standard, but they must also convince the fact finder that their narrative is true. This implicates a whole host of legal concepts—testimonial and narrative capacities, truth-telling and verification—concepts that might not be at the forefront of one who is escaping life-altering trauma.

Moreover, legal hearings are complex, and particularly disadvantage those who, through cultural or social practice, may not have been exposed to the methodologies of the hearing process. They favour the articulate and the forthcoming. In the context of societies where women are socialised not to speak up and to bear pain silently, and especially in instances where they have been violently separated from partners, it puts them at a specific disadvantage. Women's disadvantage before the refugee law regime is compounded by the fact that the "reasonable man"—the legal standard by which rationality in common law jurisdictions is measured—is in the context of refugee status a "traditional male paradigm, of the refugee as the courageous dissident" (Musalo 2007, 119).

Women's fears in flight are often, therefore, not only required to be true and sound true, but also judged by the extent to which they conform to a masculinised ideal of necessity. Thankfully, as the refugee status determination process has grown more complicated, so too have strategies developed by putative refugees to navigate the seen and unseen challenges. One of these strategies is what I call "performative vulnerability"—a strategy that is at its starkest during the process of status determination. The best introduction to this strategy is in considering the particular experience of women with flight.

WHEN WOMEN FLEE

British-Somali poet, Warsan Shire (2011), offers a stark reminder of the complex stories that refugees, asylum seekers, or internally displaced persons carry with them when they leave home: "No one leaves home unless home is the mouth of a shark."[2] Yet the process of advocacy and protection inevitably whittles down the essence of these narratives into stock pieces as advocates try to balance the needs of displaced persons with the demands of the state from which the protection is demanded. Although significant efforts have been made in recent years to personalise or humanise the experience of flight, significant work remains to be done, particularly at the intersection of refugee protection and the law.

According to UNHCR (2014) estimates, there are currently 10.4 million refugees around the world, living in conditions ranging from established camps to makeshift shelters and open air camps. Only a small minority of these refugees will have their official status recognised by a third party host country. The majority live in limbo: recognised as vulnerable by virtue of having fled a natural or manmade disaster, but unable to integrate into the host society owing to the host state's restrictions. Part of the reason why so many displaced persons remain in limbo is a pervasive "culture of disbelief" (Sigfreid 2014), wherein potential host states have become increasingly suspicious of the motivations of asylum seekers, accusing them of being economic migrants taking advantage of the refugee protection scheme, and therefore, turning what should be a positive process of narration into a negative process of testifying.

When women flee, especially, various chauvinisms collide that render them vulnerable to double persecution at the point of origin, throughout the process of flight, and into the process of admission into a country of refuge. In an essay titled "Silence is a Woman," Wambui Mwangi (2013) writes in the context of Kenya's post-election violence of power dynamics in which "some bodies impose their forms on the public, and other bodies are denied a public presence." In any society, and on any given day, women are struggling for their public presence—for the independence to present and articulate their personhood on their own terms.

War, one of the most masculinised discourses out there, aggravates these chauvinisms by relegating the concerns of women to a secondary status. The International Committee of the Red Cross, the guardian of the laws of war, recognises that conflict creates specific vulnerabilities for women simply by virtue of their gender. The threat of sexual violence and the use of rape as a weapon of war are the most obvious manifestations of these vulnerabilities, but so are the lack of access to maternal healthcare, the use of women's bodies as human shields, the risks of separation, the lack of access to identification and registration documents, increased vulnerability to domestic violence, forced marriages and the burden of witnessing and surviving egregious violence in conflict in the context of all this (ICRC 2010).

At the point of status determination, these chauvinisms often collide to render women mute, binding the horrors they endure in a discourse of shame, or in the idea that a woman's strength must never be seen to waver. Discourse on sex and sexual violence demonstrates some of these vulnerabilities. Unlike many Western countries, sex in many non-Western societies is still couched in a shame culture: it is still couched in euphemism and generally shunted out of the public sphere. In addition, across all societies and even during peacetime, rape is chronically underreported (Allen 2007, 623–41). In some countries, rape victims are not only subject to their initial sexual violence, but also exposed to subsequent assault by the police.[3] More broadly, the social costs of reporting sexual assault include lost privacy or communal recriminations, especially in communities where a woman's value is correlated to her sexual purity (623–41). These costs are exacerbated where the consequences have financial or material impact on the victim. For instance, in cultures were women are expected to rely on men for financial provision and/or excluded from certain types of work, rape and being ostracised can mean loss of income or material security. The incentive thus exists for women to hide the extent of the sexual violence they have endured in order to diminish the potential costs of revealing it. Where women are forced to barter sexual favours for passage, sexual assault can become a point of trauma that they are unwilling to revisit.

Testimonies provided during refugee status determination hearings are confidential, but evidence submitted to humanitarian actors in other contexts can be used to highlight some of the issues. Consider the testimony below, offered by a Somali refugee for a project by the Jesuit Refugee Services (2015):

> I went to Ethiopia. I didn't have any documents, so I hid from police, crossed the border illegally and arrived in Sudan. There I found and joined a group of migrants and we decided to try to cross the desert together. I spent two months there, with very little food and water, in a very hot cave. We came to Sabha, in Libya, where we were brought before this man—anyone who crossed the border had to see him—who

> abducts people and asks for ransom money. Whoever doesn't obey will stay there, where there is beating, torture. *This man also takes any woman he likes*. Unless every one of the group pays, they all stay there. It took three months for all of us to pay and then he transferred us to Tripoli. In Tripoli, I was detained for three months and was finally released because I was sick. Then I managed to come here. (9, emphasis added)

This testimony affirms that this woman, at least, witnessed some form of sexual assault, if not enduring it herself in Libya. The phrase "takes any woman he likes" is a euphemism for rape that linguistically functions to create cognitive distance between the speaker and the rape(s). Taken at face value, it does not state any crime or violence. But the preceding statement on beatings and torture raises the spectre of unspeakable horrors, and followed by such a euphemism, we are left imagining that in "taking any woman he likes," the man in question subjects them to similar, but gendered forms of violence.

In the context of a status determination hearing, this sentence is critical to the factfinder, as sexual violence is considered by some judges as a specific type of persecution for which refugee status can be obtained.[4] Yet, by not offering specific testimony, information provided in this way would likely go against the putative refugee as not reaching the increasingly high threshold of proof required to demonstrate persecution. The challenge is, therefore, creating a status determination procedure that accommodates these and other vulnerabilities. How can we create a space where women can openly bear witness to the gendered struggles they suffer in the process of flight and in their experience of becoming refugees? To answer this question, we must first deconstruct the process of status determination, specifically the legalistic approach to status determination as a hearing.

DECONSTRUCTING THE STATUS DETERMINATION HEARING

Today, the refugee status determinations process is in the form of hearings, in the same vein as criminal or civil procedures in the countries in question. In Kenya, for example, Somali refugees are entitled to prima facie recognition of their refugee status, provided they register with authorities within thirty days of arrival (Refugee Consortium of Kenya 2012, 26). In practice, Somali refugees are subjected to hearing-like conditions at the Department of Refugee Affairs in order to determine worthiness, particularly for the issue of refugee identity cards which permit access to several key services (27). Increasing tension with Somalia have further securitised the situation, and the government has created hearing-like processes that have no basis in law in order to determine who is worthy, for instance, of leaving Daadab to receive medical attention (28).

The question of evidence or proof is at the heart of these hearings. The UNHCR guidebook, used globally in RSD hearings, provides a methodology of the standard for the evaluation of evidence, a guidebook that supports the assertion that the epistemology of criminal adjudication has seeped into the process of refugee status determination. As stated, the handbook refers to *evidentiary submissions,* offering that "allowances for the lack of evidence does not . . . mean that unsupported statements must necessarily be accepted as true if they are inconsistent with the general account put forward by the applicant" (UNCHR Handbook, 39). UNHCR acknowledges that "untrue statements by themselves are not a reason for the refusal of refugee status," but insists that "the benefit of the doubt should . . . only be given when all the available evidence has been obtained and checked and when the examiner is satisfied as to the applicant's general credibility" (39).

For the refugee, this is a two-part process in which she must first provide evidence, and then ensure that the evidence provided rises to the standard of truth held by the fact finder. The role of the fact-finder is to discern the truth of the claimant's assertions, to balance these in relation to extrinsic facts that the fact-finders can research on their own, and somehow test through the hearing process by subjecting them to standardised procedures of information collection, including surveys and interviews (40). This approach is reminiscent of the negative process of evidence submission in the criminal adjudication process, where the defendant is required to show reasons why they should *not* be punished through the denial of their rights to freedom.

Significantly, the seeping legalisation of refugee status determinations leads to a reversal of the traditional balance of interests within the refugee status hearing to reflect the balance of interests in the criminal adjudication process. Where the refugee is attempting to access the protections owed to him by virtue of his status, the factfinder raises the threshold on evidence and "truth" results by using a hearing to withhold these benefits. Ideally, the interest of the state should be in providing protection for refugees against persecution, and the hearing should be about identifying the best means of providing this protection. Exclusion from refugee protection should be the exception. But the increasing influence of criminal law approaches serves the state's interest in keeping refugees out, and the refugee's task is to provide evidence why he should be granted exceptional leave against the presumption of exclusion (Kassindja and Miller Bashir 1990).

"PERFORMATIVE VULNERABILITY"

So, what is "performative vulnerability" and why? To get at this, we must first reject the ontologically questionable proposition that there is such a thing as an objective truth. Derrida proposes that the process of History entails reorganising empirical instances into a larger discourse: ordering individual moments into a bigger picture that tells a bigger story (Stocker 2006, 168). The idea is that the things that we take as "apparent" are actually iterations of parallel concepts, given the mediating forces (language, interpretation, self-deception) that lie between consciousness and the expression of consciousness (169–76). So, when building a refugee's story as part of a bigger arc of history, we must be sensitive to the interpretive forces that lie between events, the refugee's experience of an event, their interpretation of said event, their translation of said event, and, finally, the fact finders interpretation of the translation presented. When testimony is offered in court, it is not simply an expression of the person's experience of a fact, but rather a version of the truth conditioned by intrinsic and extrinsic factors. There is no "truth." There is a narrative building process that we have to engage with, critically, to offer individuals the kind of protection they need.

A discussion on deconstruction in the context of law is incomplete without considering power. If the Law (specifically, in this instance, refugee law) is a discursive process of construction, then law is not an independent moral reality, but a system of constructed norms or principles (Blackburn 2008, 76), where a norm is a "standard of behaviour created through mutual expectation in a social setting" (Brunnee and Toope 2012, 1). Norms are malleable over time; some social norms are not legal norms; and only the norms that a society holds to be most universal and sacrosanct are codified as law. Norms are both prescriptive—seeking to shape future behaviour—and descriptive, since they are derived from the current status quo, although the extent to which one subscribes to either viewpoint depends on one's theoretical framework on the law (1).

In short, the refugee status determination process is the interplay between the agency of the putative refugee and that of the factfinder, in the framework of sets of norms designed by the society exited, that which the refugee is attempting to enter, and the specific context of the refugee status determination hearing. It is a freestyled play in which the cast of characters has broadly defined, but not specifically pinned down roles. A putative refugee could, therefore, either be boxed in by the power structures and a limited comprehension of their roles, or they can employ strategies of resistance that allow them to navigate the conflicting demands of their social context with those of the hearing process.

Performative vulnerability is, therefore, the process of constructing a narrative of vulnerability around phenomena which the putative refugee—rightly or wrongly—believes the fact-finder will be most responsive to, in the context of the refugee status determination. Performative vulnerability involves everything from selective narration, in which certain elements of the process of flight are intentionally omitted in order to preserve social dignity in the broader context of the society the refugee has exited, to lies told in order to appeal to the sympathy of the fact-finder. Performative vulnerability is reading the exigencies of the refugee status determination process in the context of the putative refugee's abilities and responding to them in a way the refugee deems appropriate. Performative vulnerability isn't lying—it is recognising that where receiving countries have created the unattainable and unrealistic spectre of the "ideal refugee," even those with genuine need for protection can be denied. In the context of hostile governments that would stand by and let thousands of refugees drown to death in the name of national self-interest, performative vulnerability is survival.

Performative vulnerability must be understood in the context of hegemony. Hegemony seeks to construct a story of society that preserves its interests, silences dissent and mutes contradictions. The phenomenon of the refugee is a counter-hegemonic identity, constantly negotiating and writing against hegemony in an effort to survive. As a social force, hegemony is persistent and consistent: it functions within speeches and silences, in what is said and done and in what remains unsaid and undone (Lazarus-Black and Hirsch 1994, 7). As such, to hear refugees, we must use counter-hegemonic listening devices—read against the dominant narrative, investigate silences etc. Consider the following testimony taken from the JRS (2015) report:

> I used to live with my mother and father, we had a farm and we fed our family from this. We were very poor and had no crops because of the fighting in our area. We had nothing. We were getting poorer and poorer, so my father decided to marry me off to this man who had a "better life." That was when my problems started but I cannot talk about them here. (12)

The speaker has used multiple ways to figuratively redact phenomena from her lived experience. Note the sentence, "but I cannot talk about them here," especially, which allows the refugee to allude to the fact that her experience in her country was difficult without naming anything. Hegemony creates hostile spaces in which specific testimonies become unacceptable—for instance, the implicit distinction that men can speak about political violence, but women cannot speak about domestic violence. This woman's poverty does not shame her; she testifies to that openly, but whatever dark experiences characterised her marriage does. This suggests a form of negotiation. She alludes to the experience, because they are integral to her lived experience as a refugee, but she keeps the particulars to herself. The private violence that women endure and the indignity of being bartered like a farm animal are the stories that power prefers to keep hidden.

Nonetheless, hegemony and power do not exist without resistance—the ideologies that inspire subaltern groups to reject the dominance of power and to reframe issues in ways that resonate more closely with their lived experiences (Lazarus-Black and Hirsch, 7–8). Resistance could be rejecting participation in hegemonic structures, or by adapting or modifying the structures to suit the goals of the subordinate classes (10). The same refugee as above continues:

> Then I came to Tripoli. What I remember most is seeing how migrants used to sleep in their shoes at night because they were afraid the police would come and catch them. Some migrants broke their legs when they jumped the walls to get away when there was a raid. *I didn't want to be always living in fear,* hiding from the police or from civilians who might tell the police I am there. *This is what made me cross the sea to come here.* (10, emphasis added)

Language can highlight moments of resistance in a hearing, where members of a subordinate group appropriate the language of power to articulate their concerns. Language can be used to resist, either by the choice of language used or not used (the whole), the manipulation of language through different stylistic choices (the first level), or the manipulation of the content of the language. "I didn't want to always be living in fear . . . this is what made me cross the sea to come here"—this is the language of resistance to a narrative of victimhood. It is the language of action—displacement as an active choice to move forward, rather than a passive consequence. Again, it may seem counterintuitive for a refugee to reject such a narrative given how starkly it contrasts with the dominant narrative. However, it is important to emphasise that this is a process of negotiation. The refugees must intellectually retain the status they believe themselves to hold in the context of their society, but still conform to whatever ideas of refugeehood exist in the society they wish to enter. Where states seek to humiliate refugees into exit, refugees resist this casting, because the processes of modern refugee status determination—from flight, through detention through the process of the hearing exist to rob them of their dignity as one of the women refugees interviewed by the Jesuit Refugee Services in their report observes:

> In my country my rights were violated, I could not go to school, I could not choose who to marry. My life was not mine but dictated by someone else. In the desert, it was the same, and here too I find myself in the same situation, in detention, without any control over my life, at the dictates and mercy of someone else. (17)

Silence can also be a form of resistance, where members of the subaltern class refuse to engage with power on power's terms. Refugees can choose not to share elements of their personal narrative in order to preserve their dignity. Unfortunately, resistance to hegemony in the context of a refugee status determination hearing is risky and potentially counterproductive. Hegemony, or power, is not unresponsive to resistance. It adapts itself, either by pushing back within the immediate context of the hearing or creating and using loopholes in the amended law that allow for the same outcomes as the prior situation. In the context of the creeping legalistic approach to refugee status determination, the main response to these strategies of resistance is emphasis on credibility as the determinative factor in whether or not status should be conferred. Kagan (2003) writes that credibility is becoming "the single biggest substantive hurdle" that refugees face in the status determination process (368). Refugee organisations in the UK call this the "culture of disbelief," where the Home Office accepts and perpetuates the presumption that "large numbers of asylum claims are unfounded, mendacious or 'bogus'" (Souter 2011, 48–59).

Critically, states increasingly rely on the language of security to insidiously dismantle the principles of universality and skew outcomes in favour of a specific political and social agenda (Chimni 2000, 10). Power in this case has an interest in isolating refugees—characterized as "spoilers" in a system where human value is directly linked to economic productivity—either in societies in the periphery of the neoliberal hegemony of Western countries, or by returning them to their home countries (13). The humanitarian imperatives of the refugee protection process are increasingly subsumed in largely unfounded security claims, raising the burden of proof on the refugee, who must now not only prove that she is fleeing persecution and deserves protection, but also that she has never and will never be a threat to the security of the country of entry.

RETURN TO HUMANITY

How then, do we undo the "unhumaning" of refugees that happens when we subject their narratives of flight to criminal-like inquiry? One approach is to use the tools of literature, and oral literature specifically, to "handle" refugee narratives. Oral literature theory can provide a methodological approach that will "preserve the autonomy and integrity of the text as art and at the same time, provide a sound methodology for understanding meaning in all of its contexts" (Masinjila 1992, 3–4). Oral literature theory recognises that legal texts are performances—oral, layered with meaning beyond the words contained therein, and capable of a plurality of interpretations. Significantly, it is a method that is sensitive to social and ethical concerns of understanding power. Oral literature can be used to approach the hearing as a performance of a text, which can be analysed using literary techniques that peer behind Derrida's repetitions.

The use of literature to deconstruct the law is not a novel proposition. Despite its radical strand, the methodology of deconstruction in literature has been deployed in the field of law and literature to propose alternative ways of reading legal texts. Literature and deconstruction are closely related, because they both recognise that communication is complex, and language multifaceted, and understanding both requires decoding and inference (Carutthers 1996, 75). However, where orthodox language theory views the gap between the consciousness and the expression of consciousness as a gap to be breached, deconstruction sees signifiers that must be subordinated to the "communicated function of discourse" (Posner 1998, 213). Deconstruction places these signifiers on the same level as the concepts they are believed to signify—meaning is contained both in words and in the ways in which words are put together and presented.

Deconstruction, as a literary approach has also been used in legal contexts to challenge traditional views of "the author" as "present" in the text (Posner, 213). Posner writes that the disappearance of non-written elements in the presentation of texts like the US Constitution, including inflection or tonality, necessarily reduces the "presence," and therefore, the authority of the author as the primary interpreter of the text at hand (213). If texts are necessarily imperfect representations of the consciousness, then any substantiated inferences drawn from the text, even by people who are not the author, are in some ways correct (as much as they are wrong). Where testimony is treated as text, deconstruction opens the door to multiple readings of the same text, a tolerable proposition in the practice of common law as demonstrated by the willingness of certain judges to overturn precedent in order to achieve a particular outcome.

Literature allows for expansive readings of texts that implicate concepts beyond the narrow milieu of the hearing (Posner, 214). Literary concepts that are increasingly analysed in the study of law include: "the use of figurative language, rhyme, assonance, meter, fiction, parable, punning, etc.," and other devices that emphasise the subjective nature of meaning (214). Still, deconstruction in literature does not necessarily proceed in the same way as deconstruction in law (215).

Oral literature theory adds something specific to deconstruction in the law. The hearing, unlike a constitution or a memorandum, is a document that transitions from one form into another, and the dynamism of language is often lost in the transition from speech to writing. Written text, particularly that which is bound so tightly by procedure cannot capture the psychology of a speaker in the moment he or she expresses a thought. Translating a text from oral to written form necessarily flattens it, as the poetics and context of the spoken word cannot be efficiently communicated in writing (Finnegan 1991, 190–93).

Within the context of the refugee status hearing, there may be contradictions in the choice to leave out or include certain information in an account of one's flight from conflict or disaster, even if such information may increase likelihood of receiving refugee status; e.g. where female victims of sexual violence leave out details of their assault in fear of social consequences within their community, or even within their own perceptions of self (Johnson 2012). There is a tension between the immediate physical need for protection from persecution and the longer-term psychological and emotional need for respect and acceptance within one's community. A non-literary reading of a hearing, despite all guidance towards sensitivity and understanding, cannot unpack these extraneous elements, because it can only analyse "the facts of the case and . . . personal impression" (UNHCR Convention) of the fact-finder. More importantly, it cannot do this in service to subaltern groups, because it is a depersonalised, de-contextualised approach attuned to the needs of power. Only a literary approach—and specifically, an oral literature approach to handling these texts can accomplish these goals.

CONCLUSION

Who deserves protection? Ideally, everyone does. The principles of shared humanity demand that we give everyone who is forced to flee their homes an opportunity to build back their lives. It is absurd that individuals are being denied all such opportunities based on the fiction of the state and the inventions required to sustain it. The current bent towards using tools grounded in the law serves the state's hunger for exclusionary citizenship—narrowing the class of people who belong to those groups whose values resonate best with hegemony. But, they are contrary to the basic fact that we all must share this earth, and that factors like violence or instability are not limited to certain populations.

Legalistic approaches to refugee status determination hearings divorce the system from its humane origins, and the need for a more humane approach to reading refugee narratives of flight necessitates creativity. When we recognise performative vulnerability, we recognise the resilience and resistance as core human traits, and systems must develop tools that accommodate this, or continue to force individuals to seek increasingly desperate methods of seeking safety in the face of war. Performative vulnerability is easily misread as lying in a system that doesn't recognise it as a method of survival—something that the criminal justice system does not do. Narratives of flight may also be judged unduly harshly by a fact-finder who does not have appropriate literary tools to deal with stories of flight, humanely.

Oral literature methodology can begin the process of moving refugee status determination back towards humaneness. It allows the determiner to approach refugee narratives as what they are—rich, complex human stories—and to handle them with respect and sensitivity to the difficult circumstances in which stories are crafted, and why they are presented in certain ways. This flexible and interpretive approach will prove indispensable as international figures on conflict and displacement trend upwards, and the need to offer protection across cultural divides increases.

REFERENCES

Allen, W. David. 2007. "The Reporting and Underreporting of Rape." *Southern Economic Journal*. Vol. 73. 3 (January): 623–41

Blackburn, Simon. 2008. *The Oxford Dictionary of Philosophy*. Oxford, UK: Oxford University Press.

Brunnee, Jutta and Stephen J. Toope. 2012. "Constructivism and International Law." In *Interdisciplinary Perspectives on International Law and International Relations: The State of the Art*, edited by Jeffrey L. Dunoff and Mark A. Pollack. New York: Cambridge University Press.

Carutthers, Paul. 1996. *Language, Thought and Consciousness: An Essay on Philosophical Psychology*. New York: Cambridge University Press.

Chimni, B. S. 2000. "Globalisation, Humanitarianism and the Erosion of Refugee Protection." In *Refugee Studies Centre Working Paper*. no. 3, 10.

Finnegan, Ruth. 1991. *Oral Tradition and the Verbal Arts: A Guide to Research Practices*. New York: Routledge.

Goodwin-Gill, Guy S. 2008. "The Politics of Refugee Protection." *Refugee Survey Quarterly*, 27 (1): 8–23.

International Committee of The Red Cross. 2010. "Women Protected Under International Humanitarian Law. "In *International Committee of the Red Cross Overview*, October 29. https://www.icrc.org/eng/war-and-law/protected-persons/women/overview-women-protected.htm.

Jesuit Refugee Services. 2015. *No Giving Up; Stories of Unfinished Journeys*. Valleta, Malta. Jesuit Refugee Services.

Johnson, Ginger A. 2012. *Frozen Words: Memory and Sexual Violence amongst Sudanese Refugee Women in Cairo. UNHCR Research Paper*, no. 240. http://www.unhcr.org/4fdef5799.pdf.

Kagan, Michael. 2003. "Is Truth in the Eye of the Beholder? Objective Credibility Assessment in Refugee Status Determination." *Scholarly Works*. Paper 633. http://scholars.law.unlv.edu/facpub/633.

Kassinjda, Fauzia and Layli Miller Bashir. 1990. *Do They Hear You When You Cry?* New York: Delta Publishing.

Lazarus-Black, Mindie and Susan F. Hirsch. 1994. "Introduction, Performance and Paradox: Exploring Law's Role in Hegemony and Resistance." In *Contested States: Law, Power and Resistance*, edited by Mindie Lazarus-Black and Susan F. Hirsch. New York: Routledge.

Locke, John. 1689. *Second Treatise on Government*. In *Classics of Moral and Political Theory*, edited by Michael L. Morgan. New York: Hachet.

Masinjila, Masheti. 1992. "The Genesis of Theory: The Case of Kenyan Oral Literature." In *Reflections on Theories and Methods in Oral Literature*, edited by Okoth Okombo and Jane Nandwa. Nairobi, Kenya: Kenya Oral Literature Society.

Musalo, Karen. 2007. "Protecting Victims of Gendered Persecution: Fear of Floodgates or Call to (Principled) Action?" *14 Virginia Journal of Social Policy and Law*, 119: 107–26.

Mwangi, Wambui. 2013. "Silence is a Woman," *The New Inquiry*, June 4. http://thenewinquiry.com/essays/silence-is-a-woman/.

Posner, Richard A. 1998. *Law and Literature*. Cambridge, MA: Harvard University Press.

Refugee Consortium of Kenya. 2012. *Asylum Under Threat: Assessing The Protection of Somali Refugees in Dadaab Refugee Camps and Along the Border*. Nairobi, Refugee Consortium of Kenya.

Seigfried, Kirsty. 2014. "Culture of Disbelief Works Against Asylum Seekers," *IRIN News*, http://www.irinnews.org/report/97906/culture-of-disbelief-works-against-as.

Souter, James. 2011. "Culture of Disbelief or Denial? Critiquing Refugee Status Determination in the United Kingdom." *Oxford Monitor of Forced Migration*. Vol. 1 (1): 48–59.

Stocker, Barry. 2006. *Derrida on Deconstruction*, Abingdon, Oxford: Routledge.
UN General Assembly. 1951. "Convention Relating to the Status of Refugees," July 28. *United Nations, Treaty Series,* vol. 189, 137. http://www.refworld.org/docid/3be01b964.html
———. 1967. "Protocol Relating to the Status of Refugees," January 31. *United Nations, Treaty Series*, vol. 606, 267. http://www.refworld.org/docid/3ae6b3ae4.html
United Nations High Commissioner for Refugees. 2011. *Handbook and Guidelines on Procedures and Criteria for Determining Refugee Status: Under the 1951 Convention and the 1967 Protocol Relating to the Status of Refugees*
———. 2014. *Refugee Figures* UNHCR.org. http://www.unhcr.org/pages/49c3646c1d.html

NOTES

1. "[N]o refugees or displaced persons who have finally and definitely, in complete freedom and after receiving full knowledge of the facts, including adequate information from the Governments of their countries of origin, expressed valid objections to returning to their countries of origin . . . shall be compelled to return." UNGA res. 8(I), February 12, 1946.

2. Warsan Shire, *Conversations about home (At the Deportation Centre) Teaching My Mother To Give Birth* (2011).

3. For testimonies of sexual assaults by police officers, see e.g. "Saron," *Abused from Ethiopia to England: My Story as a Raped Refugee*, for the Women Under Siege Project, October 25, 2012 (accessed 1 June 2015) http://www.womenundersiegeproject.org/blog/entry/abused-from-ethiopia-to-england-my-story-as-a-raped-refugee; Carlotta Gall, *Women in Tunisia Tell of Decades of Police Cruelty, Violence and Rape* in *The New York Times,* May 28, 2015 (accessed June 1, 2015). http://www.nytimes.com/2015/05/29/world/africa/women-in-tunisia-tell-of-decades-of-police-cruelty-violence-and-rape.html?_r=0.

4. See, e.g., *Sofia Campos-Guardado v. Immigration and Naturalization Service,* 809 F.2d 285, United States Court of Appeals for the Fifth Circuit, March 9, 1987, available at: http://www.refworld.org/docid/47fdfb0e0.html [accessed 2 June 2015].

Index

About the Contributors

Pauline Ada Uwakweh, the editor of *African Women Under Fire,* is associate professor of literature and graduate coordinator in the Department of English, North Carolina A&T State University, Greensboro, North Carolina. She earned her PhD from Temple University, Philadelphia. She is coeditor of *Engaging the Diaspora: Migration and African Families* (Lexington, 2014). Several of her articles appear in professional journals, such as *Research in African Literatures, African Literature Today,* and *Journal of African Literature Association,* and books on literary criticism, including *Emerging African Voices, Emerging Perspectives on Buchi Emecheta, Emerging Perspectives on Ama Ata Aidoo, Nwanyibu: Womanbeing in African Literature.* Her research interests include the transnational female identities, female militancy in African and African Diaspora literature, trauma and literary representations of war and conflict. She maintains active interest in children's literature and is author of a children's novel—*Running for Cover* (Onwubiko, Nigeria: Africana First Publishers)—based on the Nigerian civil war. Uwakweh is a 2016 Fellow of the Carnegie African Diaspora Scholars Program.

Jessie Sagawa is a senior ESL facilitator at the University of New Brunswick, Fredericton, Canada. A two time Canadian Commonwealth scholar, she is a graduate of the University of Malawi, Chancellor College, and the University of New Brunswick, Fredericton. Her doctoral thesis was a feminist post-colonial analysis of the representation of women and feminism in selected Malawian novels written in English. She has taught at the University of Malawi, UNB, and Saint Thomas University. Her research interests are African and Diasporic African Literature, Women's Studies, Canadian Literature, ESL, Literacy and African Oral Literature.

Tendai Mangena lectures in the Department of English and Media Studies of Great Zimbabwe University. She holds a PhD in literary studies from Leiden University (of Netherlands) and has published papers in peer-reviewed journals on Zimbabwean literature and cultures. She currently sits on the Executive Board of the Names Society of Southern Africa (NSSA) as its Vice President. She has been awarded a Georg Forster Postdoctoral Fellowship to be hosted by Prof. Dr. Kerstin Knopf at the University of Bremen in Germany for the period May 2016 to April 2018.

Melissa R. Root, educator, writing adviser, writer, and editor, lives in Denver, CO. She has a PhD in English literary studies and currently teaches at Metropolitan State University of Denver.

P. Julie Papaioannou is a senior lecturer in the Department of Modern Languages and Cultures at the University of Rochester, in Rochester, NY. Her teaching and research interests include French and Francophone literature and film, literary and postcolonial theory, feminist and film theories.

Paul N. Touré is assistant professor of French and Francophone Studies at Millikin University, Decatur, Illinois. He received his PhD in Romance Languages and Literatures at the University of Cincinnati, Ohio. His research interests are Francophone African studies with a focus on migrant and translational narratives and film, ethics, emotions, resilience studies, violence, genocide, and postcolonial theory. His articles and book chapters have appeared in various academic journals such as *Nouvelles Etudes Francophones, African Literatures Association,* and *L'Harmattan*. He is currently editing a book on Francophone African literature and films, entitled *L'imaginaire africain francophone et le miroir de la culture globale.*

Emilie Diouf is a PhD candidate in African American and African Studies at Michigan State University. Her research interests include African Women's Literature and Cinema, especially narratives of violence, trauma, and displacement. She explores the ways in which sociocultural conditions affect African women's expressions of trauma caused by civil war and genocide. She is currently writing her dissertation which examines testimonial narratives, including novels and memoirs by refugee women from the Democratic Republic of Congo, Rwanda, Uganda, Togo, and Cameroon. Emilie earned her Master's degree in Literatures in English from Michigan State University in 2010 and Bachelor's in African Literature and Culture from Cheikh Anta Diop University, Dakar, Senegal in 2006.

Moussa Issifou, is coordinator of student success in the English Department at North Carolina Agricultural and Technical State University. He also teaches composition, critical theory, and literature courses. He has taught in Togo and Gabon. Dr. Issifou received his PhD in Postcolonial Literature and Theory at the University of North Carolina, Greensboro.

H. Nanjala Nyabola is a feminist writer, humanitarian advocate and political analyst currently based in Nairobi. Her work has appeared in print and online for *Foreign Policy, Foreign Affairs, The BBC, The Guardian, New African Magazine, Al Jazeera, African Arguments* and many other publications. Her academic publications focus on issues of conflict, post-conflict reconstruction and the law. Nanjala holds a BA in African Studies and

Political Studies from the University of Birmingham (UK), an MSc in African Studies and an MSc in Forced Migration, both from the University of Oxford, and a JD from Harvard Law School.

Lightning Source UK Ltd.
Milton Keynes UK
UKHW010056270420
362290UK00010B/78

9 781498 529204